The Latino Threat

The Latino Threat

CONSTRUCTING IMMIGRANTS, CITIZENS, AND THE NATION

SECOND EDITION

Leo R. Chavez

Stanford University Press
Stanford, California

Stanford University Press
Stanford, California

Printed in the United States of America on acid-free, archival-quality paper

Library of Congress Cataloging-in-Publication Data

Chavez, Leo R. (Leo Ralph), author.
   The Latino threat: constructing immigrants, citizens, and the nation / Leo R. Chavez. —
Second edition.
      pages cm
   Includes bibliographical references and index.
   ISBN 978-0-8047-8351-4 (cloth : alk. paper) — ISBN 978-0-8047-8352-1 (pbk. : alk. paper)
   1. Hispanic Americans—Press coverage—United States.   2. Mexican
Americans—Press coverage—United States.   3. Immigrants—Civil rights—United
States.   4. Citizenship—United States.   5. Emigration and immigration law—United
States.   6. Prejudices in the press—United States.   7. United States—Emigration and
immigration.   I. Title.
   PN4888.H57C43 2013
   305.868'073—dc23

                                                                                2012040902

Typeset by Newgen in 10/14 Minion

For those generations who came before and made my life possible, and the generations to come—may their dreams be fulfilled.

And for my wife, Cathy, and my children, Koji and Andrea— for fulfilling all my dreams.

CONTENTS

PREFACE AND ACKNOWLEDGMENTS

I WOULD NOT HAVE GUESSED in 2008, when the first edition of this book was published, that the story line I called the Latino Threat Narrative would become so quickly and commonly referenced in political discourse. The Latino Threat Narrative consists of a number of taken-for-granted and often-repeated assumptions about Latinos, such as that Latinos do not want to speak English; that Latinos do not want to integrate socially and culturally into the larger U.S. society; that the Mexican-origin population, in particular, is part of a grand conspiracy to take over the U.S. Southwest (the *reconquista*); and that Latin women are unable to control their reproductive capacities, that is, their fertility is out of control, which fuels both demographic changes and the alleged *reconquista*.

Advocates for reduced immigration, media pundits, and politicians pushing tough immigration laws routinely characterize Latinos, both immigrants and citizens, along the lines of the Latino Threat Narrative. For example, Pat Buchanan has warned of Mexican-origin Americans having "no desire to learn English" and creating a "nation within a nation." Even respected scholars such as Samuel P. Huntington have espoused the Latino Threat Narrative: "Mexicans and other Latinos have not assimilated into mainstream U.S. culture"; "Demographically, socially, and culturally, the reconquista of the Southwest United States by Mexican immigrants is well underway."

Such views have exploded into politics in Arizona, Alabama, and many other states where harsh anti-immigration laws have been passed. As I will show, images and rhetoric used in the politics surrounding get-tough state laws which seek to increase surveillance of immigrants, even to the point of having teachers and medical personnel alert authorities to "suspected" undocumented immigrants, express taken-for-granted assumptions of the Latino Threat Narrative. In Arizona, these assumptions led lawmakers to ban Mexican American studies classes because they allegedly fomented an overthrow of the United States, the *reconquista*.

Presidential politics, especially the Republican presidential candidates' debates in 2012, focused on the threat Latinos pose to the nation. For example, candidate Rick Perry, the governor of Texas, was attacked for his support for a state DREAM Act to help young people who were brought to his state as undocumented immigrants as young children. The U.S.-born children of undocumented immigrants also had the legitimacy of their citizenship questioned; most of the Republican candidates called them "anchor babies," meaning they were part of a plot to help their parents take advantage of the United States. Even sports events have not been immune to the Latino Threat Narrative, as Latino high school and college players, all American citizens, have been subjected to opposing fans chanting "USA" and "Where's your papers?" The pervasiveness of these public displays toward Latinos pushed me to move forward with the second edition of *The Latino Threat*.

Readers will find that this second edition is fully revised, updated, and extended to include events since 2008. A new chapter focuses on the children of undocumented immigrants. As the above discussion indicates, heated political debate has emerged over both undocumented youth who have spent most of their lives in the United States and U.S.-born children, citizen children, of undocumented immigrants. This new chapter explores two important questions: Should undocumented immigrants who have spent their formative years in the United States be provided a path to citizenship or be deported? Should we throw out the Fourteenth Amendment to the Constitution so that undocumented immigrants cannot give birth to U.S.-citizen children? The public debate over both questions invokes the Latino Threat Narrative in ways that are unsettling and that undermine public attitudes toward Latinos. Throughout the book, I've updated the statistics to show how the trends elucidated in the first edition have continued apace. Evidence of use of English, marriage patterns, religious behavior, and other patterns exhibited by both Latino immigrants and citizens that challenge the veracity of the Latino Threat Narrative has been expanded to include research on the greater Los Angeles area where appropriate.

As in the first edition, this new edition keeps issues of citizenship and media spectacles front and center. After all, debates over citizenship are really about whom we, as a nation, judge eligible to become one of "us." And the stories that become media fodder provide essential information—or sometimes misinformation—on the nature of immigrant and citizen Latino lives. Unfortunately, media stories that espouse the tenets of the Latino Threat Narrative cloud the judgments we, as a nation, must make about immigration reform and how to encourage mutual respect as we all pursue the dreams that have been the promise of America.

.   .   .

Although I alone am responsible for any misrepresentations or errors of judgment found in these pages, many people contributed in some way to the development of my thoughts and this work. I would like to thank my local UC Irvine support group: Victor Becerra, Gil Conchas, Cynthia Feliciano, Manuel Gomez, Michael Montoya, Leticia Oseguera, Henry Pontell, Vicki Ruiz, Diego Vigil, and many others. Roberto Gonzales, Juliet McMullin, Cathy Ota, Frank Bean, Louis DeSipio, Mei Zhan, Kamal Sadiq, and Rubén Rumbaut also contributed to this work in various and invaluable ways. I am particularly indebted to Rebecca Martinez for her careful reading of the manuscript and her many insightful suggestions. William Maurer and Norma Miranda provided the Anthropology Department's support at crucial moments. Stella Ginez is always a stalwart and ready accomplice. This work has also been influenced greatly, from afar, by Carolyn Brettell, Patricia Zavella, and Nina Glick Schiller. I am indebted to Loretta J. Williams, director of the Gustavus Myers Center for the Study of Bigotry and Human Rights, for alerting me to *Time* magazine's ad on the issue of nonwhite fertility. The University of California Committee on Latino Research provided funding that made possible the 2006 survey research examined here. I would also like to thank the anonymous reviewers for their generous suggestions. Finally, I am grateful for Kate Wahl for encouraging me to write the original book and this second edition. I would also like to thank all those at Stanford University Press whose hard work has made *The Latino Threat* possible.

The Latino Threat

INTRODUCTION

ON MARCH 24, 2009, Pat Buchanan stated on MSNBC: "Mexico is the greatest foreign policy crisis I think America faces in the next 20, 30 years. Who is going to care, 30 years from now whether a Sunni or a Shia is in Baghdad or who's ruling in Kabul? We're going to have 135 million Hispanics in the United States by 2050, heavily concentrated in the southwest. The question is whether we're going to survive as a country."[1] Buchanan's apocalyptic pronouncement went beyond immigrants from Latin America to warn about the threat posed by their children and subsequent generations.

A report from the Southern Poverty Law Center in August 2009 warned of the rapid growth in militia groups across the United States.[2] There were various reasons for this rise, with the stress of the recession and a liberal administration led by a black president being the most important. But the center also cited "conspiracy theories about a secret Mexican plan to reclaim the Southwest" that are part of the public debate about immigration.

On April 23, 2010, Arizona's governor Jan Brewer signed the United States' toughest immigration law. What soon followed were similar laws in Georgia, Alabama, Mississippi, Indiana, South Carolina, and Utah, as various states seemed to compete to pass the most draconian anti-immigration legislation. Although in June 2012 the U.S. Supreme Court struck down most of Arizona's immigration law, it did allow police to continue asking anyone suspected of being in the country illegally for their immigration papers.[3] In Arizona, passage of the immigration law was followed by attacks on teaching Chicano studies in high school. Arizona's banning of Chicano studies and textbooks was based on

Figure I.1. Sharron Angle political ad, using a photograph of Mexicans taken in Mexico.
SOURCE: Andrew Price for www.good.org.

the argument that such classes fomented anti-Anglo (non-Latino white) hatred and promoted the idea of a Latino takeover of the U.S. Southwest.[4]

In the 2010 U.S. Senate race in Nevada, Republican Sharron Angle ran against Democrat Harry Reid. Angle's campaign aired an advertisement that featured three Latino-looking male youth (Figure I.1). Each was standing looking directly at the camera, wearing casual clothing, sweatshirts and jackets. One wore a baseball hat backwards. Across the image were the words, in bold, "ILLEGAL ALIENS." One would think that these three Latino males were the hardest-working models in political ads that year, as they turned up in other advertisements as well. What's important here is that the ad did not provide identifying information on the young men, such as where they were born or even if they really were "illegal aliens." For all we knew, they could have been well-paid actors, college students, or immigrant workers. The reality is that these three Mexican men were photographed in Mexico. There is no evidence they were ever in the United States as undocumented immigrants.[5] However, being "Mexican looking" was enough to create the message that Latino immigrants represented a problem and that a vote for the political candidate would help fix the problem.

Republican presidential candidate Herman Cain was in Tennessee on October 15, 2011, where he responded to a question about his views on erecting a fence between the United States and Mexico. Cain replied that if elected president, he would build a border fence: "It's going to be 20 feet high. It's going to have barbed wire on the top. It's going to be electrified. And there's going to be a sign on the other side saying, 'It will kill you—Warning.'"[6] Mr. Cain said later that he was joking but then quickly added, ". . . but not really." How could a presidential candidate joke about electrifying human beings?

This book grew out of my attempt to unpack the meanings of these views about Latinos. Rather than considering them in isolation, I began to see them as connected, as part of a larger set of concerns over immigration, particularly from Mexico and other parts of Latin America; the meaning of citizenship; and the power of media spectacles in contemporary life. The Latino Threat Narrative provides the raw material that weaves these concerns together.

The Latino Threat Narrative posits that Latinos are not like previous immigrant groups, who ultimately became part of the nation. According to the assumptions and taken-for-granted "truths" inherent in this narrative, Latinos are unwilling or incapable of integrating, of becoming part of the national community. Rather, they are part of an invading force from south of the border that is bent on reconquering land that was formerly theirs (the U.S. Southwest) and destroying the American way of life. Although Mexicans are often the focus of the Latino Threat Narrative, public discourse, as I elaborate in Chapter 1, often includes immigration from Latin America in general, as well as U.S.-born Americans of Latin American descent. Thus, the broader and more inclusive term *Latino* is used throughout this book, while recognizing that Latinos actually vary greatly in terms of their historical backgrounds and success in integrating into U.S. social and economic life.

The contemporary Latino Threat Narrative has its antecedents in U.S. history: the German language threat, the Catholic threat, the Chinese and Japanese immigration threats, and the southern and eastern European threat. In their day, each discourse of threat targeted particular immigrant groups and their children. Each was pervasive and defined "truths" about the threats posed by immigrants that, in hindsight, were unjustified or never materialized in the long run of history. And each of these discourses generated actions, such as alarmist newspaper stories (the media of the day), anti-immigrant riots, restrictive immigration laws, forced internments, and acrimonious public debates over government policies. In this sense, the Latino Threat Narrative is part of a grand tradition of alarmist discourse about immigrants and their perceived negative impacts on society.[7]

However, the Latino Threat Narrative recognizes that Latinos are different from past immigrants and other ethnic groups in America today. Latinos have been in what is now the United States since the late sixteenth and early seventeenth centuries, actually predating the English colonies. Since the Mexican-American War, immigration from Mexico and other Latin countries has waxed and waned, building in the early twentieth century, diminishing in the 1930s, and building again the post-1965 years. These migrations paralleled those of other immigrant groups. But Mexicans in particular have been represented as the quintessential "illegal aliens," which distinguishes them from other immigrant groups. Their social identity has been plagued by the mark of illegality, which in much public discourse means that they are criminals and thus illegitimate members of society undeserving of social benefits, including citizenship. Latinos are an alleged threat because of this history and social identity, which supposedly make their integration difficult and imbue them, particularly Mexicans, with a desire to remain socially apart as they prepare for a reconquest of the U.S. Southwest.

The Latino Threat Narrative is pervasive even when not explicitly mentioned. It is the cultural dark matter filling space with taken-for-granted "truths" in debates over immigration on radio and TV talk shows, in newspaper editorials, and on Internet blogs. Unquestioned motives and behavior attributed to Latino immigrants and their children permeate discussions over amnesty for undocumented immigrants, employer sanctions, driver's licenses, prenatal care, education for the children of immigrants, citizenship for "anchor babies" (U.S.-born children with undocumented-immigrant parents), and even organ transplants for immigrants. Although some aspect of the Latino Threat Narrative can be found in almost any discussion of immigration in contemporary public discourse, what I attempt here is a more systematic elaboration of this narrative. I will also contest the basic tenets of this narrative, an ambitious aspiration for a cultural critic admittedly not unlike Don Quixote's attacking windmills.[8]

In addition, I want to connect the Latino Threat Narrative to what I see as the contemporary crisis in the meaning of citizenship. The Minuteman Project's activities in Arizona in 2005 (see Chapter 6) were about more than drawing attention to the perils of an uncontrolled border and unauthorized immigration. The Minutemen were also decrying what they perceived as the dilution of the rights and privileges of U.S. citizenship because of massive immigration. The Latino threat is profoundly implicated in the second theme of this book, the contested terrain of citizenship in a world where national borders are increasingly permeable. What citizenship means in this changing landscape is not clear. But what is certain is that a legalistic definition of citizenship is not enough. Other meanings of citizenship—economic, social, cultural, and even emotional—are being presented in debates, marches, and public discourse focused on immigrants, their children, and the nation.

"Citizen" and "noncitizen" are concepts used to imagine and define community membership. According to Benedict Anderson, members of modern nations cannot possibly know all their fellow members, and yet "in the minds of each lives the image of their communion. . . . It is imagined as a community, because, regardless of the actual inequality and exploitation that may prevail in each, the nation is always conceived as a deep, horizontal comradeship."[9] Anderson eloquently argues for the importance of print media in the construction of "imagined communities" and subjectivities that lay the foundation for nationalism and modernity.[10] In a similar vein, Jürgen Habermas has argued that the public sphere relies on the circulation of print commodities.[11] I extend this thinking to the image-producing industries in order to explore how the media help construct the imagined community through representations of both inclusion and exclusion.[12]

Both the Latino Threat Narrative and struggles over the meaning of citizenship pervade media-infused spectacles where immigration or immigrants are the topic. Broadly speaking, events or public performances that receive an inordinate volume of media attention and public opinion become media spectacles.[13] It is difficult to escape media coverage and the incessant "talk" about immigration.[14] Border surveillance, reproduction, fertility levels, fears of immigrant invasions and reconquests, amnesty programs, economic impacts, organ transplants, and the alleged inability to assimilate Latino immigrants and their offspring are all fodder for media attention.

Immigration-related media spectacles force us to reconsider what we mean by the word *spectacle*. *Spectacle* comes to us from Middle English and is an Anglo-French term with roots in the Latin *spectaculum*, derived from *spectare*, to watch, and *specere*, to look at. In other words, a spectacle is something watched or looked at. It is the object of the viewer's gaze. The *Merriam-Webster Online Dictionary* includes this sense of the word in its definition but adds more connotations: a spectacle is "something exhibited to view as unusual, notable, or entertaining; especially an eye-catching or dramatic public display" or "an object of curiosity or contempt."[15] These definitions of *spectacle* may capture, to a certain extent, what occurred in the immigration marches and other immigration-related events considered here. However, these events push us to think about the meaning of spectacles in society and how they help construct subjective understandings of "citizens" and "noncitizens."

When immigration-related events or issues receive extensive media focus and become media shows, there is more going on than merely relating the news. As Guy Debord has observed, in modern technological societies, life has become "an immense accumulation of *spectacles*" and "all that once was directly lived has become mere representation."[16] The images we constantly consume not only inform us of life around us but also help construct our understanding of events, people, and places in our world.[17] In short, media spectacles are productive acts that construct knowledge about subjects in our world. This is particularly the case for how we internalize who we are as a people. How we, as a nation of diverse people, derive our understanding of who to include in our imagined community of fellow citizens is a product of many things, not the least of which is what we glean from the media.[18] Debates over immigration, citizenship, and national belonging are informed by the events we witness through the media's representation of immigrant spectacles, whether they are promoting concern for the plight of immigrants or anti-immigration events.

How newcomers imagine themselves and are imagined by the larger society in relation to the nation is mediated through the representations of immigrants' lives in media coverage. Media spectacles transform immigrants' lives into virtual lives, which are typically devoid of the nuances and subtleties of real lived lives (see Chapter 1).[19] It is in this sense that the media spectacle transforms a "worldview"—that is, a taken-for-granted understanding of the world—into an objective force, one that is taken as "truth."[20] In their coverage of immigration events, the media give voice to commentators, pundits, informed sources, and man-on-the-street observers who often invoke one or more of the myriad truths in the Latino Threat Narrative to support arguments and justify actions. In this way, media spectacles objectify Latinos. Through objectification (the process of turning a person into a thing) people are dehumanized, and once that is accomplished, it is easier to lack empathy for those objects and to pass policies and laws to govern their behavior, limit their social integration, and obstruct their economic mobility. Portraying Latinos as objects or things makes it easier to see immigrant marchers as a chaotic mass rather than as people struggling to be recognized as contributing members of U.S. society (Chapter 7), or Latinas represented in advertisements as beer bottles—literally things—rather than human beings (Chapter 3).

Through its coverage of events, the media produce knowledge about, and help construct, those considered legitimate members of society as well as those viewed as less legitimate, marginalized, and stigmatized Others.[21] Thus media spectacles—such as those that occurred around organ transplants for noncitizens, Minuteman Project activities, and immigrant marches examined in the chapters that follow—help define what it means to be a "citizen," a task that can be undertaken only by also defining its contrasting concepts: "alien," "illegal alien," "foreigner," and "immigrant." Where do Latinos stand in relation to these concepts? Are Latino immigrants worthy of the rights and benefits of citizenship if they are supposedly unwilling to integrate into U.S. society? Are Latinos who were born in the United States suspect as citizens because of the disloyalty to the nation implied by the Latino Threat Narrative? The very act of asking such a question casts U.S.-born Latinos as "alien-citizens," perpetual foreigners despite their birthright.[22]

Before proceeding, we need to clarify the context within which the Latino Threat Narrative gains tremendous currency and which has provoked a crisis over the meaning of citizenship. Adding to this necessary contextualization is a brief overview of recent legislation to control immigration. Debates over immigration reform provide ample opportunities for the Latino Threat Narrative to be invoked. In addition, immigration reform legislation is an exercise in inclusion and exclusion when it comes to defining who is legitimately able to join the community of citizens.

IMMIGRATION AND THE NATION

The number of immigrants to the United States has been growing steadily since 1960 (Figure I.2). The proportion of foreign-born in the U.S. in 2005 was 12.4 percent, which is approaching the historic high of 14.7 percent foreign-born in 1910, during the peak years of immigration during the early twentieth century.[23] Estimates of undocumented immigrants currently living in the country range from 10 to 12 million, with most coming from Mexico (57 percent) and other Latin American countries (23 percent).[24] These trends have led to public concerns over immigration and legislative proposals to reform the nation's immigration laws.[25]

The U.S. Congress seems to be on a ten-year cycle for taking up major immigration reform legislation. After passage of the monumental 1965 immigration

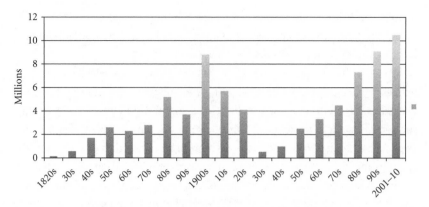

Figure I.2. Immigration to the United States by decade, 1820–2010.
SOURCE: *2011 Yearbook of Immigration Statistics* (Department of Homeland Security, 2012).

law, President Jimmy Carter, in the 1970s, floated the possibility of an amnesty for undocumented immigrants and sanctions for employers who hired undocumented workers, neither of which gained much political ground at the time.[26] Almost a decade later, Congress passed, and President Ronald Reagan signed into law, the Immigration Reform and Control Act of 1986 (IRCA). The major provisions were sanctions for employers who hired undocumented immigrants and an amnesty program for over a million undocumented immigrants. Although touted as legislation to end undocumented immigration, IRCA was relatively ineffective.

The Immigration Act of 1990 made some adjustments to immigration law, such as increasing from 500,000 to 700,000 the number of legal immigrants allowed into the United States each year. It also created a lottery program for visas to help lure immigrants from countries that had not been part of recent immigration flows, especially countries in Europe. But major immigration reform came six years later.

In 1996 the U.S. Congress passed the Illegal Immigration Reform and Immigrant Responsibility Act. This law toughened the requirements for undocumented immigrants to adjust their status to that of a legal immigrant and streamlined the judicial process by turning deportation decisions over to an immigration court, thus reducing the levels of judicial review open to immigrants. It also streamlined the deportation of criminals and widened the range of deportable offenses. Among the changes to the nation's immigration law included in this act was a provision making immigrants' sponsors responsible for public benefits used by immigrants. This provision, according to Sarita Mohanty et al., "created confusion about eligibility and appeared to lead even eligible immigrants to believe that they should avoid public programs."[27]

It should be noted that Congress also passed welfare reform in 1996 that targeted immigrants. The Personal Responsibility and Work Opportunity Reconciliation Act of 1996 ended the federal government's sixty-one-year commitment to provide cash assistance to every eligible poor family with children.[28] This law was expected to save the government $54 billion over the following six years, with nearly half of those savings, or $24 billion, to come from restricting legal immigrants' use of food stamps, Supplemental Security Income, and aid for low-income elderly, the blind, and the disabled. Legal immigrants were barred from using Medicaid for five years after their entry.[29] Undocumented immigrants, who already were denied virtually all federal assistance, continued to be barred from assistance except for short-term disaster relief and emergency medical care. Benefits, however, were soon restored to some at-risk populations, especially the elderly.[30]

On December 15, 2005, the House of Representatives passed HR 4437, the Border Protection, Antiterrorism, and Illegal Immigration Control Act.[31] The bill represented yet another expression of the "get tough" attitude toward undocumented immigration.[32] Among its many provisions were more border fences and surveillance technology, increased detention provisions, employer verification of employees' work eligibility, and increases in the penalties for knowingly hiring undocumented immigrants. Moreover, it would have made living in the country as an undocumented immigrant a felony, thus removing any hope of becoming a legal immigrant. The bill also broadened the nation's immigrant-smuggling law so that people who assisted or shielded illegal immigrants living in the country would be subject to prosecution. Offenders, who might include priests, nurses, social workers, or doctors, could face up to five years in prison, and authorities would be allowed to seize some of their assets. The House's bill was clearly an exercise of exclusion, whereas the immigrant marches it generated were public displays of a desire for inclusion.

The U.S. Senate, in May 2006, passed its own version of immigration reform that included a guest worker program for immigrants and a legalization program, a "path to citizenship," for some undocumented immigrants. Importantly, many of the draconian measures in the House bill did not become part of a final version of immigration reform promulgated under the George W. Bush administration, but the willingness of the House of Representatives to pass such measures sent a clear message to undocumented immigrants about their stigmatized status in the United States.[33]

Through the media, politicians desiring to restrict immigration have been able to represent undocumented immigrants as undeserving criminals and possible terrorists. Sometimes it seems that the spectacle surrounding immigration reform is more important than enacting new laws. For example, rather than arriving at a compromise bill on immigration, the House of Representatives sponsored more than twenty public meetings throughout the nation to discuss immigration reform, in what one newspaper editorial called the "endless summer" of 2006.[34] After that round of immigration reform failed to result in a new law, Congress, with President Bush's support, again took up immigration in May 2007, where it met a similar fate.[35]

Immigration reform laws and the politics surrounding reform proposals frame the public discourse over immigration. If the decibel levels in the debate are sometimes high, it is because the stakes are too. Who we let in to the nation as immigrants and allow to become citizens defines who we are as a people. Conversely, looking at who we ban from entry, or for whom we create obstacles to integration into society and to membership in the community of citizens, also reveals how we imagine ourselves as a nation—that is, as a group of people with intertwined destinies despite our differences.

CONCEPTUALIZING CITIZENS AND NONCITIZENS

The Latino Threat Narrative, immigration patterns, and the contemporary crisis over the meaning of citizenship are a triple helix of mutual influences.[36] However, what is meant by "citizen"—who is eligible for citizenship and who qualifies for the rights and benefits of citizenship—has always been a matter of contention, at least in U.S. history.[37] Consider the types of questions surrounding citizenship that were debated early in this nation's history: All *men* may be created equal, but are they equally eligible for citizenship?[38] Should only white males with property have the privileges of citizenship? What about women, slaves (three-fifths of a person for enumeration purposes), and Native Americans? Not all immigrants were deemed eligible for citizenship. Asians were ineligible during much of the twentieth century.[39] Historically, poor, unmarried single women, whose morality was thus questionable, and the sick and infirm were deniable as immigrants and thus also ineligible for citizenship.[40] The legacies of these issues continue to be found in contemporary immigration policies.

The intertwined logics of race and national hierarchies based on theories of social evolution framed struggles over definitions of citizenship and immigrant desirability during the late nineteenth and early twentieth centuries.[41] Although race continues in importance, the crisis over citizenship in today's world has moved to a different register, one complicated by globalization—a term that refers to how the world and its people are increasingly becoming integrated into one giant capitalist system. The spread of world capitalism also carries with it a spread of Western—often American—culture. Anyone who travels notices how common American fast-food restaurants have become in the world, a process sometimes referred to as the McDonaldization of society.[42] But globalization is more than the movement of capital and the search for cheap labor. It is also about the movement of people, ideas, material culture, and commodities (e.g., movies, music, "traditional" Chinese medicine), as well as a whole host of flows unmoored from fixed nation-states.[43]

Globalization has led to questions about the rights and privileges of citizenship and whether citizenship extends beyond the limits of the nation-state.[44] Indeed, the proliferation of types of citizenships now under consideration is an indication of the current crisis surrounding the meaning of citizenship. Some argue that there are "economic citizens," who through their labor contribute to the well-being of society.[45] Others argue for transnational citizenship, postnational citizenship, transmigrant citizenship, transborder citizenship, or flexible citizenship, each of which recognizes that migrants often maintain lives that extend across the borders of nation-states.[46] Then there are "denizens," legal residents of a country who are not naturalized citizens but enjoy some economic and political rights.[47] Victoria Bernal observes that an "emotional citizenship" emerges through the use of the Internet by the widely dispersed Eritrean refugees.[48] Others point to social inequalities that create a segmented citizenship, as some members of society are more valued than others, who often become stigmatized.[49] Some also argue that immigrants and minorities are engaged in a struggle for cultural citizenship, reflecting their claims for inclusion in society.[50]

What, then, do we mean by citizenship? As a key concept in American culture, citizenship can, and does, have many meanings.[51] It can range from the notion of being a "good citizen," implying responsible membership in a social group, to strict legal definitions of rights and privileges. Incorporating immigrants into society entails a transformation from "other" to "us." However, becoming part of the "us," or to be included as part of the "we," as in "we the people," is a contested process partly because it is not clear what this process entails.[52] Meanings of such seemingly concrete and objective terms as "citizen" and "citizenship" fluctuate over time and place. And immigration always complicates the notion of citizenship.[53] Should immigrants and their children be included as citizens? Under what conditions should they be included in the national body? How we answer these questions depends on the way we perceive immigrants, which in turn is often based on what we know of them through their "virtual" lives, which are constructed through media representations.[54] The problem is that real lives of immigrants and their children may not correspond to their media-constructed virtual lives, as Chapter 2 suggests.

In a thorough review of the literature, Linda Bosniak found that there are four distinct understandings of citizenship: as legal status, as rights, as political activity, and as a form of collective identity and sentiment.[55] It is from the last of these definitions of citizenship that issues of cultural citizenship emerge. These four elements of citizenship find their analogues in the public debates and events focused on immigration, whether the actors are immigrants themselves or those posturing for restrictive immigration policies and greater surveillance of borders. Through the interplay of these four elements in daily discourse, the media, and government policies, we construct and define "citizens" in contrast to "noncitizen" subjects, as well as put pressure on society to broaden the definition of citizenship (the immigrants and their supporters' agenda).

Citizenship as Legal Status

Simply put, for many, citizenship is about legal recognition. In this sense, citizenship refers to formal membership in an organized political community.[56] But, as Bosniak observes, problems arise over defining who is entitled to acquire citizenship and deciding where to draw the line between citizens and "aliens" when it comes to allocating rights and privileges (voting, education, health care, driver's licenses, etc.).[57] For the millions of undocumented immigrants in the United States, as well as other countries, the lack of a formal legal status becomes a salient factor in this framing of citizenship.[58] Moreover, collapsing a lack of legal status with criminality adds another justification for denying undocumented immigrants legal recognition or amnesty, which would, the argument goes, be tantamount to rewarding criminals with a path to citizenship.

Citizenship as Rights

For many, especially anti-immigration groups such as the Minuteman Project, citizenship is also about rights, privileges, and responsibilities. What distinguishes citizens from aliens are precisely the rights and privileges reserved for citizens. However, immigrants, including undocumented immigrants, also have rights in many nations, including the United States, where the Constitution speaks of "persons," not citizens, when describing inalienable rights.[59] Consequently, immigrants have enjoyed rights to juridical due process, fair labor standards and practices, education, emergency medical care, and more.[60] Complicating this issue further are claims to basic human rights or rights based on universal or extranational agreements, such as the United Nations' Universal Declaration of Human Rights.[61]

Rights accorded to immigrants put pressure on the concept of citizenship, extending it beyond a narrow legal definition to include economic and cultural rights as part of the conceptualization of citizenship.[62] However, since rights are part of a process of defining citizens and aliens, affording rights to immigrants can reflect, for some, a dilution of citizenship, reducing its value in a calculus of privileges.[63] Not surprisingly, anti-immigrant discourse and actions are often framed around rights and privileges—that is, reducing the rights and privileges afforded to immigrants, an idea that has found its place in immigration policy. For example, the 1996 immigration law made it more difficult to become a legal resident, broadened the criteria for deportation even for permanent legal residents,[64] and lessened opportunities for due process in deportation cases. The 1996 welfare law removed immigrants from eligibility for many social services. In addition, there are persistent calls to deny undocumented children access to public education, to deny citizenship to the U.S.-born children of undocumented immigrants, and to deny public housing and medical care to undocumented immigrants. Undocumented immigrants are refused driver's licenses in many states. In effect, these policies redefine the value of citizenship by reducing the rights and privileges accorded to immigrants. The controversy over organ transplants for immigrants, especially those illegally in the country, is particularly revealing of the battle over citizenship rights and privileges and is examined in Chapter 5.

Citizenship as Political Activity

Regarding citizenship as political activity is common among political theorists going back to Aristotle, and its meaning in this sense refers to "active engagement in the life of the political community."[65] But what is the meaning of "community?" Is the political activity of citizens possible only within the confines of the nation-state? Or has globalization produced new forms of citizenship to include political organizations and activities that traverse national boundaries? It is here that pressures to expand notions of citizenship come into play, with new forms of global citizenship and transnational citizenship becoming part of political discourse.[66] As the sites of citizenship expand, there has been a rejection of the state as the only site of citizen participation and a move toward a more pluralistic view of citizenship located in the groups and communities where people live.[67] As Bosniak has noted, these alternative sites of citizenship practices have increasingly been considered as part of "civil society."[68] This new conception of citizenship provides an opening for immigrant practices of citizenship. Immigrants, even the undocumented, engage in political coalitions, movements, mobilizations, and other practices that would constitute political citizenship in their communities.[69]

Nina Glick Schiller has argued that this opening up of citizenship has led scholars to distinguish between political citizenship and social citizenship.[70] Claims of social citizenship occur through social practice rather than law, "when people make claims to belong to a state through collectively organizing to protect themselves against discrimination, or receive rights and benefits from a state, or make contributions to the development of a state and the life of people within it."[71] Citizenship as social practice is different from a more cultural or identity-based approach to citizenship.

Citizenship as Identity/Solidarity

Understanding citizenship as based in identity and solidarity recognizes that subjective experiences color how people understand the concept of citizenship. The practices of natives and immigrants alike produce citizen-subjects who have affective ties of identification and solidarity with social groups maintained through direct contact or merely imagined as communities.[72] Feelings of citizenship, belonging, and social integration can extend from the very local to the transnational. Such sentiments are not entirely determined by legal definitions of citizenship or by the borders of nation-states.[73] As Susan Coutin has noted, feelings of belonging arise despite the "legal nonexistence" of undocumented immigrants.[74] In other words, to feel part of a community is determined not solely by immigration status but also by sentiments influenced by social relationships and cultural beliefs and practices.[75]

It is within this sense of citizenship that claims for cultural citizenship become grounded in experiences and subject-making.[76] Flores and Benmayor define cultural citizenship as the result of a broad range of activities that disadvantaged groups use to claim space and rights in society.[77] More specifically, Rosaldo and Flores define cultural citizenship as "the right to be different with respect to the norms of the dominant national community, without compromising one's right to belong."[78] The immigrant marches during the spring of 2006 were instances of claims for cultural citizenship. Immigrants, if only for a brief time, claimed the "town square" as a place for their public performances of civic participation and cultural citizenship.[79]

However, Rosaldo and Flores's definition of cultural citizenship, as claiming the right to be different, may not be enough.[80] Feelings of belonging and desire for inclusion in the social body exist in a dialectical relationship with the larger society and the state, which may or may not find such claims for cultural citizenship convincing. In this sense, cultural citizenship as subject-making is not a unilateral act, as Ong argues when she refers to it "as a dual process of self-making and being made within webs of power linked to the nation-state and civil society." She adds, "Becoming a citizen depends on how one is constituted as a subject who exercises or submits to power relations."[81]

Ong's emphasis on the nation-state's role in defining cultural citizens builds on Michel Foucault's observations on governmentality.[82] Foucault argues that subjects are created through the modern regimes and practices of governance, such as inscription, inspection, registration, statistics, and in this case, restrictions on immigration and citizenship.[83] For Ong, the nation-state, through a process of individuation, constructs people in specific ways as citizens, so that one can speak of citizen-taxpayers, consumers, and welfare dependents.[84] The practices of governance also define the noncitizen.[85]

In addition to the state, civil society also plays a role in disciplining immigrants with proper normative behavior and constructing their identity.[86] For example, the many groups organized around the politics of restricting immigration are constantly engaged in individuating different types of immigrants from citizens, defining citizenship, and limiting immigrants' claims to cultural citizenship.[87] A way to challenge citizenship claims is through discourse that calls into question a group's loyalty to the nation, danger to the nation, and legitimate claims to membership in the nation. The Latino Threat Narrative is such a discourse.

As this discussion suggests, *citizen* and *citizenship* have various meanings that move us away from overreliance on legalistic definitions. Citizenship as social participation and as subjective understandings of cultural identity also must be taken into account when trying to understand notions of belonging in today's world. The objective here is to explore these questions in various sites where issues of immigration and citizenship have become contested terrain. Of interest are such seemingly disparate subjects as the Minutemen in Arizona, immigrant marches, Latina reproduction, and organ transplants. All of these subjects raise serious debate over who is a legitimate member of society and deserving of the rights and privileges of citizenship. Importantly, the Latino Threat Narrative pervades these sites of contestation over belonging to the nation.

OVERVIEW OF CHAPTERS

Part 1 examines the development, over the last forty years or so, of a set of taken-for-granted assumptions or "truths" about Latin American, mainly Mexican, immigrants and their offspring. This first part takes an admittedly empirical approach because sometimes critiquing discourse is not enough; at times counterevidence must be brought to bear on the truth claims being put forward in the Latino Threat Narrative. However, I pursue this cultural criticism, knowing that it is difficult to destroy myths that have developed over a long time and in some respects go back to the nineteenth century.[88] Such myths have organic-like lives of their own.[89] Once given birth, they grow and take on ever more elaborate and refined characteristics until they are able to stand on their own as taken-for-granted "truths."

Chapter 1 focuses on how popular discourse and the media represent Latinos as an invading force that is conspiring, in Quebec-like fashion, to reconquer the U.S. Southwest. Moreover, Latinos, according to this discourse, are unable, or unwilling, to learn English and generally integrate into U.S. society. These representations constitute the "virtual" lives of immigrants and their imagined threats to the nation. The Latino Threat Narrative underlies much of the public debate over immigration and immigration policy, as well as the struggle over citizenship examined in subsequent chapters.

Chapter 2 moves to a different register, one that interrogates the veracity of various premises of the Latino Threat Narrative. According to the narrative, Mexicans (and other Latin American immigrants are often lumped with Mexicans here) are unable or unwilling to integrate into U.S. society, preferring to remain linguistically and socially isolated, and, in the narrative's more sinister renditions, they and their offspring are part of a conspiracy to take over the southwestern United States. I examine these issues, using data on immigrants and the children of immigrants in Orange County, California.

Chapter 3 looks at reproduction and fertility as sites of political debate over the nation and citizenship. In the Latino Threat Narrative, Latina fertility is represented as a threat to the nation, and Latinas and their children are a key component of the reconquest hypothesis. Issues range from population explosions to birthright citizenship, but at the core of the politics of reproduction are representations of the "hot" Latina and her "out-of-control" fertility. Latinas are represented as locked into a cultural tradition and Catholic religious doctrine that renders them slaves to childbearing. Through such representations, Latinas are integrated into a stratified system in which their reproduction is feared rather than valued. Their very bodies symbolize key aspects of the Latino Threat Narrative. Not surprisingly, the politics of reproduction does not stop at Latinas' bodies but also focuses on their children.

Chapter 4 reconsiders Latina fertility and reproduction through the lens of empirical findings from two research projects in Orange County, California. Although it may be impossible to refute deeply held beliefs, Latina reproductive behavior and fertility levels do in fact change in response to new historical contexts and life circumstances and across generations in the United States. Latina sexuality and reproduction are not out of control. Latinas have, on average, fewer children over time in the United States within the first generation, and the trend continues across generations.

Part 2 focuses on media-infused spectacles surrounding organ transplants for undocumented immigrants, Minutemen along the Arizona-Mexico border, and immigrant marches. These cases became spectacles because of the public performances of the actors involved and because of the large volume of media attention and public opinion they generated.[90] Each case was the topic of myriad news stories on radio, television, newspapers, magazines, and the Internet. Pundits in each of these media explored the politics of these events, sometimes in reasoned debate but more often pandering to anti-immigrant sentiment. Evident in these cases is the way in which the Latino Threat Narrative informs struggles over the meaning of citizenship—that is, who is a legitimate member of society and thus deserving of the privileges of citizenship.

Foucault's ideas about biopolitics, surveillance, discipline, and governmentality—that is, the techniques for control of the conduct of populations—frame the analysis of events in these chapters.[91] Immigrants internalize a subject status as a result of the pervasive Latino Threat Narrative, media representations of their lives, debates over their inclusion or exclusion from the community of citizens, and government policies targeted at them. Immigrants and their families also resist the pervasive negative representations of their lives. At the same time, the targeting of immigrants allows citizens to reaffirm their own subject status vis-à-vis the immigrant Other.

Chapter 5 examines organ transplants as a site of biopolitics over citizenship and its privileges. The body of the nation and the body of the citizen merge metaphorically and literally when considering organ transplantation. The particular case of Jesica Santillan, the unfortunate recipient of a "bungled transplant," reveals the way in which undocumented immigrants, in particular, raise intense debate over who constitute legitimate recipients of "citizen organs."[92] Characterizing "illegal alien bodies" as undeserving of citizen organs actually increases the biovalue of immigrant bodies, in that this disciplinary discourse ensures a net flow of organs from immigrants to citizen bodies.

Chapter 6 takes a critical look at the Minuteman Project's surveillance in the Arizona desert in the spring of 2005. Emerging out of nowhere, the Minuteman Project quickly captured the imagination of those who believed that immigration was a problem and that illegal Mexican immigration in particular had to be stopped. The Minutemen created a media spectacle on the Arizona-Mexico border as a way to both reaffirm the privileges of citizenship and influence policy makers to enhance border surveillance and promote anti-immigration reform. The taken-for-granted "truths" of the Latino Threat Narrative developed in Chapter 1 form the backdrop for the Minuteman Project's activities.

Chapter 7 explores the cultural and political significance of the large marches and demonstrations by immigrants and their supporters in the spring of 2006. The marches were a response to the proposed bill HR 4437, especially the provisions that would have made felons of all undocumented immigrants in the country. In addition, however, the marches were also about something much grander, the immigrants' laying claim to social and cultural citizenship and to respect, even for those lacking authorization to be in the country. Marginal groups in a society can use spectacles as a way of defining citizenship from the bottom up because it is through such public events that citizenship is performed and constructed.[93] What we find is that organized public events are not restricted to the strong and powerful; though perhaps more difficult for those without resources, the weak also can perform citizenship through public spectacles.[94] Through acts such as the immigrant marches, citizenship is performed and becomes part of an identity represented to the larger society.[95] When immigrants marched en masse, they performed the role of citizen-subjects, but citizens of a particular sensibility: the economically contributing, entrepreneurial, government services–avoiding neoliberal citizen-subject.

Finally, Chapter 8 moves from Latina reproduction to the media spectacles surrounding the children of immigrants. Of increasing political interest are undocumented immigrants brought as children by their parents. Referred to as the 1.5 generation, they have been raised and educated in the United States. A social movement has emerged around immigration reform known as the DREAM Act, which would allow some of the 1.5 generation to gain legal residency and thus a path to citizenship. Called DREAMers, these young undocumented immigrants have come out of the shadows to advocate for their cause, amid a vitriolic debate framed by the Latino Threat Narrative. The U.S.-born children of immigrants, who are U.S. citizens, have also witnessed the legitimacy of their citizenship being questioned. They have become the targets of media discourse that labels them "anchor babies," and are said to be part of a nefarious plot to get their parents legal status. Such rhetoric has spurred attempts to change the Fourteenth Amendment to the U.S. Constitution by removing birthright citizenship. As unlikely as such drastic changes might be, the media spectacle focusing on anchor babies and citizenship underscores the pervasiveness and inherent stigma-producing power of the Latino Threat Narrative.

CONSTRUCTING AND CHALLENGING MYTHS **Part 1**

1 THE LATINO THREAT NARRATIVE

> *It is time we stopped thinking of our nearest neighbors*
> *[Canada and Mexico] as foreigners.*
>
> **Ronald Reagan**

> *By a psychological and cultural mechanism of association [with*
> *'alien' and 'illegal' undocumented workers] all Latinos are thus*
> *declared to have a blemish that brands us with the stigma of being*
> *outside the law. We always live with the mark indicating that*
> *whether or not we belong in this country is always in question.*
>
> **Renato Rosaldo**

DESPITE RONALD REAGAN'S PLEA for a more civil political discourse,[1] the tone of the public debate over immigration became more alarmist between 1979 and 1999, when the anthropologist Renato Rosaldo commented on the stigma accorded all Latinos,[2] and this trend has continued up the present time.[3] The events of September 11, 2001, heightened a public discourse on the dangers the United States faces in the contemporary world. President George W. Bush developed a general strategy for the national security of the United States while critics focused on the dangers inherent in forging an empire in the modern world.[4] Americans seemed willing to allow the constitutional rights of foreigners and immigrants to be diminished so long as those of citizens appeared to remain intact, a dangerous bargain at best.[5] But if there has been one constant in both pre- and post-9/11 public discourse on national security, it has been the alleged threat to the nation posed by Mexican and other Latin American immigration and the growing number of Americans of Mexican descent in the United States. The themes in this discourse have been so consistent over the last forty years that they could be said to be independent of the current fear of international terrorism. However, the events of 9/11 "raised the stakes" and added a new and urgent argument for confronting all perceived threats to national security, both old and new.

The Latino threat, though old, still has currency in the new, post-9/11 world. Consider Samuel P. Huntington's views expressed in an article in the March–April 2004 issue of *Foreign Policy*. Huntington compared Latinos, especially Mexicans, with earlier waves of European immigrants and found that "unlike past immigrant groups, Mexicans and other Latinos have not assimilated into mainstream U.S. culture, forming instead their own political and linguistic enclaves—from Los Angeles to Miami—and rejecting the Anglo-Protestant values that built the American dream."[6] He also made these assertions: "Demographically, socially, and culturally, the reconquista (re-conquest) of the Southwest United States by Mexican immigrants is well underway"; "In this new era, the single most immediate and most serious challenge to America's traditional identity comes from the immense and continuing immigration from Latin America, especially from Mexico, and the fertility rates of those immigrants compared to black and white American natives."[7]

Huntington's statements are all the more remarkable given the historical context in which they were made. At the time, the United States was waging war in Iraq, deeply involved in the war on terrorism in Afghanistan, and still searching for Osama bin Laden and Al Qaeda operatives worldwide. And yet amidst all these crises, Huntington singled out Latin American, particularly Mexican, immigration as America's most serious challenge. But this threat did not suddenly surface after 9/11; Huntington had raised the alarm a year before the attack on the World Trade Center. In 2000, Huntington wrote in the *American Enterprise*: "The invasion of over 1 million Mexican civilians is a comparable threat [as 1 million Mexican soldiers] to American societal security, and Americans should react against it with comparable vigor. Mexican immigration looms as a unique and disturbing challenge to our cultural integrity, our national identity, and potentially to our future as a country."[8]

Rather than discarding Huntington's rhetorical excesses as bombastic hyperbole, we are better served by attempting to clarify the social and historical context of such pronouncements. How did Mexican immigration, the Mexican-origin population, and Latin American immigration in general come to be perceived as a national security threat in popular discourse? Such ideas do not develop in a vacuum. They emerge from a history of ideas, laws, narratives, myths, and knowledge production in the social sciences, the natural sciences, the media, and the arts. In other words, they exist within a "discourse," a formation or cluster of ideas, images, and practices that construct knowledge of, ways of talking about, and forms of conduct associated with a particular topic, social activity, or institutional site in society.⁹ As Stuart Hall has noted, "These *discursive formations*, as they are known, define what is and is not appropriate in our formulation of, and our practices in relation to, a particular subject or site of social activity; what knowledge is considered useful, relevant and 'true' in that context; and what sorts of persons or 'subjects' embody its characteristics."[10]

Mexico, Mexican immigrants, and the U.S.-born of Mexican origin are the core foci of the Latino Threat Narrative, but the threat is often generalized to all Latin American immigrants and at times to all Latinos in the United States. In the discursive history of Mexican immigration, specific themes of threat emerge, become elaborated, and are often repeated until they attain the ring of truth. This is a story with a number of interwoven plot lines, or narrative themes: the construction of "illegal aliens" as criminals, the Quebec model, the Mexican invasion and *reconquista* (reconquest) of the United States, an unwillingness to learn English and integrate into U.S. society, out-of-control fertility, and threats to national security. An examination of these themes provides the necessary context for understanding the debates over citizenship and immigrants' rights in the United States that are discussed in the following chapters.

CONSTRUCTING THE "ILLEGAL ALIEN"

Restrictions on immigration and citizenship have always been about how we imagine who we are as a people and who we wish to include as part of the nation, whether this is explicitly recognized or not. Underscoring this observation is Mae Ngai's authoritative history, *Impossible Subjects: Illegal Aliens and the Making of Modern America*, which concentrates on the early twentieth century but illuminates much that is being debated in the early twenty-first century. The immigration reforms of the 1920s created major restrictions in the flow of immigrants, in the process producing hierarchies of people and nationalities. Western and northern Europeans were the desired immigrants, and their movement hither was the goal of the national origins quotas. Southern and eastern Europeans, Asians, Africans, Mexicans, and other Latin Americans were less desirable, even when demand for their labor made their immigration necessary. The 1920s also witnessed a profound new importance placed on the territorial imperative of national borders, which coincided with new techniques of surveillance, the creation of the Border Patrol, and immigrant health examinations. Out of this new order of border control emerged the "illegal aliens," those who bypassed border controls and found ways to enter the country. The large-scale restrictions of the 1924 immigration law "generated illegal immigration and introduced that problem into the internal spaces of the nation." As Ngai argues, "Immigration restriction produced the illegal alien as a *new legal and political subject*, whose inclusion within the nation was simultaneously a social reality and a legal impossibility—a subject barred from citizenship and without rights."[11]

Mexican immigrants quickly became associated with the term *illegal alien*. According to Ngai, "As numerical restriction assumed primacy in immigration policy, its enforcement aspects—inspection procedures, deportation, the Border Patrol, criminal prosecution, and irregular categories of immigration— created many thousands of illegal Mexican immigrants."[12] However, it was ironic that Mexicans became so closely identified with the term *illegal*, since they were not subject to numerical quotas and were defined as "white," unlike Asians, and thus were not excluded as racially ineligible for citizenship. The "whiteness" of Mexicans was a legal definition that was a by-product of Mexico's signing of the Treaty of Guadalupe Hidalgo at the end of the U.S.-Mexican War. Mexicans living in what was now U.S. territory were allowed to become U.S. citizens, a privilege reserved for "white" immigrants at the time. Despite such legal definitions, Mexicans were still considered "not-white" in the public imagination.[13] Italian immigrants in the late nineteenth and early twentieth centuries had a similar problem. Their racial designation was ambiguous in that they were viewed as undesirable and inferior to earlier waves of northern and western European immigrants, yet Italian "whiteness" in contrast to African, Asian, and Mexican Americans was never in doubt.[14]

Asians and Mexicans became legally racialized ethnic groups.[15] I use *racialized* here to indicate that these are not genetic-based categories of race but, rather, labels that are socially and culturally constructed based on perceived innate or biological differences and imbued with meanings about relative social worth.[16] Asian immigrants were denied a pathway to citizenship, and Mexicans were associated with illegal alien status and subjected to Jim Crow segregation throughout the U.S. Southwest. Legally racialized because of their national origin, Mexican and Asian immigrants found themselves cast as permanently foreign and faced obstacles to their integration into the nation.[17] For example, in 1925, David Starr Jordan, past chancellor of Stanford University and an ardent eugenicist, commented that "the Mexican peon, who for the most part can never be fit for citizenship . . . is giving our stock a far worse dilution than ever came from Europe."[18] As a result, these racial formations produced "alien citizens"—"Asian Americans and Mexican Americans born in the United

States with formal U.S. citizenship but who remained alien in the eyes of the nation."[19]

Such perceptions complicated debates over legalization programs for undocumented immigrants at the time. Some believed that undocumented immigrants should be allowed to legalize their status, while others wanted them deported. Not surprisingly, therefore, legalization programs in the early twentieth century were applied unevenly, reflecting hierarchies of nationality and race. At that time, hundreds of thousands of undocumented immigrants, primarily from Europe, were allowed to adjust their status to that of legal immigrants and eventually citizens. Americans viewed as unjust the deportation of ordinary immigrants with homes and families in the United States. Deportation was justifiable for criminals, but not for otherwise law-abiding immigrants who had established roots in the country. This reasoning, however, did not apply to Mexicans, who also desired to adjust their status. They were subject to a different logic that began with the premise of criminality because of their illegal entry into the nation. As Ngai observed, "By contrast [to European undocumented immigrants], walking (or wading) across the border emerged as the quintessential act of illegal immigration, the outermost point in a relativist ordering of illegal immigration."[20] The current opposition to allowing undocumented immigrants to become legal immigrants (the "pathway to citizenship") begins with the same association of illegal entry with criminality, and Mexicans are still the prototypical "illegal aliens."[21]

Also prevalent in the early twentieth century was the belief that providing immigrants with rights, even the equal protection guaranteed by the Fourteenth Amendment, diminished the value of citizenship.[22] This belief still has currency in contemporary debates over allowing undocumented immigrants access to driver's licenses and publicly funded education, medical care, and housing.[23] To some, such rights and privileges appear as rewards for illegal entry. Rather than rewarding "illegals," public opinion often declares that they should be punished and removed from the country. Thus, for some, universal access to these rights and privileges blurs the line between citizen and noncitizen and thus cheapens citizenship.

The historical lesson is that "illegality" is socially, culturally, and politically constructed.[24] As people move across ever porous national boundaries, their status is determined by policies in those nation-states, not by some essential quality inherent in the migrant's genetic code or personal philosophy of life. Policy makers, using Foucauldian techniques of governmentality, construct classifications to further bureaucratic control of populations, including, and perhaps most especially, migrants.[25] Being an unauthorized migrant, an "illegal," is a status conferred by the state, and it then becomes written upon the bodies of the migrants themselves because illegality is both produced and experienced. But illegality itself is a status resulting from political decisions made by governmental representatives who could just as well have decided to allow migrants to enter under the sanction of law, as legal immigrants, legal workers, or legal guest workers. The migrants themselves are the same people, whether deemed legal or illegal by their receptive states. What marks the illegal is the receiving state's unwillingness to recognize the conditions that create a demand for labor, most notably falling fertility rates, aging populations, and values that construe certain jobs as "immigrant jobs." As a result, a legal fiction emerges, one that recognizes that x number of migrant laborers will be attracted to most of the industrialized nations but also recognizes that politicians will respond to the fears of immigration among their constituents by allowing in far fewer legal immigrants/workers than the actual flow.[26] The surplus could have been allowed to enter legally, but instead the "illegal" entrant is constructed. The total flow, the x number of in-migrants, continues, albeit under these constructed categories of legal and illegal migration. What follows is an examination of the condition of illegality, not so much in the actual lives of "illegal aliens" but in the representations of that condition in public discourse.

INVASION, RECONQUEST, AND THE QUEBEC MODEL

Since its formation in the 1920s, the idea that Mexican undocumented immigrants are "criminals" has continued in public discourse, but in the 1970s a new trope was added: Mexican immigration as an invasion of the United States.[27] Over time, the invasion theme evolved, with the elaboration of the notions of a Mexican reconquest of the U.S. Southwest and what I call the Quebec model. In the Quebec model, the Quebecois independence movement among French-speaking Canadians is held up as an example of the threat posed by Spanish-speaking Mexican immigrants and their descendants, who supposedly maintain linguistic and socially separate lives from the rest of U.S. society. These themes are repeated so often that they become a taken-for-granted set of assumptions about the inability and unwillingness of Mexican immigrants and their children, extending for generations, to become part of society. Huntington's observations, above, are among the latest renditions of these assumptions, but as we will see, they build upon a long history of such assertions about the threat of Mexican immigration, Mexican Americans, and Latinos in general.

As legal immigration began to increase after 1965, public anxiety over un-documented immigration was also increasing. Although it was difficult to es-timate the actual numbers of unauthorized immigrants in the United States in the 1960s and 1970s, Leonard F. Chapman Jr., then-commissioner of the Immi-gration and Naturalization Service (INS), publicly announced that alarmingly high numbers (as many as ten to fifteen million or more) of "illegal aliens" were "flooding" into the country at the time.[28]

The media's display of such large numbers carries meanings apart from their mathematical references. Because it is difficult to assess the accuracy of such numbers and what they mean—for example, their relative impact in a na-tion as large as the United States—such numbers become images. They jump off the page or the television at the reader or viewer, but these numerical images are flat, in that they lack the depth of understanding that comes with historical context, economic explanations, and social science elaboration. Consequently, numbers such as these invoke simplified responses—low/high, good/bad, affirmative/alarmist, assurance/fear—depending upon the prevailing senti-ment toward immigration. An assured response to such purportedly large numbers might be that the nation's economy is doing so well that it is attract-ing and absorbing many eager new workers. However, in this case, at that time, the media's display of these numbers underscored beliefs that there were "too many" undocumented immigrants. Thus, even though these numbers turned out to be exaggerated, the authority of their source—the INS—meant that they entered public discourse as a symbol of alarm.[29]

For example, the December 1974 cover of the *American Legion Magazine* depicted the United States being overrun by "illegal aliens" (Figure 1.1). Most of the cartoon people in the image are Mexicans storming, en masse, across the U.S.-Mexico border, breaking down a sign that reads "USA BORDER" and another one reading "KEEP OUT." Other immigrants are landing by boats along the East Coast, flying in and swimming from the Caribbean, parachuting across the Canadian border, and all of them are converging upon, and inundat-ing, the nation's institutions, most notably welfare, education, housing, jobs, and medical care. Such images were to become more frequent in the nation's magazines over the next three decades, contributing to an increasingly alarmist discourse on Mexican immigration.[30]

The Quebec model first surfaced, ever so subtly, on the cover of the Decem-ber 13, 1976, issue of *U.S. News and World Report*, which featured the headline "Crisis across the Borders: Meaning to U.S." The cover illustration was a map of North America with two arrows, both beginning in the United States, one

Figure 1.1. Cover of the *American Legion* magazine, December 1974. Illustration by James Flora. © Jim Flora Art LLC. Used by permission.

pointing to Mexico and one pointing to Canada. The crisis in Mexico was the potential for increased migration to the United States. The problem in Canada was Quebec, where many French-speaking residents were pushing for greater sovereignty and even separation from the English-speaking provinces. The Quebec movement was, perhaps, particular to the Canadian context, especially the effect of the 1967 Canadian law concerning bilingualism and biculturalism put into place by Prime Minister Pierre Elliot Trudeau.[31] The particularities of the Canadian context undermine the comparison with Mexican immigration's implications for the United States, but, as we will see, the Quebec independence movement came to serve as a metaphor, or civics lesson, for the threat of national division inherent in the "Mexican problem."

The invasion theme continued to be represented in the nation's magazines for the next three decades. The April 25, 1977, issue of *U.S. News and World Report* featured the cover headline: "Border Crisis: Illegal Aliens Out of Control?" The specific "out of control" behavior was clarified in the accompanying article as Mexican immigrants' use of welfare and medical services, displacing citizens from jobs, and turning to crime, all of which threatened the economic security of the nation. The article also referred to Mexican immigrants as "invaders" and asserted that the "U.S. has lost control of its borders" (p. 33).

On January 29, 1979, the same magazine published yet another cover on the "invasion," with the headline "Illegal Aliens: Invasion Out of Control?" The magazine notes that "up to 12 million" undocumented immigrants might have been in the United States at the time and that by the year 2025 they could account for 10 percent of the population. The negative implications of undocumented immigration raised by the magazine included displacing U.S. citizens from jobs, use of welfare, and crime. But even more important was the internal threat posed by the children of immigrants, an idea that is central to the reconquest theme and the Quebec model. Labor secretary Ray Marshall was quoted as saying that illegal immigration "sows the seeds of a bitter civil-rights struggle in the 1990s by the children of today's illegal aliens" (p. 41). The magazine story asserted that the threat was magnified because "the traditions of Mexican Americans remain undiluted, refreshed daily by an influx of illegal immigrants from the mother country" (p. 42). "Undiluted traditions" was another way of saying that Mexican Americans did not assimilate into American society and culture. They remained separate and apart—so separate and apart, in fact, that there was no mixture, no dilution. Characterizing Mexican Americans as foreigners who remain foreign (undiluted) gave added urgency to the invasion metaphor of the article and the cover.

The 1980s witnessed continued repetition of the invasion theme and an elaboration of the Quebec model. *U.S. News and World Report*'s issue of March 9, 1981, featured an illustrated map of the North American continent, including Mexico. The United States was the focal point of the map, and the stars and stripes of the U.S. flag covered it. To the north was Canada, with the image of a Mountie holding the Canadian flag and a French Canadian holding the Quebec flag in one hand and raising his other hand in a defiant, closed-fisted gesture toward the Mountie. To the south was Mexico, where a line of men emerged from the mountains and walked single file toward California. The man in front had his left foot ready to step on the red and white of California, at about San Diego. The headline read "Our Troubled Neighbors—Dangers for U.S." The Quebec "problem," the magazine made clear, was a model for what was prophesied to become the Mexican "problem," a reconquest of the United States.

The reconquest theme was reiterated in the early 1980s. *Time*'s June 13, 1983, issue featured an article on Los Angeles titled "The New Ellis Island." *Time* warned its readers that "Los Angeles is being invaded" (p. 18); that "the statistical evidence of the immigrant tide is stark" (p. 19); and that there was a "staggering influx of foreign settlers" (p. 20). Immigration, according to the magazine, had caused dramatic changes in the ethnic composition of Los Angeles. But *Time* singled out Mexicans, who, because the Southwest was once part of Mexico, ar-rived "feeling as much like a migrant as an immigrant, not an illegal alien but a *reconquistador*," or reconqueror (p. 24).

The now fully elaborated triple threat of invasion, reconquest, and a Quebec-like separatist movement soon took on even greater currency in public discourse. *U.S. News and World Report*'s cover on March 7, 1983, announced: "Invasion from Mexico: It Just Keeps Growing." And in the April 1, 1985, edi-tion of the *New Republic*, House majority leader Jim Wright worried about "a Balkanization of American society into little subcultures" (p. 25). In that same issue, Richard Lamm, the ex-governor of Colorado, feared that immigration would result in "a vast cultural separatism" and that the children of Latino im-migrants would not grow up as loyal Americans but might instead lead "seces-sionist" riots in the Southwest to "express their outrage at this country" (p. 25).

The reconquest and separatist inclinations of Mexican immigrants and their offspring were also the theme of the August 19, 1985, cover of *U.S. News and World Report*, which announced: "The Disappearing Border: Will the Mex-ican Migration Create a New Nation?" The accompanying article, titled "The Disappearing Border," stated the "reconquest" theme as if it were a fact, with little need of supporting empirical evidence:

> Now sounds the march of new conquistadors in the American Southwest. The heirs of Cortés and Coronado are rising again in the land their forebears took from the Indians and lost to the Americans. By might of numbers and strength of culture, Hispanics are changing the politics, economy and language in the U.S. states that border Mexico. Their movement is, despite its quiet and largely peaceful nature, both an invasion and a revolt. At the vanguard are those born here, whose roots are generations deep, who long endured Anglo dominance and rule and who are ascending within the U.S. system to take power they consider their birthright. Behind them comes an unstoppable mass—their kin from below the border who also claim ancestral homelands in the South-west, which was the northern half of Mexico until the U.S. took it away in the mid-1800s. Like conquistadors of centuries past, they come in quest of fabled cities of gold. America's riches are pulling people all along the continent's His-panic horn on a great migration to the place they call El Norte. (p. 30)

Importantly, in the *U.S. News and World Report* narrative of invasion and re-conquest, it was not just recent Mexican immigrants who posed a threat but even those Americans who were descended from the first Spanish-speaking explorers of the Southwest. Not even 400 years of living in the Southwest, and over 150 years of that period as U.S. citizens, reduced the threat posed by Latinos (note the quote's reference to Hispanics, not Mexican Americans) in the Southwest. Apparently, according to this argument, they had remained socially and linguistically separate, biding their time for a "revolt" and takeover. In other words, the conspiracy for the reconquest of the Southwest had been in operation for generations and spanned centuries. That so far-fetched and unsupported a scenario could be seriously presented in a national magazine attests to how deeply the taken-for-granted assumptions about invasion and reconquest had, by this point, entered into public discourse. No critical perspective on the assumption of difference was put forward here, a difference so great and incommensurable that the people so designated were not even subject to the normal expectations of social and cultural change.[32] It was as if Mexican Americans and other Latinos existed in an ahistorical space apart from the life that took place all around them. They were cast as "alien-citizens," perpetual foreigners with divided allegiances despite being U.S. citizens by birth, even after many generations.[33] Such notions became an acceptable part of public discourse even among otherwise learned scholars.

Indeed, during the 1990s, the Mexican invasion and reconquest were at the heart of a veritable publishing industry that emerged, playing on the public's fears of immigration. Among the many books on the topic that have appeared since the early 1990s are Arthur M. Schlesinger Jr.'s *Disuniting of America*; Peter Brimelow's *Alien Nation*; Georgie Anne Geyer's *Americans No More*; Patrick J. Buchanan's *Death of the West: How Dying Populations and Immigrant Invasions Imperil Our Country and Civilization*; Victor Davis Hanson's *Mexifornia: A State of Becoming*; Samuel Huntington's *Who We Are: The Challenges to America's National Identity*; Tom Tancredo's *In Mortal Danger*; Jim Gilchrist and Jerome R. Corsi's *The Minutemen: The Battle to Secure America's Borders*; and Patrick Buchanan's second book on the topic, *State of Emergency: The Third World Invasion and Conquest of America*. These works often explicitly refer to the Mexican invasion, the Quebec model, and the Mexican reconquest of the U.S. Southwest.

Schlesinger's *Disuniting of America* was an important contribution to the literature on the threat of immigration to the nation. Here was the archetypical Harvard liberal intellectual raising the alarm about the social separatism caused by bilingual education, the cult of ethnicity promoted by multiculturalists, and the disintegrative effects that would occur if immigrants and their offspring did not assimilate. He also cited the example of Canada (the Quebec model) and its inability to make a federal multiethnic state work. Schlesinger's observations were not entirely novel, but they carried great weight, and his ideas were echoed in the writings of many other authors, including those mentioned below. He was also the first of three prominent professors, the others being Samuel Huntington and David Kennedy, who warned of the disuniting potential of Latin American immigrants, especially from Mexico.

In 1994 Patrick Buchanan, a nationally recognized conservative politician, expressed his deep concern that a Quebec-like threat loomed large in America's future. In an opinion article in the *Los Angeles Times*, Buchanan reasoned that sometime in the near future the majority of Americans would trace their roots not to Europe but to Africa, Asia, Latin America, the Middle East, and the Pacific islands.[34] He thus asked: What would it mean for "America" if, for example, South Texas and Southern California became almost exclusively Latino? He provided the following answer: "Each will have tens of millions of people whose linguistic, historic and cultural roots are in Mexico," and thus, "like Eastern Ukraine, where 10 million Russian-speaking 'Ukrainians' now look impatiently to Moscow, not Kiev, as their cultural capital, America could see, in a decade, demands for Quebec-like status for Southern California."[35] For Buchanan, Latino immigrants and their children posed the risk of a separatist movement, which would very likely seek to take over U.S. territory and return it to Mexico's control.

In *Alien Nation*, Peter Brimelow argued that Hispanics were particularly troublesome, going so far as to claim that they were "symptomatic of the American Anti-Idea," an idea that is neither defined nor clarified.[36] But Brimelow leaves no doubt what he means: "Symptomatic of the American Anti-Idea is the emergence of a strange anti-nation inside the U.S.—the so-called 'Hispanics.'" The growth of an anti-nation inside the nation is a way of retelling the threat characterized by the Quebec model. In this case, in addition to Hispanic population growth, Brimelow asserted that the various groups of people lumped together as "Hispanics" had, in effect, an artificial identity because of their differences. But because U.S. government agencies treated them as a homogenous "protected class" and encouraged bilingualism and the teaching of Spanish, Hispanics were now much less encouraged to assimilate to American culture. "In effect," Brimelow noted, "Spanish-speakers are still being encouraged to assimilate. But not to America."[37]

In *Americans No More*, Georgie Anne Geyer argued that excessive immigration, especially unauthorized immigration, and the rights accorded immigrants were diluting the meaning of U.S. citizenship. Mexicans, in particular, posed a threat to California, and thus the nation, because their "high" birth rates were changing the demographic and political landscape. Geyer worried that "illegal aliens, with no commitment to the country and no respect for its common principles," were forming "their own political power groups to challenge the old citizens' America."[38] In her version of events, reconquest through reproduction would lead to disastrous demographic and political changes: "By the end of the 20th century, America itself had changed—it was in danger of drifting toward becoming a Third World nation, and crucially important parts of it, like once-glorious California, were actually moving backwards in time and backwards in development."[39]

In November 1996 the eminent Stanford historian David M. Kennedy wrote in the *Atlantic Monthly* about the Quebec model and "the Reconquista."[40] Despite the seeming interdependence between Mexico and the United States, Kennedy argued that Mexican immigration did not follow the pattern of pluralism supposedly exhibited by European immigrants. Mexicans were from a single cultural, linguistic, religious, and national source, and they concentrated in one geographical region, the Southwest. The United States, according to Kennedy, had had no experience comparable to this regional concentration of Mexican Americans. According to Kennedy, the possibilities of this trend were that Mexican Americans could, if they chose to do so, "preserve their distinctive culture indefinitely":

> They can challenge the existing cultural, political, legal, commercial, and educational systems to change fundamentally not only the language but also the very institutions in which they do business. . . . In the process, Americans could be pitched into a soul-searching redefinition of fundamental ideas such as the meaning of citizenship and national identity. . . . If we seek historical guidance, the closest example we have at hand is in the diagonally opposite corner of the North American continent, in Quebec. The possibility looms, that in the next generation or so we will see a kind of Chicano Quebec take shape in the American Southwest, as a group emerges with strong cultural cohesiveness and sufficient economic and political strength to insist on changes in the overall society's ways of organizing itself and conducting its affairs.[41]

By using the word "Chicano," Kennedy was expanding the threat to include U.S.-born Mexican Americans, who, in this scenario, would maintain a distinctive culture and language "indefinitely." The heretical idea that U.S.-born Chicanos were steeped in U.S. culture and spoke English was not a part of the scenario—otherwise where would be the threat? Kennedy simply assumed that U.S.-born Chicanos had so little social, cultural, political, or economic capital in U.S. society that they would want to form a separate country. Otherwise, if these "truths" were not self-evident, proof of a reconquest conspiracy and proof of Latino unwillingness to integrate socially and culturally would have to be provided in no uncertain detail. But because these taken-for-granted truths were self-evident, merely invoking the Quebec example served as ample evidence that a certifiable Latino threat existed.

Douglas S. Massey and Karen A. Pren also found an increase in alarmist rhetoric and imagery in their analysis of the *New York Times*, *Washington Post*, *Wall Street Journal*, and *Los Angeles Times* between 1965 and 1995. They searched for the words "undocumented," "illegal," or "unauthorized" paired with "Mexico" or "Mexican immigrants" and the words "crisis," "flood," or "invasion." Massey and Pren found that "the use of the negative metaphors to describe Mexican immigration was virtually nonexistent in 1965, at least in major newspapers, but thereafter rose steadily, slowly at first and then rapidly during the 1970s to reach a peak in the late 1970s, roughly at the same time illegal migration itself peaked."[42] They attributed the increase in negative rhetoric to politicians, who discovered the advantages of raising fears about Latino immigrants and illegal immigration, and to the media's realization of how much could be gained through continued use of verbal and visual images of the border under siege.

It must be noted that not all public discourse on immigration was alarmist, especially during the latter half of the 1990s, which experienced an economic boom. With low unemployment rates and significant job growth, suddenly immigrant labor was in demand. It was as if Ross Perot's warning of a "giant sucking sound" finally took place, except the jobs created were in the United States and not in Mexico, as he predicted would occur as a result of the North American Free Trade Agreement of 1994. So many undocumented workers were drawn to jobs in the United States that about 8.8 million were estimated to be there in 2000 and 10.3 million in 2004.[43] Moreover, the expanding economy created a hyper-demand for immigrant labor that pulled Mexican immigrants to ever more "exotic" locations in the Midwest and the southeastern United States, including North Carolina, Tennessee, Mississippi, Arkansas, and Georgia.[44] It was also perhaps due to economic expansion and the need for immigrant labor that alarmist public discourse was superseded, if only for a few years, by more moderate views on immigration. George Will, in *Newsweek*, argued that today's immigrants, including Mexicans, were no different from Italians and other earlier waves of immigrants.[45] The AFL-CIO suddenly changed its policy to one that favored legalizing and unionizing undocumented immigrants.[46] Federal Reserve chairman Alan Greenspan noted that immigrants were good for the economy.[47] And George W. Bush, shortly after assuming the presidency in 2001, put forward an ambitious immigration reform plan that would have legalized Mexican undocumented immigrants and created a new guest worker program for Mexican workers.[48] Negative reactions to Bush's proposals dredged up the reconquest theme, as evidenced by a cartoon of the U.S. president with Mexico's president, Vicente Fox (Figure 1.2).

Time magazine's June 11, 2001, cover image illustrated just how subtly the idea of reconquest, or a Mexican takeover of the United States, could be evoked (Figure 1.3). Here were two smiling Latino children dressed like American children anywhere might be dressed. Although the image of the children might have evoked a sense of pleasantness, the text raised an alarm about Mexican immigration: "Welcome to Amexica: The border is vanishing before our eyes, creating a new world for all of us." Because the term *Amexica*, made up by

Figure 1.2. Cartoon of George W. Bush and Mexican president Vicente Fox, in response to Bush's immigration reform proposals, by Rick Tuma. Courtesy of CNSNews.com.

Figure 1.3. Cover of *Time*, June 11, 2001. © 2007 Time Inc. Reprinted courtesy of the editors of Time Magazine.

blending parts of the words *America* and *Mexico*, was framed by the "vanishing border" statement, it was Mexico that was intruding on America, slowly taking it over or obliterating it. Colors were used to reinforce the message; the letters are in red, white, and blue, except the *C*, which is in green, a key color of the Mexican flag. Suddenly the rather pleasant-looking children were revealed as part of a reconquest of America, which was occurring because the "vanishing border" was letting them, and others like them, into the country, thereby creating a "new world."

POST-9/11 AMERICA

In the wake of the tragedy of September 11, 2001, the U.S.-Mexico border became associated with a new threat, the gateway through which possible terrorists might enter.[49] On January 25, 2002, President Bush released a statement from the White House, *Securing America's Borders Fact Sheet: Border Security*: "America requires a border management system that keeps pace with expanding trade while protecting the United States and its territories from threats of terrorist attack, illegal immigration, illegal drugs, and other contraband." *Time* magazine's cover for September 20, 2004, showed the U.S. flag being torn apart by two light-brown hands. The text stated: "Special Investigation—America's Border: Even after 9/11, it's outrageously easy to sneak in." In this image, the flag represented both the fabric of the nation, which was being torn apart, and the border between safety and terrorists trying to enter the country. The implicit message was that this shredding of the nation's border and the flag must be stopped.

The new threat of terrorism resulted in calls for controlling the border as a means of improving homeland security. As Mark Krikorian, executive director of the Center for Immigration Studies, put it: "Blocking the enemy's ability to enter our country must be a central objective of homeland security."[50] That none of the terrorists involved in the 9/11 carnage crossed the U.S.-Mexico border illegally was beside the point. Post-9/11 concerns with "the terrorist threat" and national security resulted in greatly increased funding for border surveillance and control, including passage of a bill to build a seven-hundred-mile fence along the U.S.-Mexico border. Despite the added urgency of the new terrorist threat, the old triple threat posed by Mexican immigration has continued to play a key role in public discourse on immigration after 9/11.

Not long after 9/11, Patrick J. Buchanan's book *The Death of the West* was published. The book's subtitle laid bare the author's perspective: *How Dying Populations and Immigrant Invasions Imperil Our Country and Civilization.* In a chapter titled "La Reconquista," Buchanan continued arguments he had published in the *Los Angeles Times* almost a decade earlier. Not only was the Mexican population in the United States growing rapidly, but there was also the problem of assimilation: "Mexicans not only come from another culture, but millions are of another race. History and experience teach us that different races are far more difficult to assimilate" (p. 125). So this "Mexican race" had difficulty assimilating for reasons that were biological, what Buchanan perceived as their inherent difference. This racial problem was different from a supposed lack of desire to assimilate, which was cultural. But Buchanan added this to the mix as well:

Unlike the immigrants of old . . . [m]illions of [Mexicans] have no desire to learn English or to become citizens. America is not their home; Mexico is; and they wish to remain proud Mexicans. They have come here to work. Rather than assimilate, they create Little Tijuanas in U.S. cities. . . . With their own radio and TV stations, newspapers, films, and magazines, the Mexican Americans are creating an Hispanic culture separate and apart from America's larger culture. They are becoming a nation within a nation. (pp. 125–26)

Notice how quickly and easily Buchanan's focus on immigrants had expanded to include their children, and even later generations of Mexican Americans, who were creating a separate culture and nation. A few pages later, Buchanan put forward the Quebec model as the "predictable" future of California: "America's largest state is on its way to becoming a predominantly Third World state. No one knows how this will play out, but California could become another Quebec, with demands for formal recognition of its separate and unique Hispanic culture and identity" (p. 140).

Victor Davis Hanson published *Mexifornia: A State of Becoming* in 2003. Hanson, a fifth-generation Californian from a farming family, lamented for times gone by, for the good old days when "the offspring of Selma's immigrant farmers learned English, they intermarried, and within a generation they knew nothing of the old country and little of the old language":

> Now Selma is an edge city on the freeway of somewhere near twenty thousand anonymous souls, and is expanding at an unclenched pace, almost entirely because of massive and mostly illegal immigration from a single country: Mexico. . . . I was deeply attached to the old town, now vanished. It was by no means perfect, but it was a society of laws and customs, not a frontier town like the current one, in which thousands reside illegally, have no lawful documentation, and assume that Selma must adapt to their ways, not the reverse. (p. 2)

Hanson found that in America today schools were not interested in assimilating immigrants and their children. He deplored the "identity politics" of Chicano studies programs. He believed that the children of Mexican immigrants lacked an interest in becoming part of U.S. society, which led to their dropping out of school, becoming gang members, and causing problems. Compounding the problem, as Hanson saw it, was that Mexican immigrant families adhered to a culture that stressed having many children.

Both Hanson and Buchanan pointed to the cultural politics of Chicano studies programs and professors and to the student organization MEChA (Movimiento Estudiantil Chicano de Aztlán), a college student organization, for perpetuating an ideology that claims the U.S. Southwest as Aztlán, the mythical homeland of the Aztecs. This so-called ideology of Aztlán became fused with the Quebec model in public discourse surrounding the 2003 race for governor of California. Cruz Bustamante, the lieutenant governor, ran against actor Arnold Schwarzenegger and Schwarzenegger won. One of the key issues raised about Bustamante was his participation in MEChA when he was an

undergraduate student.[51] Opponents characterized MEChA, and thus Bustamante by association, as an organization that advocated the Chicano takeover
of the American Southwest because it was once Aztlán and thus rightfully
theirs.[52] An image that appeared on the September 5–11, 2003, cover of the *OC
Weekly*, published in California's Orange County, satirically represented Bustamante as an Aztec warrior, a representation the magazine was critiquing, not
advocating. The illustration had Bustamante wearing an eagle headdress complete with large feathers and large Aztec earplugs, as he stared off into space.
The text read: "Fear of a Brown Planet: Cruz Bustamante Rises, Conservatives
Freak Out." Thus, Cruz Bustamante, despite his protestations, had become an
Aztec warrior, a separatist, a member of the "Brown Klan," and a militant intent
on "reconquering" the American Southwest.

   Business Week's March 15, 2004, issue raised the possibility that a separate
Hispanic nation might emerge within the United States. The bold headline
on the issue's cover visibly shouted "Hispanic Nation," followed by "Hispanics
are an immigrant group like no other. Their huge numbers are changing old
ideas about assimilation. Is America ready?" (Figure 1.4). Also included on the
cover was a photograph of a Latino family that stood in ironic opposition to

Figure 1.4. Cover of March 15, 2004, edition of *Business Week*. Reprinted by permission.
Copyright 2004 by The McGraw-Hill Companies.

the cover's text; the family's dress suggested that they were solidly middle class and the caption noted that they lived in Cicero, Illinois, outside the traditional areas of concentration for the Latino population—California, Texas, Florida, and New York.

Despite this visual incongruity, the cover's text represented the Latino population as unique in contrast to other immigrant groups, who did not form separate independent nations in the United States and for whom assimilation was, supposedly, a smooth and linear process. Assimilation for other immigrant groups, historically and today, has been set up as a banner example of the "old ideas about assimilation." We can only assume that the Hispanics that were the subject of *Business Week*'s 2004 cover were changing these old ideas in ways that reflected not assimilation but rather the social, cultural, and linguistic separatism that would result in a separate nation. In other words, *Business Week* offered yet another rendition of the Quebec model.

That same year, Samuel Huntington published *Who We Are: Challenges to America's National Identity*, which focused on the threat of Mexican immigration. He repeated the problems with Mexican immigration found in the quotes at the beginning of this chapter. He spoke of a Mexican *reconquista*, a blurring of the border between Mexico and the United States, and the problem of a blending of cultures (p. 221). This was happening, according to Huntington, because "Mexican immigrants and their progeny have not assimilated into American society as other immigrants did in the past and as many other immigrants are doing now" (p. 222). He asserted that the areas where Mexican immigrants and their children were not assimilating were in use of English, educational attainment, occupation and incomes, and intermarriage, adding: "If this trend continues, it could produce a consolidation of the Mexican-dominant areas into an autonomous, culturally and linguistically distinct, economically self-reliant bloc within the United States" (p. 247). In short, as in the Quebec model, the *reconquista* would lead to the formation of a separate nation (p. 230).

Appearing in 2006 was Patrick J. Buchanan's second book on the topic, *State of Emergency: The Third World Invasion and Conquest of America*. With chapters titled "The Invasion," "The Aztlán Plot," and "The Return to Tribalism," Buchanan's message that a Mexican invasion was taking place was apparent. Speaking of the *reconquista*, however, Buchanan added a novel twist of transnational conspiracy to the retelling: for over a decade Mexico and its president, Vicente Fox, had pursued a strategy that "aims directly at a reannexation of the Southwest, not militarily, but ethnically, linguistically, and culturally, through transfer of millions of Mexicans into the United States and a migration of 'Anglos' out of the lands Mexico lost in 1848" (p. 125). Buchanan noted, "In California, the project is well advanced. As native-born Californians depart, Hispanics move toward dominance. As Mexicans come in the millions—one in six is already here—they are urged to seek U.S. citizenship to advance the agenda of the mother country" (p. 125). Later, he explained a bit more about how the takeover would occur: "*La Reconquista* is not to be accomplished by force of arms, as was the U.S. annexation of the Southwest and California in 1848. It is to be carried out by a nonviolent invasion and cultural transformation of that huge slice of America into a Mexamerican borderland" (p. 132).

Also in 2006, Jim Gilchrist, the founder of the Minuteman Project, and Jerome R. Corsi published *Minutemen: The Battle to Secure America's Borders*. Although the book was as much about Jim Gilchrist and the Minuteman Project as it was about undocumented immigration, it reiterated the Mexican invasion theme in a chapter titled "The Trojan Horse Invasion," and the reconquest theme in a chapter titled "The *Reconquista* Movement: Mexico's Plan for the American Southwest."

On May 11, 2010, Arizona governor Jan Brewer signed the state's law on ethnic studies, known as HB 2281. The law reflects the perceived threat of Latinos and their alleged *reconquista* of the U.S. Southwest. As the law states, "A school district or charter school in this state shall not include in its program of instruction any courses or classes that include any of the following: 1. Promote the overthrow of the United States government."[53] Anti-immigrant proponents such as John Huppenthal, Arizona's superintendent of public instruction, decided that Mexican American studies programs in Arizona's high schools promoted a takeover of the United States despite the lack of evidence supporting such a claim. According to the *Los Angeles Times*, a report undertaken by Huppenthal's own office actually found no such evidence but did find that the classes promoted ethnic and racial tolerance and increased positive school performance.[54] Nevertheless, the pervasiveness and taken-for-granted assumptions of the Latino Threat Narrative overwhelmed opposition to the school board's actions.

In 2011, Patrick J. Buchanan published his third book warning of America's impending doom: *Suicide of a Superpower: Will America Survive to 2025?* Buchanan notes that recent Mexican presidents have declared that the Mexican nation (people) extends into the United States (pp. 138–39). He also sees evidence of a conspiracy to take over the United States in Mexico's dual nationality laws. He claims Mexico is constructing a Mexican nation inside the United States, where U.S. citizens of Mexican birth and ancestry place loyalty to Mexico before allegiance to the United States (p. 138). Buchanan then returns to his oft-stated point: "Not only is our melting pot cracked, it has been repudiated in favor of multiculturalism. Immigrants are urged to keep their language, customs, traditions, culture, and national identity. And the largest cohort comes from a country, Mexico" (p. 142). The problem with Buchanan's ad hominen argument about the threat to the nation posed even by citizen Latinos is that there is no evidence to support their alleged lack of allegiance to the United States nor information on changing language use and related cultural behaviors.

In May 2012, the U.S. Justice Department sued Sheriff Joe Arpaio of Maricopa County in Arizona for "racially profiling Latinos, abusing them in his jails and retaliating against his critics."[55] These alleged unconstitutional behaviors on Sheriff Arpaio's part were directed against Latino citizens and immigrants alike. Arpaio has achieved a level of notoriety rarely bestowed on a county sheriff. But for Sheriff Joe, being hailed as "America's Toughest Sheriff" harkens back to the exploits of earlier western lawmen, such as Wyatt Earp, Bat Masterson, and Pat Garrett. Why is the sheriff so tough on Latinos? His 2008 book (co-authored by Len Sherman), *Joe's Law: America's Toughest Sheriff Takes on Illegal Immigration, Drugs, and Everything Else That Threatens America,* offers a clue. Latinos threaten America, he writes, because they are not like his own Italian immigrant parents, who did not view America as somehow once belonging to Italy. For Latinos: "A growing movement among not only Mexican nationals but also some Mexican-Americans contends that the United States stole the territory that is now California, Arizona, and Texas, for a start, and that massive immigration over the border will speed and guarantee the *reconquista* of these lands, returning them to Mexico" (p. 48).

THE LATINO THREAT NARRATIVE AS DISCOURSE

Perhaps it is only by becoming aware of the mind-numbing repetition glimpsed in the examples above that we can get a true sense of the degree to which the narratives of invasion, reconquest, and the Quebec model have become taken-for-granted assumptions about the threat posed by Mexican immigrants, by Mexican Americans with multiple generations in the United States, and at times by all Latinos. Although more could have been included, those presented above are enough to demonstrate that the pattern has been established. The discourse of these pundits, authors, and scholars is unified in its representations of

Latinos, especially Mexican immigrants and their descendants, as people who will not and cannot become part of U.S. society. The Latino Threat Narrative, as a discourse, is an example of Michel Foucault's notions of knowledge and power. The objects of this discourse are represented as the Other and as a "threat" and "danger" to the nation through such simple binaries as citizen/ foreigner, real Americans / "Mexicans" or real Americans / "Hispanics," natives/ enemies, us/them, and legitimate/illegal. Once constructed in this way, Mexican and other Latin American immigrants, and even U.S.-born Latinos, can then be represented as "space invaders"—as Nirmal Puwar has put it—whose reproduction, both social and biological, threatens to destroy the nation's identity.[56]

What I am getting at might better be understood in relation to Antonio Gramsci's notions of hegemony and common sense.[57] Hegemony is the system of values, attitudes, morality, and other beliefs that passively or actively support the established order and thus the class interests that dominate it. Common sense is the largely unconscious and uncritical way of perceiving the world that is widespread in any given historical epoch. Common sense incorporates within it the prevailing consciousness, or hegemony, that is largely internalized and taken for granted by members of society.

The Latino Threat Narrative works so well and is so pervasive precisely because its basic premises are taken for granted as true. In this narrative, Latinos, whether immigrant or U.S.-born, are a homogenous population that somehow stands apart from normal processes of historical change. They are immutable and impervious to the influences of the larger society and thus are not characterized as experiencing social and cultural change. They are uneducated, monolingual Spanish speakers, segregated into ethnic enclaves. Because they lead separate social and linguistic lives, one must assume that they marry only their own kind. They are locked into Catholic doctrine, leading to high fertility rates. In this narrative, Latinos, especially Mexican immigrants and their children, are seldom represented as agents of positive change, because their unwillingness to integrate denies them the opportunity to influence the larger society in any appreciable way, except in the negative—as a threat to existing institutions (e.g., education, social services, medical). In other words, the Latino Threat Narrative posits a neo-evolutionary scenario but in reverse, the devolution of society. Because of these characteristics, Latinos, especially those of Mexican origin, are said to be outside the practices of citizenship/subject-making and incapable of feelings of belonging.[58] In this way, the Latino Threat Narrative constructs distinctions between citizens and noncitizens, elaborating a segmented citizenship in which some members of society are valued above others. Such differences, once constructed and normalized, rationalize and justify governmental practices and policies that stigmatize and punish certain categories of immigrants and their children.

The discursive construction of Mexican immigrants and their children, and often of Latinos in general, resonates with anthropologist Mary Douglas's insights into the cultural constructions of *Purity and Danger*. She argues that culture classifies things and people into categories that make order out of an otherwise chaotic existence. When something or someone is "out of place," it or they are often considered dangerous, as pollution, threatening the purity of those in place—that is, in their "proper" category. Mexicans in the United States are constructed in the discourse examined here as people out of place and thus as a threat to the nation in which they reside. Put another way, one that Benedict Anderson might agree with, the Latino Threat Narrative does not imagine Latinos, whether immigrants or U.S.-born, as part of the national community.[59] When they do enter into the social imaginary, however, it is as an internal threat to the larger community.

Through news stories, TV and radio talk shows, movies, and more, the media construct social imaginaries, the implicit understandings that form collective subjectivities and make common practices possible.[60] Social imaginaries, argues Edward LiPuma, exist by virtue of representations and provide the taken-for-granted assumptions about identities (e.g., citizens, immigrants, consumers) and belonging in the world. For people immersed in these social imaginaries "there appear to be no genuine alternatives," for "modern agents have increasingly come to imagine these imaginaries as the unquestionably real and natural ground for acting in the world."[61]

The Latino Threat Narrative is a social imaginary in which Latinos are "virtual characters." They exist as "illegal aliens," "illegitimate recipients of organ donations," "highly fertile invaders," and "unassimilable separatists bent on a reconquest of the U.S. Southwest." Their lives are part of a virtual reality, one that is not necessarily tied to empirical evidence. Learning what we know about immigrants indirectly through the media is what anthropologists Daniel Miller and James G. Carrier call virtualism.[62] Virtualism is a critique of contemporary capitalist society and the problems that result when virtual reality is perceived as reality and then we attempt to make the world conform to that virtual vision.[63] We learn about the Latino threat through the media, but the actual lives of Latinos, whether immigrants or U.S.-born, may not correspond to those constructed, virtual lives. And yet anti-immigrant sentiment and immigration laws are in many ways a response to what we think we know about the Latino threat based on the virtual lives with which we are familiar.

The virtual lives of "Mexicans," "Chicanos," "illegal aliens," and "immigrants" become abstractions and representations that stand in the place of real lives. Rather than actual lives, virtual lives are generalized, iconic, and typified and are turned into statistical means. They are aggregate figures melded into cost-benefit analyses. They are no longer flesh-and-blood people; they exist as images. Because of this, a "global card trick" occurs between virtual personas and real-life personas.[64] The virtual personas of Latino immigrants—represented as a threat to the nation—make the authority that has accumulated for real immigrants in their role as workers and consumers vanish. The positive contributions of Latino immigrants often disappear in public discourse by means of this card trick. Through their very visible marches and demonstrations, immigrants have attempted to subvert the taken-for-granted truths accorded to virtual immigrants and to assert what they believe are their very real, material contributions to society.

As we make this critique of modern culture, we must always keep in mind that real immigrants do exist. Undocumented immigrants have lives. Immigrants and their children eat, breathe, and dream in cities and towns across America. How their actual lives "live up to" their virtual lives as represented in the Latino Threat Narrative is the subject of the next chapter.

2 CULTURAL CONTRADICTIONS OF CITIZENSHIP AND BELONGING

AS THE PRECEDING CHAPTER TESTIFIES, Latino immigrants and their children constantly find themselves the object of a discourse in which they are represented as a threat and a danger to the nation. This discourse defines them as outside the practices of citizenship/subject-making and feelings of belonging. But do the objects of this discourse internalize these representations? What are the lives of Latino immigrants and their children like across generations in the United States? Do legal status and citizenship make a difference in their lives? Do their lives resemble the way in which the Latino Threat Narrative represents them? These questions guide this chapter. Let us begin with three cases.[1]

ROCÍO'S CASE

I interviewed Rocío in 2003, when she was 22 years old. She had come with her parents from Argentina to the United States when she was 9 years old. Although she is now a legal resident of the United States, she had only had this status for about two years at the time of the interview and was entering her senior year of university. Her case reflects the obstacles to mobility faced by undocumented immigrants who arrived as young children, and their perseverance and determination for mobility despite these obstacles. Throughout high school, Rocío focused on academics, but at the same time she realized that her immigration status would make going to college difficult. As an undocumented immigrant, she would have to pay foreign-student tuition to attend a college or university in the United States, thousands of dollars above in-state tuition. As she said, "I just felt very impotent. I felt like, 'Oh, my God. What was I going to do?' I wanted to study. That's when I started realizing my legal status affected my life. I wanted to study, but it was limiting my goals." Rather than attend California State University, which she was scholastically prepared to do, she went to a junior college as a cheaper alternative, hoping to buy time for acquiring permanent residency status or perhaps for seeing a change in the law concerning tuition and undocumented students.

Rocío and her parents had made strategic decisions over the years that influenced their mobility along various dimensions. For example, her parents decided to move from one part of Anaheim to another so that she could attend a "better" school. As she said, "We used to live in another part of Anaheim, east of Lincoln, lots more crime, so my parents didn't want us to go to high school there. So they did what they could to move us into an area that is a little better."

Rocío's father also managed to acquire legal residence status. This allowed him to get a better-paying job as an interpreter with a local department of education. He worked in construction when he first came to the United States and then became a community worker. Although his position as an interpreter was a "good" job from the standpoint of benefits, it was less than secure. When the economy took a downturn in California, he lost his job. Rocío's mother, however, was able to support the family through her entrepreneurial work. She hires and manages employees who provide housecleaning services.

Rocío's educational mobility was aided by her father's legalization because she was then able to apply for legal residency, which she acquired while in college. Also, changes were made in California's law regarding undocumented students: Assembly Bill (AB) 540 allows undocumented students like Rocío to qualify for in-state tuition, though not for financial aid. Rocío graduated from a University of California campus and pursued postgraduate education as well.

JUAN'S CASE

Twenty-two years old at the time of his interview, Juan had moved with his family from Puerto Vallarta, Mexico, to California when he was 7 years old, crossing the border clandestinely with his mother and older siblings. He is the youngest of nine children, four of whom live in the United States. Only an older, unmarried sister is a legal resident (she has not, however, helped any of her family members to naturalize). Shortly after moving to the United States, Juan's mother married a man who is also unauthorized. Without papers or any formal education, she has worked as a babysitter, earning little money. Steady income and affordable housing have always been an issue for the family.

Juan's educational career began to go off track when he was kicked out of high school and the entire school district during his sophomore year, for excessive truancy and troubles with drugs. Although he did not graduate from high school, he earned his general equivalency diploma (GED) at Taller San Jose, a community outreach program in Santa Ana, California, a few years later and took classes at Santa Ana College. Juan lived on his own since he was 19, after his family was evicted from an apartment in Anaheim. Rather than burden his mother any longer, Juan moved into a small room in the back of someone's house, for which he paid $200 a month at the time of the interview.

Juan's economic mobility was hampered by his immigration status and his criminal record. In addition to his unauthorized status, Juan served a three-year probation for attempted robbery, for which he also served jail time. He had two part-time jobs, one doing clerical work for an anger management program and the other setting up carnival rides for events on weekends. He made $8 an hour with his weekend job and less than that in the clerical job. The two jobs added up to less than full-time work and were not steady. The income from his weekend job provided Juan enough money for rent, but not much more. His meager earnings were, however, more than his mother ever made.

Juan worked using someone else's Social Security number but was fearful of being caught. At the time of the interview, Juan had just received a letter from the Internal Revenue Service, stating that his Social Security number did not match the name he was using. He was fearful that his employer at his clerical job would learn of his problem with the IRS. Besides being scared, Juan was frustrated and angry about his status and felt that he did not have any freedom. He could not drive because he could not get a California driver's license, and he could not get financial aid to further his education.

.   .   .

As Rocío and Juan's vignettes suggest, experiences of social integration vary. Rocío faced major obstacles to integration (low income, unauthorized status) but had enough resources to begin to overcome them (family support, a means to acquire legal residency). Juan also faced obstacles (low income, unauthorized status, criminal record). His resources (social, cultural, and economic capital), however, were not as helpful as Rocío's. Juan faced major obstacles to social integration and economic mobility. Rather than giving up, however, he constantly struggled to improve his situation. He was not as fortunate as Rocío, in that he had not found a way to legalize his immigration status, which would remove one of the major intervening factors influencing his economic mobility. Nor did he seem to have a social support system to help him improve his chances for social mobility and acquire the privileges of citizenship. Moreover, his criminal record constituted another obstacle that will take time and a great deal of effort to overcome. Juan's story is one of arrested social integration and economic mobility, but it was and still is hard to predict his future. He was still relatively young and taking steps to improve his skills and raise his education level, and he might even become eligible to become a legal resident in any future change to the nation's immigration laws.

CARLOS'S CASE

Carlos's case suggests the dramatic and often poignant ways in which governmental policies can affect members within the same family differently because of varying immigration and citizen statuses.[2] Carlos was 26 years old at the time of his interview and came to the United States when he was 6. Although born in Guatemala, he has spent most of his life in the United States, speaks English well, and is culturally integrated into American life. However, Carlos came to the United States as an unauthorized immigrant, joining his mother, who had left for the States when Carlos was a year old. Carlos's brother, age 24, was born in the United States. Even though both Carlos and his brother shared some of the same obstacles, their different citizenship status has resulted in inequalities in opportunity and mobility.

Carlos's mother is now a legal resident of the United States, but she was unauthorized for most of Carlos's childhood. Because of her status, she worked long hours cleaning houses. Carlos spent very little time with his mother, with whom his relationship became antagonistic. He came to resent her, leading him to turn to the streets for social relationships, where he became involved in using and selling drugs. He dropped out of high school his senior year.

Carlos had yet to gain legal residency status, although he had initiated the process for acquiring it. He had trouble finding steady employment and was out of work. He frequently found temporary jobs. Carlos used many different aliases in order to get jobs, cash checks, and even obtain a driver's license. He did not own a car. He lived in a trailer park, where he rented a room from a woman with two children.

Carlos's brother has had the benefit of U.S. citizenship from birth. He went to junior college and then a California state university. His work involved data entry, but he had earned a teaching credential and was looking for work as a teacher. Carlos referred to his brother as his inspiration. Speaking of his brother and his own future, Carlos noted, "He is very smart. He's a fast learner. I think it's going to be hard for me. . . . I'd like to go to college. But right now, I want to focus on this [finishing his GED]. I want to be realistic. I would like to have the capability of. . . . For example, I see many kids that went to college, but they had supportive families. I want to take it to the extent that I can. But at the same time, I am not going to give up!"

The experiences of Carlos and his brother demonstrate that, even within a family, inequalities of opportunity can exist, especially between siblings who are U.S. citizens and those who are undocumented. Carlos's case reflects how hard it can be for undocumented family members to overcome such obstacles. Carlos struggles to achieve even a modicum of educational mobility, and he is only marginally integrated into the labor market. On the other hand, his brother, not having to carry the social stigma of being "illegal" nor being closed off from the resources and benefits of citizenship, has achieved educational mobility and experienced economic mobility.

.   .   .

Latino immigrants and their children are struggling to gain a foothold in American society in the face of government policies that make their lives exceedingly difficult. Their immigration status or that of their parents makes getting an education, a job, a driver's license, or medical care both a daily effort and something that requires the development of long-term strategies. The privileges of citizenship are not easy to come by, but such privileges are neither renounced nor undesired.

Rocío, Juan, and Carlos are struggling to become part of the larger society. If they find it difficult to gain a modicum of security, upward mobility, and social integration, the fault is not entirely their own. The deck is stacked against them. And yet they persevere and evaluate what they can do to obtain the keys to successful participation in society, such as a GED, a high school diploma, or a college degree. At the same time, they are aware of the odds against them for successfully achieving their goals.

It is important to note that these young, disadvantaged Latinos did not offer evidence of a takeover of the United States, a desire to reconquer California to return it to Mexico, or any of the other imagined fears presented in the Latino Threat Narrative. Although their presence alone is enough to cause some to raise an alarm, they themselves are too busy trying to make it in a society that has constructed the rules of the game against them. And yet they are fully aware of the simple binaries that construct and constrain their lives. They know that if they are not legal immigrants, they are not citizens, not legitimate, and thus not worthy, in society's view, of a driver's license or financial aid for school. Many live at the juridical border between citizens and noncitizens. These hard realities are clear to them, especially to those for whom the privileges of citizenship are embodied in a U.S.-born sibling. In stark relief are the privileges and opportunities enjoyed by the citizen-sibling that Carlos both envies and strives to emulate.

LATINOS: STATIC LIVES OR AGENTS OF SOCIAL AND CULTURAL CHANGE?

This chapter challenges the basic premises of the Latino Threat Narrative that are so pervasive in the discourse about Latino immigrants and their offspring. If we are to believe this discourse:

Latinos are a reproductive threat, altering the demographic makeup of the nation.

Latinos are unable or unwilling to learn English.

Latinos are unable or unwilling to integrate into the larger society; they live apart from the larger society, not integrating socially.

Latinos are unchanging and immutable; they are not subject to history and the transforming social forces around them; they reproduce their own cultural world.

Latinos, especially Americans of Mexican origin, are part of a conspiracy to reconquer the southwestern United States, returning the land to Mexico's control. This is why they remain apart and unintegrated into the larger society.

The Latina reproductive threat is examined in Chapters 3 and 4. This chapter explores the other politically charged and historically constructed elements of the Latino Threat Narrative by drawing on survey data I collected in 2006 in Orange County, California.[3]

Orange County is the third most populous county in California, with an estimated 302,048 inhabitants in 2005.[4] It covers an area of 789 square miles, is largely urban, and contains 34 cities and numerous unincorporated communities. Latinos accounted for 32.5 percent of the county's population in 2005. Most Latinos are of Mexican heritage, but Latino immigrants from other nations in

Table 2.1. Respondents in CRLGS Orange County survey, 2006

	Males		Females		Total	
Interviewees	N	%	N	%	N	%
Mexican immigrants	215	41.5	282	41.3	497	41.4
Salvadoran immigrants	7	1.4	12	1.8	19	1.6
Other Central American immigrants	17	3.3	15	2.2	32	2.7
Other Latin American immigrants	9	1.7	14	2.0	23	1.9
Other foreign-born Latinos	2	0.4	0	0	2	0.2
U.S.-born of Mexican descent	95	18.3	90	13.2	185	15.4
Other U.S.-born Latinos	21	4.1	26	3.8	47	3.9
Whites	152	29.3	244	35.7	396	32.9
Total	518	100	683	100	1201	100

NOTE: CRLGS = Center for Research on Latinos in a Global Society.

Latin America, particularly Central America, also live in the county. Latinos are found in greater concentrations in the northern half of the county, which includes Santa Ana, where about 80 percent of the residents are Latino. The southern half of the county has been an area of rapid growth in new middle-class, upper-middle-class, and exclusive residential communities. Latino immigrants often work in south county communities but find less expensive housing in the many working-class communities in the northern part of the county. Of the 805 Latinos surveyed, most were Mexican immigrants or of Mexican origin (Table 2.1). There were, however, Salvadoran and other Central American immigrants, some South Americans, and a few immigrants from the Caribbean.

I will also refer to a study I was part of, the Immigration and Intergenerational Mobility in Metropolitan Los Angeles (IIMMLA) study, that collected data on the adult children of immigrants throughout the greater Los Angeles area, from Ventura County in the north to San Bernardino County in the south.[5] I refer to these data, where appropriate, because they show that patterns in Orange County also exist throughout Southern California.

I used two key variables—generation in the United States and citizenship status—to analyze various dimensions of Latino integration into Orange County life (Table 2.2). Both variables reflect change, one across generations in the United States, and the other in relation to citizenship/immigration status. When other variables are compared in relation to both of these variables, a pattern of increasing integration into U.S. society emerges.

Table 2.2. Social and economic variables by generations and citizenship-immigration status

	Age (median)	Years in U.S. (median)	Years of schooling (median)	Family income $35,000 or more (%)	Private or government medical insurance (%)
Latino generations					
First generation (migrated age 15 or older, N = 445)	39	16	9	25.8	53.5
1.5 generation (migrated under age 15, N = 128)	29	23	12	53.6	61.4
Second generation (N = 131)	31	—	13	71.1	65.9
Third-plus generation (N = 95)	46	—	14	73.3	80.0
Whites (N = 396)	57	—	16	79.2	90.1
Latinos and immigration-citizenship status					
Undocumented (N = 241)	33	12	9	15.2	44.5
Legal permanent residents (N = 205)	41	20.5	11	31.4	56.1
Naturalized citizens (N = 116)	45	27	12	65.7	75.0
U.S.-born Latinos (N = 232)	37	—	13	73.6	72.2

SOURCE: Center for Research on Latinos in a Global Society's 2006 survey of Orange County.

Of the Latinos surveyed, 573 (71.7 percent) were first generation, meaning that they were born in a foreign country and migrated to the United States.[6] The first generation can be further differentiated according to those who migrated to the United States at less than 15 years of age—the so-called 1.5 generation—and those who migrated at age 15 or older. It must be noted here that because the 1.5 generation came to the United States as young children, it was their parents who made the decision to migrate. The 1.5 generation experienced their formative years in the United States, including most or all of their schooling, and thus much of their cultural and social development occurred in the U.S. context. Rocío, Juan, and Carlos, whose vignettes began this chapter, were all of the 1.5 generation. The 128 interviewees in the 1.5 generation accounted for 22.4 percent of the first-generation Latino respondents.

The second generation, those born in the United States with at least one foreign-born parent, accounted for 16.4 percent ($N = 131$) of the Latinos sampled. Latinos designated as third-plus generations were born in the United States, as were both of their parents, and accounted for 11.9 percent ($N = 95$) of the sample.

Latinos in the survey were, on average, 39.5 years old. However, their age varied depending on their generation. The 1.5 generation were the youngest, and the third-plus generations the oldest. However, the 1.5 generation had more years in the United States (median, 23 years) than other first-generation Latinos (median, 16 years).

Latinos acquire more years of education with each generation in the United States. The 1.5 generation tended to have more years of schooling than those who were older when they migrated to the United States. Latino immigrants who migrated at 15 years of age or older had a median of 9 years of schooling, which is typical of Latin American, especially Mexican, immigrants.[7] Latino immigrants raised in the United States, the 1.5 generation, had a median of 12 years of schooling, and many (44 percent) had one or more years of college experience. In comparison, only 19 percent of those who migrated at age 15 or older had schooling beyond high school, reflecting that they had come to the United States ready and willing to work.

About a third (32 percent) of the Latino 1.5-generation interviewees, and 47 percent of the first generation who had migrated at age 15 or older, were not legal residents of the United States, a statistically significant difference.[8] The 1.5 generation's undocumented status had significant ramifications for their education. For example, although they were able legally to attend a college or university in California, they were not eligible for government-sponsored financial aid and thus often found meeting the costs of higher education difficult. Not surprisingly, given the financial obstacles, only 30.3 percent of the undocumented 1.5 generation had 13 or more years of schooling, whereas 50 percent of their legal resident counterparts did.

Second- and third-plus-generation Latinos had medians of 13 and 14 years of schooling, respectively. Relative to the first generation, subsequent generations of Latinos had made significant gains in schooling. From this perspective, Latinos are an educational success story. However, there was still an education gap between Latinos and the dominant non-Latino population, evidence of the need for continued attention to improving educational opportunities for Latinos. But contrary to the negative characterizations of the Latino Threat

Narrative, educational attainment across generations of Latinos was found to be moving in the right direction.[9]

Latinos also made significant gains across generations in terms of income. Thirty-two percent of all first-generation Latino immigrants (including the 1.5 generation) had a family income (interviewee's income plus spouse/partner's income, if applicable) of $35,000 or more, whereas 71 percent of second-generation Latinos, and 73 percent of the third-plus generations, were in this higher-income category. There was a gap, however, between U.S.-born Latinos and Anglos in terms of total family income.

Within the immigrant generation, the 1.5 generation was more than twice as likely as the other first-generation Latinos to be in the higher-income category, a statistically significant difference.[10] However, citizenship status among the 1.5 generation must be considered. Undocumented 1.5-generation immigrants could not work legally in the United States and so were not able to fully apply their U.S.-acquired education. Consequently, among Latinos who migrated at a young age but were still undocumented at the time of the interview, only 23.5 percent had a family income of $35,000 or higher, whereas two-thirds (67.6 percent) of the legally resident 1.5 Latinos had attained that income level, also a significant difference.[11]

Access to medical insurance, through both employment and government-sponsored programs, is an indication of acquiring "better jobs" and integration into social programs. As Table 2.2 indicates, both first- and second-generation immigrants fared less well in acquiring medical insurance than third-plus-generation Latinos and whites in Orange County. They were still in the less advantageous sector of what Portes and Bach have called a segmented labor market, one that is split between jobs with few or no benefits such as medical insurance and better jobs with medical insurance, paid vacations, pension plans, and/or opportunities for mobility.[12] By the third-plus generations, Latinos were much more likely to have medical insurance than other Latinos, but they still lagged behind whites. (The issue of medical insurance is examined further in Chapter 5.)

Latinos experienced similar gains in home ownership. Once again, there was a linear progression across generations: homeowners made up 33.9 percent of first-generation Latino immigrants who migrated at age 15 or older, 51.9 percent of 1.5-generation Latinos, 68.7 percent of second-generation Latinos, and 72.6 percent of third-plus-generation Latinos. Proportionally more whites (85.6 percent) in the sample owned their own homes, but they were also older and thus more likely to be in the higher-income category. Home ownership can be part of a family's strategy for economic and social mobility. Another recent research project on Latinos in Southern California found that, by the third generation, Latinos had moved into communities that were less spatially segregated (a higher percentage of white residents) and into neighborhoods with higher property values.[13]

Up to this point, the Latino Threat Narrative does not coincide very well with the trends in education and income among Latinos in the Orange County study. These findings suggest that in terms of education, income, and home ownership, each subsequent generation of Latinos is increasingly integrated into U.S. society and its economy. This does not mean that inequalities in access to education or the job market cease to exist. But despite structural obstacles to social and economic mobility, Latinos manage to make important gains over time.

However, as the data on the 1.5 generation suggest, immigration/citizenship status makes a difference. Among the Latinos in the Orange County study, nearly a third (30.4 percent, $N = 241$) did not have an immigration status to report.[14] Another 25.8 percent ($N = 205$) were legal permanent residents, 14.6 percent ($N = 116$) were naturalized citizens, and 29.2 percent ($N = 232$) were U.S.-born Latinos. The overwhelming majority of whites (94.4 percent) in the sample had been born in the United States.[15] One Anglo was an undocumented immigrant, 9 were legal permanent residents, and 12 were naturalized citizens.

Examining Latinos along the path to citizenship reveals a linear progression in age, years living in the United States, years of schooling, and income. Undocumented immigrants were the youngest Latinos overall, had lived the least amount of time in the United States among the immigrants, and had the least education relative to legal permanent residents (legal immigrants) and naturalized citizens. This makes sense in that often the permanent legal residents were formerly undocumented immigrants who found a way to obtain legal status after many years in the United States. With increasing time in the United States, the legal permanent residents had the opportunity to seek formal citizenship and additional schooling.

Acquiring legal status significantly increased earning opportunities. Only 15 percent of the unauthorized Latino immigrants had a family income of $35,000 or more at the time of the interview in 2006. The proportion earning $35,000 or more doubled for Latinos moving from unauthorized status to legal permanent residence and doubled again among the naturalized citizens.

Looked at another way, a U.S.-born Latino was about five times more likely than an undocumented immigrant to have a family income over $35,000.

These findings suggest significant gains in education and income as Latinos move along the path to citizenship. Without a doubt, however, a lack of immigration status is the biggest obstacle to more rapid economic integration among Latino immigrants. These patterns were not occurring only among Latinos in Orange County but were also found among Latinos in the greater Los Angeles area, from Ventura to San Bernardino.[16]

What about social and cultural integration? The Latino Threat Narrative insists on the inability or unwillingness of Latinos to learn English and integrate socially into the larger U.S. society. However, Latinos are also experiencing increased integration in terms of language use, friendship networks, and intermarriage patterns.

When asked about the language spoken at home, Latinos in Orange County showed tremendous changes over generations in the United States (Figure 2.1). First-generation Latinos were the most likely (76.9 percent) to speak all or mostly Spanish at home. However, almost one-fourth used English as often as Spanish (bilingually) or mostly English. Many in this category were the

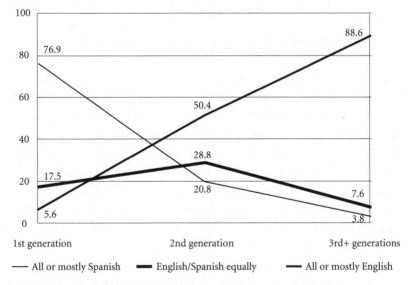

Figure 2.1. Languages spoken by Latinos at home, by percentages of generations.
SOURCE: CRLGS Orange County Survey, 2006.

1.5 generation, who had grown up in the United States and were comfortable with English. In the second generation, only a fifth of the respondents spoke all or mostly Spanish at home. Half (50.4 percent) used all or mostly English at home, a dramatic increase in one generation. Almost 30 percent used Spanish and English equally, reflecting their bilingual capabilities. By the third-plus generations, the overwhelming majority used all or mostly English at home, a statistically significant change over generations.[17] Bilingualism at home persisted but dropped to less than 10 percent (7.6 percent). Only 3.8 percent in the third-plus generations continued to use all or mostly Spanish at home.

The IIMMLA study on Latinos in the greater Los Angeles area showed almost identical results.[18] Whereas few (2 percent) first-generation Mexican immigrants preferred speaking English at home, 37 percent of the 1.5-generation children of immigrants preferred English, with another 22 percent speaking both English and Spanish. By the second (60 percent) and third-plus (85 percent) generation, the majority of Mexican-origin interviewees preferred speaking English at home. Similarly, nationwide, the vast majority of second generation (88 percent) and third-plus generation (94 percent) of Latinos report being fluent in English.[19]

The language spoken with friends followed a similar pattern. Seventy-one percent of the first generation in Orange County spoke all or mostly Spanish with their friends, as one might expect. However, even among the first generation, 18.2 percent used English as much as Spanish, and another 10.8 percent used all or mostly English with their friends. In other words, even among immigrant Latinos, English was not uncommon. By the second generation, only 11.3 percent of Latinos spoke all or mostly Spanish with their friends. Bilingualism continued in this generation, with 17.3 percent speaking both English and Spanish equally with their friends, but those who used all or mostly English rose to 71.4 percent. By the third-plus generations, again the overwhelming majority (85.7 percent) of Latinos in Orange County used English all the time or most of the time with their friends, a statistically significant change over generations.[20] Bilingualism continued, however, among almost one-tenth of Latinos (9.1 percent), while only a few (5.2 percent) spoke all or mostly Spanish with friends.

Language spoken at work showed even more of a penetration of English into Latino lives (Figure 2.2). Among first-generation Latinos, the immigrants, only a little more than half (55.1 percent) spoke Spanish all or even most of the time at work. One out of four spoke all or mostly English at work and another

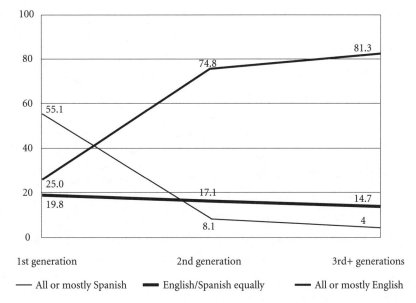

Figure 2.2. Languages spoken by Latinos at work, by percentages of generations.
SOURCE: CRLGS Orange County Survey, 2006.

one out of five spoke English and Spanish equally. Three out of four Latinos spoke all or mostly English at work in the second generation, and more than four out of five do so in the third-plus generations. Spanish at work shows a similarly dramatic change but in the reverse direction, from less than 10 percent in the second generation who used all or mostly Spanish at work to only 4 percent in the third-plus generations. Bilingualism diminishes, but less dramatically, and continues at about 15 percent even in the third-plus generations. Changes in the use of language at work were also statistically significant.[21]

Citizenship status also influenced language use at the workplace (Figure 2.3).[22] About two-thirds of undocumented immigrant Latinos spoke all or mostly Spanish at work, while about a third of undocumented Latinos spoke English at work, either using English and Spanish equally or speaking all or mostly English. Some of these undocumented immigrants were of the 1.5 generation, who had grown up in the United States but had not found a way to legalize their status. About half of legal permanent resident Latinos spoke all or mostly Spanish at work; for the other half, English was already part of their work experience. Only about a third of the naturalized Latino citizens spoke all or mostly Spanish at work. That Spanish was still spoken at work among

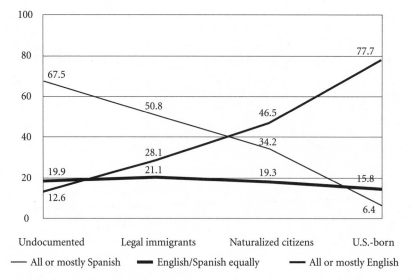

Figure 2.3. Languages spoken by Latinos at work, by citizenship status (in percentages). SOURCE: CRLGS Orange County Survey, 2006.

many of the legal immigrants and naturalized citizens indicated that many were probably employed in occupations that generally hire many immigrants. Citizenship status, however, correlated strongly with increased English use at the workplace. Among all U.S.-born Latinos, over three-quarters used English only or mostly at work. Bilingual usage at work continued for about 16 percent, indicating that they were probably working in firms that also employed immigrants and their language skills were important.

The rapid decline in use of Spanish in the Latino second and third-plus generations suggests that concerns about a threat to the prevalence of the English language are unfounded.[23] This pattern not only is occurring among the children of Mexican and other Latin American immigrants but also is widespread among the children of most immigrant groups in the United States today.[24] Indeed, the linguistic threat is misguided, in that the real concern should be with the loss of a major resource, languages other than English, during a time of increasing global economic, cultural, and political relationships.[25] Moreover, the decline in Spanish usage also increases the risk of losing a language with a rich literary tradition that was present in what is now the United States before the arrival of the English-speaking Pilgrims. The positive finding here, from this perspective, is that Spanish continues to be used bilingually at work by

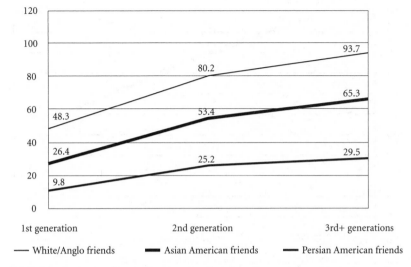

Figure 2.4. Non-Latino friends of Latinos, by ethnicity and percentages of Latino generations.
SOURCE: CRLGS Orange County Survey, 2006.

about 16 percent of Latinos even in the third-plus generations. Rather than a negative, bilingualism may be one of the greatest advantages of growing up in a family with immigrant parents or grandparents.

Work was not found to be the only factor influencing language use. Friendship patterns were also important, not just for language use but also because the Latino Threat Narrative characterizes Latinos as living in their own social world. However, when asked about friends with whom they socialized outside of work, Latinos indicated that they had non-Latino friends (Figure 2.4). Latinos in each generation have friends among the demographically largest groups in Orange County: whites, Asian Americans, and Persian Americans. First-generation Latinos had Anglo friends (48.3 percent), Asian American friends (26.4 percent), and Persian American (9.8 percent) friends. Among second-generation Latinos, the percentage of Anglo and Asian American friends almost doubled, and Persian American friends increased two and a half times. By the third-plus generations, almost all Latinos had white friends, most had Asian American friends, and more than one-fourth had Persian American friends. For a group that is allegedly insular in its social outlook—a prerequisite, it would seem, for a group conspiring to reconquer the area—Latinos in Orange County seem to have a very vibrant set of friendship networks.

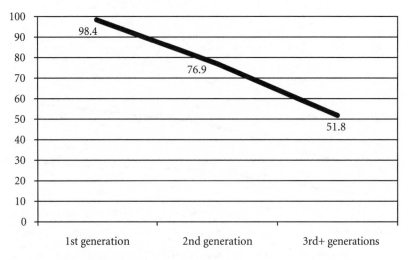

Figure 2.5. Latino-Latina marriages by generation (in percentages).
SOURCE: CRLGS Orange County Survey, 2006.

Perhaps because of these increasing social relationships over generations, Latinos have tended to marry non-Latinos over time (Figure 2.5). As one might expect, most first-generation Latinos married other Latinos, typically from the same country of origin. However, by the second generation, almost one in four Latinos was married to or living with someone who was not Latino, typically a white. By the third-plus generations, only half of Latinos were married to other Latinos, a statistically significant change.[26] The other half of third-plus-generation Latinos were married to or living with non-Latinos, mostly whites. In contrast, most whites surveyed (85.7 percent) were married to or living with other whites. Not just in Orange County, but throughout Southern California, 60 percent of Latinos of Mexican origin were married to non-Latinos, according to the IIMMLA study.

The Latino Threat Narrative characterizes Latinos as unwilling to integrate into the larger society. However, intermarriage is a strong indicator of integration, as are friendship networks.[27] How can a group be insular—that is, limited to living within its own social world—and be preparing for a reconquest of U.S. territory, while at the same time developing friendships and intermarrying with others outside their own ethnic group? It is difficult to construct a narrative that reconciles the Latino threat with the friendship and marriage patterns found in the Orange County study.

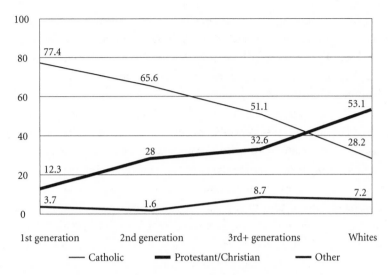

Figure 2.6. Religions of Latinos, by generation, and of whites (in percentages). SOURCE: CRLGS Orange County Survey, 2006.

In addition, the Latino Threat Narrative characterizes Latinos as unchanging, as slaves to tradition. Perhaps there is no area of cultural life that is characterized as being less amenable to change and such an essential part of Latino identity as religion. Surely, if the Latino Threat Narrative has any currency at all, it must be in terms of Catholicism among Latinos. However, here, too, Latinos exhibited significant changes (Figure 2.6). Slightly more than three-quarters of first-generation Latinos were Catholics. That almost one-fourth were not Catholic reflects the inroads made by evangelical and Mormon missionaries in Latin America.[28] By the second generation the percentage of Latinos claiming to be Catholic dropped to slightly less than two-thirds. By the third-plus generations, only about half of Latinos were Catholic, a statistically significant pattern across generations.[29] Protestant sects have increased dramatically among Latinos. Although more than a quarter of whites in the area are Catholic, most belong to a Protestant sect. The direction of the lines in Figure 2.6 suggest that Latinos, over time, are changing religious preferences toward those of the larger non-Latino community, a pattern also found throughout Southern California.[30]

In short, religious preferences among Latinos are not static; rather they are subject to contextual influences, a pattern occurring nationwide.[31] Moreover, participation in evangelizing Christianity can have other benefits, as Schiller and Caglar have argued, such as facilitating immigrants' claims for social citizenship.[32] For example, over generations Latinos are also more likely to attend a place of worship with proportionately fewer people of their own ethnic background.[33]

Latinos also increased their civic engagement across generations (Table 2.3).[34] For example, the proportion of Latinos who belonged to labor unions, work-related associations, fraternal groups (such as the Rotary Club, Lions Club, or Kiwanis Club), sports teams like soccer or bowling leagues, groups working on political issues, or neighborhood, community, or school groups, as well as many other kinds of organizations, increased from less than a tenth of the first generation (8.4 percent) to more than a fourth of the third-plus generations (27.4 percent).[35] They were also more likely to contact a government office for help with a problem or for information.[36] Latinos in each succeeding generation were more likely to attend political meetings, rallies, speeches, or dinners in support of a political candidate[37] and to contribute money to political candidates or organizations.[38] They were similarly more likely to volunteer

Table 2.3. Civic engagement of Latinos, by generation, and of whites (in percentages)

	First generation	1.5 generation	Second generation	Third-plus generations	Whites
Belongs to civic organization, club, union, etc.	8.4	10.1	13.0	27.4	32.8
In past 12 months, contacted a government office	12.2	14.0	16.3	23.4	30.3
In past 12 months, attended political meeting, rally, speech, or dinner to support political candidate	1.6	4.7	4.6	8.4	10.1
In past 12 months, contributed money to political campaign	1.8	8.5	11.5	9.5	22.0
In past 12 months, volunteered time to organization	11.7	17.8	21.4	23.4	42.7
In past 12 months, took part in protest, such as picketing or a march, demonstration, or boycott	1.1	4.7	4.6	4.2	7.1

SOURCE: CRLGS Orange County Survey, 2006.

their time to a civic organization.[39] Relatively few (less than 5 percent of any generation) said they had taken part in any form of protest, such as picketing or participating in a march, demonstration, or boycott.[40] However, the Orange County survey was conducted before the immigrant marches in the spring of 2006. In sum, Latinos were increasingly engaged in the civic life of their communities. Their civic engagement grew from 29.3 percent in the first generation to 54.7 percent of the third-plus generation engaged in one or more of these examples of civic activities,[41] by which time Latinos were much closer to the civic involvement of whites (69.4 percent). Latinos were not leading socially isolated lives.[42]

Latinos in this study also became more engaged in civic life as they moved along the path to citizenship. Unauthorized immigrants (26.1 percent) and legal permanent residents (26.3 percent) engaged in one or more of the civic activities examined here. Civic engagement increased among naturalized Latinos (41.4 percent) and among those who were U.S.-born (47 percent).[43]

The Latino Threat Narrative characterizes Latinos, especially Mexicans, as being too tied to their countries of origin to want to, or to be able to, integrate into U.S. society. Indeed, immigrants today are able to maintain social, emotional, and even political contacts back in their country of origin because of the ease of travel and of multiple forms of communication, including the Internet.[44] If they so desire, they can lead lives that extend beyond the borders of particular nation-states, occupying what social scientists call transnational social fields.[45]

Four variables in the survey indicated participation in a transnational social field: sending money to a relative or friend in another country, visiting a parent's country of origin, participating in an organization associated with a parent's state or hometown in the parent's country of origin, and using a computer to communicate with a relative or friend in another country.[46] Each of these transnational activities was found to vary by generation (Table 2.4). The first generation was the most likely to remit money to relatives or friends in another country, and remittances dropped off precipitously in the second and third-plus generations. Second- and third-plus-generation Latinos did not have the same experience in their parents' country of origin and consequently used their resources to survive economically in the United States.

The second generation was more likely than the first to visit the parents' country of origin, which in most of these cases was Mexico. Many in the first generation did not have the freedom to travel back and forth across the

Table 2.4. Latino transnational behaviors by generations (in percentages)

	First generation	Second generation	Third-plus generations
In past year, sent money to a relative or friend in another country	64.6	39.4	8.6***
In past year, visited parent's home country at least once	65.0	83.7***	—
In past year, participated in any kind of organization associated with parent's state or hometown in country of origin	4.2	9.9*	—
In past year, used a computer to communicate with a relative or friend in another country	33.5	37.7	16.3**

SOURCE: CRLGS Orange County Study, 2006.
$*p < .05; **p < .01; ***p < .001.$

U.S.-Mexico border because they lacked formal immigration/citizenship status. Of the 1.5 generation without legal status, 58 percent had not visited their parents' country of origin, which meant that, since migrating as young children, they had experienced life only in the United States.

Second-generation Latinos were citizens, making it easier for them to participate in a hometown or home state association, typically a voluntary organization that raises funds for local community development in the country of origin. However, Latino first- and second-generation interviewees engaged the least in this form of transnational activity. The computer has become a highly useful mechanism for communicating with relatives and friends in another country, and both first- and second-generation Latinos used it in similar proportions. Transnational computer contact dropped off, however, for third-generation Latinos.

What influence do transnational activities such as these have on integration into U.S. society? Do they inhibit integration because they reinforce interests in a foreign country rather than fostering a desire to integrate into U.S. life? Or is it possible for people to engage in transnational activities and maintain emotional relationships and interest in events "back home" while still developing a sense of belonging to their social world in the United States?

To explore the influence of transnational activities, I undertook two ordinary least squares (OLS) regression analyses using a five-point scale developed from the study's questions regarding languages.[47] The language used as a child and the language used now at home, with friends, and at work provided a measure of acculturation and integration into society.[48] The independent variables were length of time in the United States, total years of education, family income, transnational activities, and immigration/citizenship status. The transnational variable was a sum of the positive responses to the transnational questions.[49] The citizenship variable had four values representing a path to citizenship: 1 for no immigration/citizenship documents, 2 for legal permanent resident, 3 for naturalized citizen, and 4 for U.S.-born citizen.

In Model 1, only first-generation Latinos were included; Model 2 included both first- and second-generation Latinos. Third-plus-generation Latinos were excluded because questions about parents' country of origin were irrelevant. In Model 2, length of time in the United States was excluded because for the U.S.-born the values would be their age.

Table 2.5 shows the results of the analyses. Among immigrant Latinos in Orange County, language acculturation was significantly influenced by years in the United States, education, income, and their movement along a path to citizenship. Engaging in transnational activities, holding these other variables constant, also significantly influenced language acculturation, but in a positive direction. In other words, among first-generation Latinos, those who were

Table 2.5. OLS regression with language acculturation (five-point scale) as the dependent variable

	Model 1 (first-generation Latinos)		Model 2 (first- and second-generation Latinos)	
	B	SE	B	SE
Years in United States	.008	.004*	—	—
Years of schooling	.060	.011***	.069	.010***
Family income of $35,000 or more	.260	.099**	.228	.086**
Transnational activities	.104	.041*	.008	.034
Citizenship status	.174	.064**	.510	.036***
Constant	.223	.145	−.023	.128

SOURCE: CRLGS Orange County 2006 Study.
NOTE: OLS = ordinary least-squares; B = beta; SE = standard error.
Summary statistics for Model 1: $N = 389$; $R^2_{adj} = .267$; SE = 0.77263; $F < .0001$.
Summary statistics for Model 2: $N = 536$; $R^2_{adj} = 0.482$; SE = 0.81706; $F < .001$.
*$p < .05$; **$p < .01$; ***$p < .001$.

Table 2.6. OLS regression with the sum of civic engagement variables (seven-point scale) as the dependent variable

	First- and second-generation Latinos	
	B	SE
Years of schooling	.033	.012**
Family income of $35,000 or more	.159	.097
Transnational activities	.170	.039***
Language-acculturation (five-point scale)	.129	.043**
Constant	−.693	.148***

SOURCE: CRLGS Orange County 2006 Study.
NOTE: OLS = ordinary least squares; B = beta; SE = standard error.
Summary statistics: $N = 541$; $R^2_{adj} = 0.135$; SE = 0.95491; $F < .0001$.
*$p < .05$; **$p < .01$; ***$p < .001$.

more transnational in their behavior were also more likely to be higher in the language acculturation index. Consequently, among first-generation Latinos, engaging in transnational activities did not inhibit change or integration along the language acculturation variable.

Model 2 indicates that for first- and second-generation Latinos in Orange County, education, income, and citizenship status were significant influences on language acculturation. However, transnational activities were not significant—that is, they did not matter statistically either way.

Transnational activities also did not impede civic engagement in the United States among first- and second-generation Latinos.[50] An OLS linear regression analysis using the sum of all the examined types of political engagement as the dependent variable found that transnational activity was a positive and significant influence on civic engagement (Table 2.6). Years of schooling and language acculturation were also significant predictors of civic engagement among first- and second-generation Latinos.

FINAL THOUGHTS

The research findings presented here contradict the premises of the Latino Threat Narrative. Latinos make impressive improvements in education, income, and use of English as they gain generational experience in the United States and as they move along a path toward citizenship. Rather than living apart from the larger society, their friendship, religious, and romantic relationships extend beyond the social borders of Latino life. They are not socially secluded, waiting for the day when they can muster a Quebec-like takeover of the U.S. Southwest. They are just like other folks, open to change and the influences of ideas and people around them. They are immersed in the flow of history, not stuck in some immutable, folkloric time warp. Given these findings, it would seem that if one were seriously concerned with the integration of Latino immigrants into U.S. society, then moving them quickly along a path to citizenship would be the public policy of choice.[51] Immigrants themselves recognize this fact, especially those of the 1.5 generation who are undocumented but educated in the United States; their fate is closely tied to immigration reform proposals in Congress, especially the DREAM Act, which would allow them to become legal permanent residents (see Chapter 8).[52]

Whether the portrayal of Latino life presented here will significantly undermine the Latino Threat Narrative is difficult to predict. The narrative has a great deal of inertia, built not only on years of constructed "truths" about Latinos but also on a basic fear of the impact of immigrants on U.S. culture and on the xenophobia that has been directed toward most immigrants to these shores. One could point out that history has witnessed similar groundless fears about the inability of immigrants, and even their U.S.-born children, to become "American."[53] But even adding historical arguments to contemporary social science information such as that presented here may not be sufficient to displace the Latino Threat Narrative. It is a narrative that is, in some important ways, similar to religious faith, in that its adherents are not necessarily concerned with the verifiability of its premises. Ultimately, the Latino Threat Narrative is about affirming legitimate claims on citizenship and undermining, or at least making suspect, the claims of Latinos. This is why, even when linear improvements in some important areas—use of English, friendship networks, intermarriage, religion—can be demonstrated, Latinos may still encounter obstacles integrating into the larger society, which can lead to their having feelings of alienation and segmented or unrealized assimilation.[54]

The idea of segmented assimilation—that assimilation can move forward, hit a wall, and then move backward or in socially nonintegrative directions such as delinquency—reflects that change is not always an easy, linear process. Many can, and do, face obstacles. However, as Rocío's, Carlos's, and Juan's cases above suggest, the children of immigrants often do not give up trying to improve their lives, despite the obstacles they encounter and the frustrations and disappointments that those obstacles cause. The Latino Threat Narrative obscures such efforts toward integration and desires of belonging. The power of the Latino Threat Narrative to obscure the actual lives of Mexican immigrants and Latinos in general is particularly observable in relation to Latina fertility and reproduction, which is the subject of the next chapter.

3 LATINA SEXUALITY, REPRODUCTION, AND FERTILITY AS THREATS TO THE NATION

ON OCTOBER 17, 2006, a woman gave birth to a baby that would take the United States population to 300 million.[1] Or an immigrant entered the United States, legally or illegally, to become the 300 millionth American. The exact date of the event was set by the U.S. Census Bureau's good but still imprecise algorithm, and the exact person achieving the title "300 millionth person" would undoubtedly never be known. But leaving such uncertainties aside, the U.S. population had reached a milestone, and it was covered in the major news outlets, on talk radio, on blogs, and in online newsletters. How did Latinos and Latino immigrants become part of this population brouhaha?

If there was one thing that appeared certain in the news coverage, it was that the 300 millionth person would probably be Latino and would probably be born or living in Los Angeles, or at least somewhere in the U.S. Southwest. This pronouncement had been made a full ten months earlier in a *New York Times* article by William Frey, a demographer with the University of Michigan's Population Studies Center: "The 300 millionth [baby] will be a Mexican Latino in Los Angeles County, with parents who speak Spanish at home and with siblings who are bilingual."[2] A senior demographer with the Population Reference Bureau explained why: "While most Americans are still Anglo-Saxon Protestants, Hispanic mothers have higher birth rates, and no state has more births than California, where most newborns are of Hispanic origin. There, Jose ranked fourth in 2004 among the most popular baby names for boys after Daniel, Anthony and Andrew."[3]

Many of the news stories chronicling the event included information on historical immigration trends, contrasts with the 200-millionth-person milestone, current immigration patterns, changing demographics and the proportional increase in Latinos, the probability that the 300 millionth person would be Latino, and a photograph of Latinos, usually either Mexican immigrants participating in the immigrant marches earlier that year or a Latino family with a baby.[4] Such reporting underscored Latino fertility and immigration as key components of population growth and other demographic changes. As the *Washington Post* put it, "Hispanics from Latin America, by far the largest share of recent immigrants, are driving the natural increase [in population] here. On average, Hispanic women have one more child than non-Hispanic white women."[5] *WorldNetDaily* put it more bluntly: "Invasion USA: Illegals Push U.S. to 300 Million Mark."

Fears of immigrants' sexuality and their reproductive capacities are not new. Race, immigration, and fertility have formed a fearsome trinity for much of U.S. history.[6] During each wave of immigration, "natives" (typically the children or grandchildren of immigrants) have feared that the new immigrants would have deleterious impacts on American culture and society.[7] During the great migration from southern and eastern Europe, for example, a wary American public perceived immigrant fertility levels as dangerously high and thus a threat to the education, welfare, and medical care systems, as well as a harbinger of demographic shifts leading to the diminishing of the power of the dominant Protestant, northern European–American racial/ethnic group.[8] In addition, immigration authorities inspected immigrant women closely, suspecting them of loose morals, engaging in prostitution, becoming public charges, and other types of moral turpitude.[9]

During the most recent, post-1965 wave of immigration, Latina reproduction and fertility, especially of Mexican immigrant women, have been ground zero in a war of not only words but also public policies and laws. Indeed, anti-immigrant sentiment during the last decades of the twentieth century and the first decade of the twenty-first century focused specifically on the biological and social reproductive capacities of Mexican immigrant and Mexican-origin (U.S.-born) women.[10] The post-1965 period witnessed a continuous fertility decline among U.S. women, which has contributed to a demographic shift such that the proportion of white, non-Hispanic Americans in the overall population has decreased. Latina reproduction and fertility have been center stage in the often vitriolic public debate over the causes and meanings of demographic change. National magazines, for example, have consistently represented the fertility levels of Latinas, especially Mexicans and Mexican Americans, as "dangerous," "pathological," "abnormal," and even a threat to national security.[11] These representations of Latina fertility and reproduction are a key component of the invasion and reconquest themes examined in Chapter 1.

As the present chapter illustrates, Latina reproduction and fertility have been the subject of not only public discourse but also of social science investigation and discourse. "Latinas" exist and "reproduction" exists, but "Latina reproduction" as an object of a discourse produces a limited range of meanings, often focusing on their supposedly excessive reproduction, seemingly abundant or limitless fertility, and hypersexuality, all of which are seen as "out of control" in relation to the supposed social norm. We will see that the biological reproduction of Latinas combines with their social reproduction in the popular imagination to produce fears about Latino population growth as a threat to the nation—that is, "the American people," as conceived in demographic and racial/ethnic terms. This threat materializes not merely because of Latino population growth, but also because Latino babies transgress the border between immigrants and citizens.[12] It is here that the metaphor of leaky national borders converges with that of porous bodies (producing babies) and the permeable category of citizenship. These transgressions contribute to immigration as a hot political issue, especially when the mother is an undocumented immigrant. Note here the convergence of metaphors: leaky national borders, porous bodies, and the permeable category of citizenship.[13]

Discourses that represent people with "dangerous," "pathological," and "abnormal" reproductive behaviors and beliefs have real political and economic consequences. In California, for example, the perceived threat of Latina fertility, especially among immigrants, was central to the "Save Our State" movement that led to Proposition 187, which sought to curb undocumented immigration by denying undocumented immigrants social services, particularly prenatal care and education for their children.[14] Bette Hammond, one of the organizers of Proposition 187, characterized Latina immigrants in her hometown in a way that emphasized the threat of reproduction: "They come here, they have their babies, and after that they become citizens and all those children use social services."[15] Pete Wilson, governor of California from 1991 to 1999, made the denial of prenatal care for undocumented immigrant women a top priority of his administration.[16] The 1996 welfare reform law also targeted medical services for immigrant women.[17] As we shall observe below, the popular discourse of Latina reproduction is decidedly alarmist in that it becomes part of a discourse of threat and danger to U.S. society and even national security, which is underscored in a post-9/11 world. Thus discourses not only filter reality but help construct what is taken for "real."

This chapter begins with a brief elaboration of the theoretical and rhetorical issues framing this discussion of Latina sexuality, fertility, and reproduction. Two key questions come out of this review and frame subsequent sections. How have Latina reproduction and fertility been represented? And are these representations accurate? To examine the first question, Latina sexuality, fertility, and reproduction are analyzed as key, intertwined concepts in a national public discourse on immigration, in a manner suggested by Fraser and Gordon's research on the keyword "dependency" in the welfare state.[18] The genealogy of Latina "fertility and reproduction" as "threats to U.S. society" are traced in popular visual and textual discourse beginning in 1965.[19] The accuracy of the representations of Latinas is taken up in Chapter 4. In Chapter 8, the focus shifts to the product of Latina fertility and reproduction, the children of immigrants.

SEXUALITY, REPRODUCTION AND LATINAS

Faye Ginsburg and Rayna Rapp argue that "to reproduce" has many meanings.[20] At the very least, it is important to distinguish biological reproduction from social reproduction. Both aspects of reproduction, as well as their intersection, are often sites of political confrontation. In societies with competing and often unequal social groups split along various lines of race, ethnicity, social class, sexuality, and immigration status, the biological and/or social reproduction of one or all of those groups can be the target of public debate and of state policies aimed at controlling reproduction.[21] As Ginsburg and Rapp note, "Throughout history, state power has depended directly and indirectly on defining normative families and controlling populations."[22] In the process, regimes of representation can emerge in which particular groups are said to be pathological, even "dangerous" to the larger society.[23] Ginsburg and Rapp utilize Shellee Colen's concept of "stratified reproduction" to describe how women's reproduction in some groups is characterized positively, while that of other women is "disempowered."[24] As they note, "The concept of stratified reproduction helps us see the arrangements by which some reproductive futures are valued while others are despised."[25]

One particularly insidious example of stratified reproduction is the image of the "black welfare mother" used so effectively in political discourse.[26] As Dorothy Roberts notes, society has blamed poor black mothers for "perpetuating social problems by transmitting defective genes, irreparable crack [cocaine] damage, and a deviant lifestyle to their children."[27] African American women pose a "reproductive threat" that is different from that posed by Mexican immigrant women and their daughters, but both groups have faced the stigma of society's surveillance of their reproductive capacities. As Roberts observes, "welfare reform measures that cut off assistance for children born to welfare mothers all proclaim the same message: The key to solving America's social problems is to curtail Black women's birth rates."[28]

Ginsburg and Rapp's observations have implications for understanding the politics surrounding Latina reproduction, which is similarly demeaned, feared, and stratified. Reproduction, as an object of discourse, is an ideological concept that defines normative fertility levels (those of white women) and their opposite: the nonnormative, stigmatized, "high fertility" of Latinas and the sexual behavior that produced it. Or put another way, not only is the fertility of white women normative, but they also possess "subject status," which Jürgen Link defines as "an autonomous, responsible, quasi-juridical person of sound mind, as in a legal subject."[29] In contrast, Latinas do not possess subject status; their behavior is viewed as irrational, illogical, chaotic, subject to tradition and superstition, and therefore threatening. The simple dualism inherent in the rendering of a social group as not possessed of subject status works well when constructing images of the "enemy," those who threaten the life and well-being of those with subject status, be they individuals or nations.

Some have argued that sexuality, fertility, and reproduction are separate issues.[30] However, Carole Vance has emphasized the politics surrounding the concept of sexuality: "For researchers in sexuality, the task is not only to study changes in the expression of sexual behavior and attitudes, but to examine the relationship of these changes to more deeply-based shifts in how gender and sexuality were organized and interrelated within larger social relations."[31] For Latinas, this means that their lives as women, wives, and mothers are subject to redefinition by the larger society, which views them in comparison to more "modern" white U.S. women.[32] In particular, Euro-American women's roles are more broadly defined to include education and work outside the home, and their sexuality and reproduction are positively viewed as opposed to the Other women of the Third World, including Mexican immigrant women and U.S.-born women of Mexican descent, with their allegedly high reproductive levels.[33]

Thus, in the discourse surrounding Mexican and other Latin American immigration, sexuality, fertility, and reproduction are often intertwined.[34] The "hot" Latina is one of two stereotypes generally applied to Latinas. They are either hypersexualized and hot seductresses or pure virginal girls or married women, selfless and obedient wives and mothers. This latter stereotype is referred to as *Marianismo*, after the Virgin Mary, and is merged with the hot Latina stereotype into one hybrid image: the hypersexuality of the hot Latina combines with the abundant fertility and uncontrolled reproduction of the Mariana mother to produce the "Latina threat."[35] In other words, sexuality, especially the image of the sexually "hot" Latina, supposedly combines with pronatalist cultural and religious values (that are static and immutable because of the lack of social integration, assimilation, and acculturation) to produce high fertility rates. A few examples will suffice to illustrate the sexuality-fertility-immigration connection.

Residents of Albuquerque, New Mexico, awoke to a Cinco de Mayo surprise in 2004. Around the city were a number of large billboards advertising Tecate beer, which were placed by Labatt USA, the company that imports the beer. The ads featured an ice-cold beer bottle, with cold water beaded upon it, tilting sideways as if falling down, perhaps into a reclining position. What raised local ire were the words attached to the image: FINALLY, A COLD LATINA (Figure 3.1).

The sexual innuendos in the Tecate ad were anything but subtle. The "cold Latina" was being offered as a visual pun, but it worked only because what was unsaid but understood was that Latinas are "hot." This reference to supposedly "hot" Latinas built upon commonly held and taken-for-granted stereotypes

Figure 3.1. Tecate beer ad on a billboard in Albuquerque, May 5, 2004. Permission granted by the *New Mexico Daily Lobo*.

of Latina sexuality and reproductive behavior. What "hot Latina" means has always been constructed in relation to other taken-for-granted assumptions about the normative behavior of non-Latina whites. Thus the unspoken "hot" of the advertisement conjured up a plethora of images and referents to Latinas as exotic, sexually aggressive, flirtatious women who engage in sexual activities at an early age and thus have babies at a younger age than white women and have more sexual partners (are more promiscuous) than their white counterparts. To finally find a "cold Latina," the ad suggested, would be a truly remarkable event, underscoring the assumed innateness of the "hot" attributes associated with Latinas. These personality and behavioral characteristics were, so to speak, part of the Latina's nature.

The assumption of an innate, or genetic, basis for the Latina's "hot" characteristics is part of common discourse, especially the "it's in their blood" observation. Consider the following exchange between Arnold Schwarzenegger, governor of California, and Susan Kennedy, Schwarzenegger's chief of staff. The topic is California assemblywoman Bonnie Garcia. The only Latina Republican in the California legislature, Garcia was born in New York, where her parents had moved from Puerto Rico. The candid conversation was tape-recorded and obtained by the *Los Angeles Times*:

> Kennedy: Bonnie Garcia is great. She's a ball-buster. She's great. Is she Puerto Rican?
> Schwarzenegger: She seems to me like Cuban.
> Kennedy: She's not Mexican.
> Schwarzenegger: No.
> Kennedy: But she said something and I thought, I thought she was Puerto Rican.
> Schwarzenegger: She maybe is Puerto Rican or the same thing as Cuban. I mean, they are all very hot. They have the, you know, part of the black blood in them and part of the Latino blood in them that together makes it.[36]

Governor Schwarzenegger had offered up a theory of genetics (blood) as the basis for cultural behavior that goes well beyond the eye of the beholder's personal views. Both Schwarzenegger and the Tecate beer advertisement were articulating assumptions and taken-for-granted "truths" about an object of discourse, Latina sexuality. Characterizing all Latinas as "hot" objectifies and sexualizes them in a way that, once again, sets them up as society's Others, in distinct opposition to the normative sexuality and morality of white women.

Latinas are reduced to their biological essence, which is narrowly defined along the lines of sexual attraction.

The "hot" Latina syndrome leads to other assumptions about nonnormative sexual behavior and out-of-control fertility, which in turn are central to the immigrant threat and reconquest narratives. Consider the Internet game *Border Patrol*. The game's opening image is rectangular, with "Border Patrol" spelled out in capital letters in green, white, and red, the colors of the Mexican flag (Figure 3.2). Underneath the title is a box with a smaller box embedded in it. The smaller box says "Play" and has ten shotgun shells lined up, representing the number of shots the player gets to take. Within the bigger box is the text "There is one simple objective to this game, keep them out . . . at any cost!" To the right of the box, from top to bottom, are three people icons, each within a circle. The first is a man with black hair and beard who is wearing a dark green shirt and a bullet belt across his shoulder and under his arm. A Mexican flag is in the background. Two pistols—one on each side beneath the icon, just outside the circle and crossing into it—point at his head. Underneath the guns is the label "Mexican Nationalist." The second icon is of a Mexican who has beard stubble on his cheeks and chin and wears a large sombrero and a sleeveless white shirt. On his back is what looks like a bag with marijuana in it. Two marijuana leaves are under the image. "Drug Smuggler" is the name given to this icon. The bottom icon is a woman and a man. Two babies are under the adults. The name given to this icon is "Breeder."

Figure 3.2. Opening screen of the online game *Border Patrol*.

The *Border Patrol* game is interactive. The player is able to point and shoot at each of the three stereotypical types of border crossers. The object is to shoot them before they can cross the border. The relevant point here is that fertility is represented in one of three icons used in the game, reflecting the taken-for-granted assumption that Latina fertility is out of control and thus poses a threat to the United States. This game was apparently produced by a college student and sent out over the Internet in 2002, but it received little attention.[37] The game became the subject of a media spectacle in April 2006, when it again became widely available on anti-immigrant websites, at the same time that large immigrant-rights marches were taking place across the country.[38]

What do the Tecate beer ad for a "cold Latina," Governor's Schwarzenegger's views on the "hot Latina," and the *Border Patrol* game have in common? They all share the premise that the logical trajectory is for the hot Latina to become the hot mama to many children. Thus, the hybrid image of the Latina materializes, melding the sexuality of the former and the fertility/reproduction of the latter. They share basic assumptions about Latina sexuality and reproductive behavior that did not just appear out of thin air. They were constructed through the evolution of a discourse, to which we now turn.

LATINA REPRODUCTION IN THE POST-1965 ERA

The expanding world population became a matter of public concern in the 1960s. *Time* magazine's January 11, 1960, cover presented world population growth in cataclysmic terms, as an "explosion." The cover's image is filled with women carrying babies. It is very *National Geographic* in style, presenting Asian, African, and Latin American women in "native" or working-class dress. Two African women are naked. Of the fourteen women, two appear to be Euro-American, and both are along the left-hand side of the cover. One woman is blond and, rather than carrying her children, she is pushing one in a grocery-store shopping cart, with the other child beside her, emphasizing her modernity relative to the more folkloric styles of the other women. The overall effect is that the women with babies are primarily Third World, nonwhite women. Across the upper right is the headline "That Population Explosion."

As the explosion metaphor suggests, the world's population growth was expected to have a disastrous effect on the environment, natural resources, and quality of life as cities grew and arable land declined. The idea of fewer children, the goal of the zero-population-growth movement, would soon permeate American culture. How did the fertility and reproduction of Latinos and

Latino immigrants become part of the discourse of fear about population growth?

Four factors helped situate one group of Latinos—Mexicans and Mexican Americans—squarely in the population threat narrative. First of all, as the image on *Time*'s cover indicates, much of the world's growth was viewed as occurring among nonwhite, Third World peoples. Mexicans qualified as a suspect class on this account alone. But it was perhaps Paul Ehrlich's seminal work on population growth that popularized the idea of an impending catastrophe and focused attention on Mexican people. Then, in the 1970s, the U.S. Immigration and Naturalization Service's representatives alarmed the U.S. public with their reports of exaggerated numbers of illegal immigrants (read: Mexicans) crossing the nation's borders. Finally, academic research since at least the mid-1960s has reinforced the distinction between the "high" fertility of Latinas and the "normative" fertility of white Americans.[39] For much of this time, the emphasis has been on high fertility levels, especially among Mexican-origin women, with less emphasis on the rapid drop in fertility rates among Mexican and Mexican American women between the 1960s and today. As Hortensia Amaro observed, "The social science literature has often portrayed Mexican-American women as sacrificed to childbearing. . . . An assumption behind these evaluations of Mexican-American women is that traditional cultural values and religious traditions promote attitudes favorable to continuous childbearing, opposition to contraception, and opposition to abortion."[40]

Paul Ehrlich, a biologist at Stanford University, struck a societal nerve when his book *The Population Bomb* was published in 1968. Ehrlich meant his book as a wake-up call about the dangers of population growth and the need to control fertility levels. His cataclysmic tone is best expressed in his own prose:

> Our position requires that we take immediate action at home and promote effective action worldwide. We must have population control at home, hopefully through a system of incentives and penalties, but by compulsion if voluntary methods fail. We must use our political power to push other countries into programs which combine agricultural development and population control. And while this is being done we must take action to reverse the deterioration of our environment before population pressure permanently ruins our planet. The birth rate must be brought into balance with the death rate or mankind will breed itself into oblivion. We can no longer afford merely to treat the symptoms of the cancer of population growth; the cancer itself must be cut out. Population control is the only answer. (p. 12)

Ehrlich leaves no doubt about the catastrophic outcomes should population growth not be controlled. What he means by the ominous-sounding control "by compulsion" is not clear, but examples might include the draconian population control programs such as the one-child rule implemented in China and forced sterilizations among Latinas in the United States.[41] Such actions may seem justified within a discourse that treats population growth as a "cancer" that will kill humankind through environmental degradation, famines, pestilence, and wars between rich and poor. Ehrlich further warned that "if the pessimists are correct, massive famines will occur soon, possibly in the early 1970's, certainly by the early 1980's. So far most of the evidence seems to be on the side of the pessimists, and we should plan on the assumption that they are correct."[42]

Ehrlich argued that re-channeling the meanings attached to sexual activity was a key goal for controlling fertility. Sexual activity, according to Ehrlich, is one of man's least animal functions.[43] Sexual activity is a "peculiarly human activity" (that is, cultural) insofar as it has functions beyond reproduction, such as reinforcing interpersonal relationships, inducing pleasurable feelings, and functioning as a means of recreation. A rational approach, according to Ehrlich, would be to emphasize these nonreproductive aspects of sexual activity and to de-emphasize the reproductive role of sex, especially the satisfaction that comes with childbearing and "excessive" fatherhood. In other words, when it comes to sex, recreate—don't procreate.

Ehrlich's views not only helped ignite a social movement—zero population growth—but they also helped establish the movement's enemy: women who had supposedly high fertility levels and who continued to value childbearing. In this way, Ehrlich's *Population Bomb* contributes to an understanding of the context that developed to stigmatize Latinas as hot (hypersexual) and as possessing abhorrently high fertility rates (not to mention the stigmatizing of "welfare mothers," discussed above).

Not too long after publication of the *Population Bomb*, images began to appear that represented a population explosion south of the border spilling over into the United States. The *American Legion*'s December 1974 cover image (shown in Chapter 1) portrayed an unregulated mass of Mexicans pouring across the U.S.-Mexico border. *U.S. News and World Report* soon followed with its July 4, 1977, cover, which carried the headline "Time Bomb in Mexico: Why There'll Be No End to the Invasion of 'Illegals.'" The accompanying article clarified that the "time bomb" was Mexico's population and its projected population growth, a foreign threat given additional meaning by being so prominently displayed on the magazine's cover for the country's Fourth of July birthday. As the allusion to Ehrlich's *Population Bomb* indicates, various elements—academic and popular—worked together through mutual referencing to produce a discourse on Latina reproduction. The *U.S. News and World Report* article stressed that the fertility of Mexicans and their inability to produce jobs for their population would lead to greater pressure for future immigration to the United States. By drawing the reader's attention to the external threat posed by the reproductive capacity of Mexican women, the magazine indicated that the threat was also internal because the supposedly high fertility levels among Mexican immigrants and their U.S.-born children were implicated in U.S. population growth.

The contribution of Latino immigrants and their children to the nation's population growth was viewed as particularly problematic, given the pressure from environmental and population groups, such as Zero Population Growth Inc. For example, Leonard F. Chapman Jr., commissioner of the Immigration and Naturalization Service (INS), made this point in a 1974 interview in *U.S. News and World Report*: "We're very close in this country to a zero population growth through births. As we get closer to that zero growth, immigration will become an even larger percentage of the population increase."[44] In addition, social science constructions of the Latina, particularly Mexican American, fertility "problem" often intersected with the characterizations found in the magazines. For example, Alvirez and Bean, citing Chapman's estimates of the growing Mexican American population, stated, "The most noticeable feature of the Mexican American family is its size relative to other groups in America. The fertility of Mexican Americans is substantially higher than other groups."[45] At the time, the average size of Mexican American families (4.4) was about one person larger than for all Americans (3.5 persons per family).[46] Alvirez and Bean also observed that Mexican women's fertility rates were subject to change from urbanization and social mobility, which was substantiated by later empirical findings (discussed below).

In 1979 Paul Ehrlich followed the *Population Bomb* with *The Golden Door*, which focused on Mexico and Mexican migration to the United States.[47] According to Ehrlich and his coauthors, Mexico's population growth was a major problem for Mexico, and thus for the United States, because it combined with social inequalities and inadequate job creation to produce intense pressures on emigration. Mexico's high fertility rate was the result of an "unusually pronatalist cultural tradition," which meant that Mexicans placed an abnormally high cultural value on having children. Because of machismo and Marianismo, the argument went, men were dominant and women were submissive, and having more children increased the social status of both men and women. "Motherhood is viewed as the essential purpose for a woman's existence," Ehrlich and his colleagues wrote, adding that these pronatalist cultural values are reinforced by the Catholic Church.[48]

However, Ehrlich was also cautiously optimistic about Mexico's future fertility patterns. Based on his travels in Mexico, he observed that the Mexican government was taking population control seriously and implementing programs to change cultural values in the direction of smaller families. He noted that such programs were already having some effect and that these efforts "will be felt in the long run."[49] Moreover, Ehrlich's overview of Mexican history and the U.S.-Mexico relationship led him to warn against alarmist anti-Mexican rhetoric. In fact, he appeared to be speaking against *U.S. News and World Report*'s cover, cited above, with the message "Why there'll be no end to the invasion of 'illegals.'" As Ehrlich noted:

> Mexico is in one of the worst demographic situations of any nation—something that should worry any humane person regardless of Mexico's geographic position. . . . But because of the myths about Mexicans, in many people concern has taken the form of outright fear of an invasion. This fear is rooted in ignorance of our southern neighbors, their past, and our past involvement with them. Some knowledge of them as a *people*, rather than caricatures, should help to calm that fear and allow legitimate concerns to be handled sensibly.[50]

Despite Ehrlich's call for calm, his work reaffirmed already-taken-for-granted assumptions about the family values and fertility rates of Mexican women. Soon after *The Golden Door* appeared, *Time* magazine's August 6, 1984, issue devoted a cover to Mexico and its population problem. The cover's image begins with the headline "Mexico City: The Population Curse" (Figure 3.3). Below the headline is a sun behind two Aztec twin pyramids. The sun the Aztecs worshipped, however, is being engulfed in smoke pouring out of chimneys from either factories or oil fields, since there are a number of oil derricks surrounding the smoking towers in the middle of the image. To the left is an urban landscape of tall buildings that continue to the edge of the image in the fashion of an infinityline (a line of people, animals, or things that seems to go

Figure 3.3. Cover of *Time*, August 6, 1984. © 2007 Time Inc. Reprinted courtesy of the editors of Time Magazine.

on without end), thus giving the appearance of endless growth.[51] To the right is another endless line of suburban-style housing. Below the buildings and smoking towers is a four-lane highway filled with cars snaking off into the distance, once again with the visual metaphor of the infinityline emphasizing that the line of cars is unending. Below the highway of cars is a mass of people flowing without end across the page. The message the *Time* cover imparts to its readers is that Mexico's population curse is also the readers' curse because of the pressure it creates for Mexican emigration.

Increasingly in the 1980s, the growth of the U.S. Latino population was mentioned in conjunction with the declining proportion of whites in the U.S. population and declines in European immigration. For example, *Newsweek*'s January 17, 1983, issue reported that between 1970 and 1980, the Latino population in the United States grew by 61 percent, largely because of immigration and higher fertility rates and because since the mid-1960s there were 46.4 percent fewer immigrants from Europe. In addition, fertility took center stage in the invasion and reconquest narratives. Both *U.S. News and World Report* (March 7, 1983) and *Newsweek* (June 25, 1984) published covers with photographs of Mexican women being carried across water into the United States. *U.S. News and World*

Report's cover announced, "Invasion from Mexico: It Just Keeps Growing," and *Newsweek*'s title read, "Closing the Door? The Angry Debate over Illegal Immigration; Crossing the Rio Grande." The message was that the invasion carried the seeds of future generations. Women would have babies, create families, and soon communities of Latinos who would remain linguistically and socially separate would be clamoring for a reconquest of the United States.

Latina fertility was also linked to demographic changes, particularly to whites becoming a proportionately smaller part of the population. For example, John Tanton, an ophthalmologist from Michigan, a former president of Zero Population Growth, the founder of the Federation for American Immigration Reform, and an ardent promoter of making English the official language of the United States, wrote a now infamous memorandum in 1988 about Latina fertility and "the Latin onslaught," in which he stated: "Will Latin American immigrants bring with them the tradition of the *mordida* (bribe), the lack of involvement in public affairs, etc.? Will the present majority peaceably hand over its political power to a group that is simply more fertile? . . . On the demographic point: Perhaps this is the first instance in which those with their pants up are going to get caught by those with their pants down!"[52]

By the late 1980s and early 1990s, the "browning of America" was a concept with increasing currency.[53] For instance, in 1990 *Time* magazine noted: "The 'browning of America' will alter everything in society, from politics and education to industry, values and culture. . . . The deeper significance of America becoming a majority nonwhite society is what it means to the national psyche, to individuals' sense of themselves and the nation—their idea of what it is to be American."[54] What is even more telling concerning the role of fertility in the "browning of America" narrative is the advertisement for this issue that *Time* created.

The image in *Time*'s advertisement consists of thirty-eight newborn babies arranged ten to a row, except for the bottom row, which has eight babies and a small copy of *Time*'s cover for April 9, 1990 (Figure 3.4). The babies are a mix of various shades of brown. Only the baby next to the magazine cover's image is white. The cover's image, though reduced in size, is still discernible as an American flag without the white stars and with three white stripes almost filled in by the colors black, brown, and yellow, representing African Americans, Latinos, and Asian Americans. The color white (representing white Americans) is barely visible on the flag. The cover text states: "America's changing colors: What will the U.S. be like when whites are no longer the majority?" Although framing the

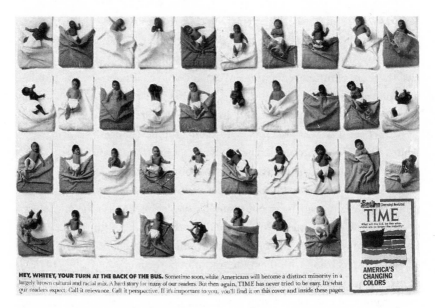

Figure 3.4. Advertisement for the April 9, 1990, issue of *Time.* © 1990 Time Inc. Reprinted courtesy of the editors of Time Magazine.

question this way, in conjunction with the flag image, is racially divisive, it pales in comparison with the words of the advertisement:

> Hey, whitey, your turn at the back of the bus. Sometime soon, white Americans will become a distinct minority in a largely brown cultural and racial mix. A hard story for many of our readers. But then again, TIME has never tried to be easy. It's what our readers expect. Call it relevance. Call it perspective. If it's important to you, you'll find it on this cover and inside these pages.

One has to wonder who exactly are "our readers" and "you," to whom the advertisement's text is directed. Can Latinos, African Americans, and Asian Americans really be among the readers that the advertisement is intended to appeal to, after they have been represented as a problem for white Americans? Are they included among the people who constitute the imagined community of the ad after they are accused of pushing whites to the "back of the bus" and metaphorically out of the nation (by excluding them from the U.S. flag)? Further targeting has been accomplished by the ad's imagery of the reproductive threat. Since most of the babies are brown, the reader can only assume that Latino reproduction is a major problem.

Most of the authors writing about the Mexican invasion and reconquest examined in Chapter 1 also focused on fertility and reproduction. For example, Peter Brimelow found that Hispanics were particularly troublesome because of biological and social reproduction issues. Using Latinos as a bully pulpit, he launched into a diatribe about bilingualism, multiculturalism, multilingual ballots, citizenship for children of illegal immigrants, the abandonment of English as a prerequisite for citizenship, the erosion of citizenship as the sole qualification for voting, welfare and education for illegal immigrants and their children, and congressional and state legislative apportionment based on populations that include illegal immigrants.[55]

Victor Hanson, who as you will recall from Chapter 1 was outspoken in his concern about the "Mexicanization" of California, blamed a blind adherence to culture for what he considered the curse of large families:

> The greatest hazard to the illegal immigrant is a large family—the truth that is never mentioned, much less discussed. Everything that he was born into—parents, priest, reigning mores—tells him to have five boys, better six or seven, to carry on the family name, ensure help in the fields, give more souls to God, provide visible proof of virility, and create a captive audience at the dinner table. In contrast, everything America values—money, free time, individual growth, secular pleasure—advises the opposite.[56]

For Hanson, Mexican identity and values were the polar opposite of American identity and values, and both were locked into unchanging, essentialized types.

Georgie Ann Geyer claimed that California's population was increasing faster than India's because of Mexican immigrant fertility rates. According to Geyer, Mexican immigrant women had six children per family and did not change over time or in response to new circumstances: "There is no truth to that bit of 'common wisdom' that says immigrant women will have fewer children as they become more prosperous."[57] Similar fatalistic views on fertility were also voiced by Samuel P. Huntington when he characterized the threat posed by Latinos. He found the fertility rates of Latin American, especially Mexican, immigrants to be the "single most immediate and most serious challenge to America's traditional identity."[58]

An appropriate end to this section is *Foreign Policy* magazine's 2001 article on "The Population Implosion."[59] It is appropriate in two senses. First of all, the article resonates with my own observations below that low fertility is no panacea for society's problems and that it generates pressure for more immigration.

Figure 3.5. Cover of *Foreign Policy*, March–April 2001. Used by permission of Karen Moskowitz / Getty Images.

Fertility levels worldwide experienced a dramatic drop of over 40 percent between the early 1950s and the end of the twentieth century. But the decline in fertility rates has been especially acute in the industrialized nations, where they are at "subreplacement" levels. When low fertility combines with rapidly aging populations, new problems emerge. The way in which *Foreign Policy* chose to represent this problem on its cover also summarizes a key point of the discussion so far. The magazine cover's headline stated: "Wanted: More Babies. Why the end of the population explosion is a mixed blessing." The sort of babies that were needed was not-too-subtly suggested by the white, blue-eyed cherubic infant that almost fills the cover (Figure 3.5). White babies were needed to counter the browning of America, a perceived threat underlying much of the anti-immigration discourse on invasions and reconquests.

John Gibson, host of Fox News's *The Big Story*, expressed similar views when he made declining fertility rates the topic of his May 11, 2006, broadcast.[60] He urged viewers, "Do your duty. Make more babies." He was responding to population statistics indicating that half of all children under age five in the United States are minorities. As Gibson said, "You know what that means? Twenty-five years and the majority of the population will be Hispanic. To put it bluntly, we need more babies." However, like the 2001 *Foreign Policy* cover discussed above, Gibson did not mean just any babies. He was specifically asking for more white babies to offset the number of babies born to Latinos and other minorities.

CRACKS IN THE DISCOURSE

I became suspicious of the veracity of this discourse on Latina sexuality and reproduction for a number of reasons. I began to ask, is the story more complicated than we are led to believe? First of all, it may be true that, overall, Latinas have more children than white women, yet one cannot help but think about the relationship between the "graying of America" discourse and fertility statistics. Is it really that surprising that Latinas have more children per 1,000 women under age 45 in a place like Orange County, California, when the 2000 census indicates that the average adult white woman is between 40 and 44 years of age and Latinas are in their 20s?[61] Latinas are in the peak reproductive ages, whereas white women, on average, are toward the end of their reproductive lives. Even using "under 45 years of age" as a category, one would find, on average, more white, non-Latinas closer to age 45 and more Latinas, on average, much younger.

Also raising suspicion was that I often ask students in class and audiences in the many talks I give around the country how many children they would like to have. Few want ten, nine, or eight children and so on. I always start at ten children, but almost all want one or two children, a preference that runs across the racial/ethnic mosaic.

Finally, I have become increasingly interested in the fertility and immigration relationship. I think of it in terms of this image of the effect of capitalism on jobs and fertility:

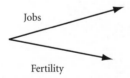

In capitalist economic systems, such as those of the United States and most of the industrialized nations of Europe as well as Japan, the basic premise is that economic growth is not only good but essential. There is tremendous pressure to maintain even a modicum of economic growth, which translates into creating more jobs today than yesterday. Creating more jobs avoids the social, political, and economic problems that come with economic recessions and depressions. For example, young people want jobs when they enter the labor market, and older people want their social entitlements, such as Social Security and medical care. Economic growth helps to accomplish these desires. However, as this simple illustration suggests, cultural values, based on economic considerations, are such that declining fertility rates are the rule in the industrialized nations and in the world more generally.

This gap between fertility and economic growth creates a demand for immigrant labor.[62] This gap will grow as U.S. baby boomers begin to retire in large numbers.[63] Why? There are only two ways to get workers for a labor market. You can either birth them or import them. This is true locally, regionally, and globally. Local labor markets can draw workers from other regions of the country, but they also draw foreign workers if the demand for labor persists. Consider the fertility rates in various countries as shown in Figure 3.6.[64] Now consider

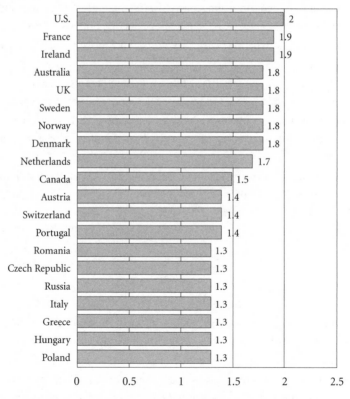

Figure 3.6. Fertility rates (children per woman) in selected countries.
SOURCE: Population Reference Bureau's 2006 Population Data Sheet.

the percentages of the foreign-born in various countries as shown in Figure 3.7.[65] What is clear is that countries with below-replacement fertility rates (less than two children per woman) often experience pressure for immigration. Only the United States is shown as being at replacement level, but its rate is actually lower if only women under 45 years of age, the reproductive years, are considered (see below). For some nations, such as Spain and Italy, fertility decline, combined with economic growth, has resulted in a rather rapid shift from being an emigrant-sending nation to an immigrant-receiving nation. Although 4 to 5 percent foreign-born in a population may not seem excessively high, the sudden visibility of immigrants can raise concerns. In Spain, for example, where the proportion of immigrants from northern Africa is relatively small,

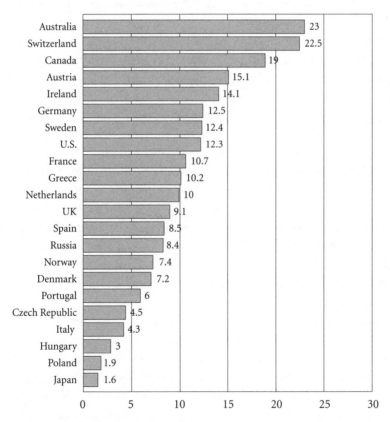

Figure 3.7. Foreign-born people as percentage of total population in selected countries.
SOURCES: Eurostat 2006; United Nations Statistics Division, 2007; Muenz, "Europe"; Kashiwazaki and Akaha, "Japanese Immigration Policy."

Spaniards view them as a threat to Spanish language, identity, and culture.[66] Japan, a nation that guards its borders carefully, has what it considers an "immigration problem," even though the foreign-born accounted for only about 1.6 percent of its population in the early 2000s.[67]

If a nation does not produce workers but has an investment in economic growth and job creation, then there is pressure to provide workers through immigration. The anti-immigration discourse blames immigrants for responding to this labor demand with little consideration given to homegrown pressures for immigrant flows. What influences the demand for immigrant labor is values, not only the value of having fewer children but also the desire for more education, a meaningful job, and more time for personal goals, as well as a desire for services such as fast food, child care, lawn care, elder care, manicures, hair care, and on and on. Along with these desires are equally strong desires not to perform certain jobs. I often ask students, "How many of you are going to spend your summer helping farmers harvest their crops?" None raise their hands. Students working on farms was once a common practice in a more rural, less urban and suburban America. We generally do not educate youth to desire low-income, semiskilled jobs in agriculture and food production, construction, manufacturing, and services. These are the default jobs for those we fail to educate properly—but that is another topic. The bottom line is that fertility is related to immigration in a way that is often not discussed in the anti-immigrant discourse.

Paul Ehrlich's call in the 1960s to engage in sexual activity in order to recreate and not procreate appears to have found its place in today's industrialized nations. However, low fertility rates have also fostered recognition of a need to procreate and not merely recreate. Many countries—among them Japan, Italy, France, Singapore, Malaysia, Poland, and Russia—are now providing tax and cash incentives for those willing to have more children.[68] In Europe the Christian Right is pressuring for more of the "right" kind of babies as fears of Muslims outbreeding whites spread.[69]

In addition to these global fertility trends, there are also some other detectable empirical contradictions. Bean, Swicegood, and Berg found that the mean number of children ever born to Mexican-origin women decreased dramatically between 1970 and 1998.[70] All Mexican-origin women in the United States between 16 and 44 years of age had 1.81 children, well below zero population growth. Non-Hispanic white women between the same ages, however, had only 1.27 children according to these data, so there is still a "gap" of 42 percent between them and Latinas.

Moreover, the few studies that have examined actual behavior among Latinas have found some important differences from stereotypical character-izations. For example, Marchi and Guendelman found that Latina girls in their study had lower rates of sexual activity than non-Latina girls, which they attrib-uted to Latino cultural norms.[71] They noted that with "increasing acculturation to U.S. norms and values, Latina girls engage in sexual activities at an earlier age and are more likely to have births out of wedlock."[72] In another study, Amaro found that most of the Mexican American women in her study favored con-traceptive use, most had used one or more contraceptive methods, and some of them desired smaller families than they actually had.[73] Similarly, Stroup-Benham and Trevino found that 61 percent of Hispanic women nationwide in 1979 has used oral contraceptives, almost as high a rate as non-Hispanics (68 percent).[74]

Finally, research in Mexico also suggests problems with common character-izations of Mexican women's fertility and reproduction. Carole Browner found that women in a rural Mexican village generally wanted fewer children than the number promoted by government policies.[75] Jennifer Hirsch found that fertil-ity rates had declined dramatically in Mexico—from 7 to 8 children per woman before 1970 to 4.4 children per woman in 1980, 3.8 children in 1986, and 3.4 in 1990.[76] By 2002, Mexico's fertility rate had dropped to 2.9 children born to a woman during her lifetime, and the rate for U.S. women was 2.1, according to the U.S. Population Reference Bureau.[77] CONAPO put the fertility rate lower—at 2.4 children per Mexican woman in 2000.[78] Clearly, Mexico has experienced a dramatic decline in fertility rates over the last few decades. Declines in fertil-ity are undoubtedly greater for younger Mexican women than these averages for fertility indicate. Hirsch attributes the drop in Mexican women's fertility to changing beliefs about marriage relationships, delaying having children, spac-ing births out more than in the past, and increased contraceptive use.[79]

These experiences and realizations led me to question the taken-for-granted "truths" of the discourse on Latina fertility and reproduction. At the very least, Latina fertility and reproduction appear to be more complex than generally characterized in public forums. The discourse on Latina reproduction would have us believe that U.S.-born Latinas and Latin American, especially Mexican, immigrants have extreme, even dangerous, levels of fertility relative to the levels among an imagined native population. The "hot" Latina stereotype is premised on assumptions of significant differences in reproductive-related behavior be-tween Latinas and white women such that Latinas are younger when they have their first sexual experience, are younger when they have their first child, have more sexual partners, and are reluctant to use birth control. What can we say about those behaviors? Differences in fertility rates may exist, but how can we understand those differences? Are Latina fertility rates immutable, or do they change in relation to contextual circumstances? What are the factors influencing the number of children Latinas have? To explore these questions, I examined data collected on Latinas and white women residents of Orange County, California, to which we now turn.

4 LATINA FERTILITY AND REPRODUCTION RECONSIDERED

ARE LATINA FERTILITY AND REPRODUCTION out of control? Do Latinas have exorbitantly high, and unchanging, fertility rates? Is there variation among Latinas because of factors such as age, education, and U.S. experience? These questions pose a challenge to the credibility and veracity of the discourse on Latina fertility and reproduction examined in Chapter 3. Here I explore these questions, using information collected among Latinas in Orange County, California.

In the early 1990s, I was part of a study designed to examine beliefs about breast and cervical cancer and the use of cancer screening examinations among Latinas and non-Latina white women in Orange County.[1] Then in 2006, I conducted another study in Orange County examining issues of social integration, the findings of which were examined in Chapter 2. Although neither study was designed to examine fertility and reproduction per se, examining the relevant findings from both of these studies suggests that there are some differences between Latinos and white women but that those differences are modest in comparison to the rhetoric surrounding Latina fertility and reproduction. Moreover, it became apparent that reproduction and fertility are not fixed and immutable but rather reflect differences among Latinas, who are often glossed as homogenous and impervious to change.

The methods followed in both studies were similar.[2] The final questionnaires asked about demographic characteristics, which included some questions related to fertility and reproduction. They also included a previously validated five-point scale that measured acculturation primarily on the use of Spanish or English (e.g., language used to speak with at home, with friends, etc.).[3] This language acculturation measure was included because it offered a greater range of variation than the dichotomous foreign-born/U.S.-born variable. Moreover many people who lack English proficiency face significant obstacles accessing medical services in the United States, including information on reproductive services.[4]

Since neither study specifically focused on reproduction and fertility, they are both limited in the data they provide. The early 1990s study included information on sexual behavior, age at birth of first child, number of children ever born, and the use of birth control pills but not other methods of contraception. The 2006 study has information on the number of children ever born. Despite these limitations, the data that are available provide interesting information on Latina reproductive behavior and allow us to examine changes in fertility among Latinas in Orange County at two moments in time, about fifteen years apart.

Another advantage of examining these two studies is that they were not undertaken with the intention of repudiating the Latina reproduction discourse. Rather, the analysis of the discourse on Latina reproduction generated questions that can be examined with data collected independently by these studies. In addition, the Orange County data can also be compared with national data to pinpoint differences and similarities between the local and the national. Questioning the factual bases of the discourse surrounding the politics of Latina reproduction may, hopefully, contribute to the formulation of a new way of thinking about reproduction, immigration, and social change.

INTERVIEWEE CHARACTERISTICS

Table 4.1 presents the nationality of survey respondents in both studies. The early 1990s study had more respondents because the sample was all women, whereas women were only part of the total number of interviewees in 2006. But both surveys captured about the same proportions of women. The majority of Latinas are of Mexican origin.

Table 4.2 provides a summary of respondents' sociodemographic characteristics. Latina immigrants tended to be younger, had fewer years of education, were less likely to have medical insurance, and had lower incomes than both U.S.-born Latinas and white women. Their language acculturation levels were also generally lower than those of U.S.-born Latinas. The women in the 2006 study were generally older, and the immigrants had been in the United States longer than women in the early 1990s study. Both of these factors meant that the women in the 2006 study were generally well into their childbearing years.

Table 4.1. Orange County surveys' respondents, women only (in percentages)

Interviewees	Early 1990s study* (N=1,225)	2006 study** (N=684)
Mexican immigrants	35	41
Salvadoran immigrants	2	2
Other Central American immigrants	3	2
Other Latin American immigrants	4	2
U.S.-born women of Mexican descent (Chicanas)	14	13
Other U.S.-born Latinas	8	4
White women	34	36

*SOURCE: Cancer and Latinas Study (Chavez et al. 1997).
**SOURCE: Center for Research on Latinos in a Global Society survey of Orange County, 2006.

Table 4.2. Sociodemographic characteristics of Orange County surveys' female respondents

	Latina immigrants		U.S.-born Latinas		White women	
	1990s (N=533)	2006 (N=323)	1990s (N=270)	2006 (N=116)	1990s (N=422)	2006 (N=244)
Age (mean)	33	39	37	42	44	58
Years of school (mean)	9	10	13	14	15	15
Years in U.S. (%)						
5 or less	28	9	—	—	—	—
6–10	21	17				
11–15	23	21				
> 15	29	53				
% married, live together	75	72	63	69	63	78
% homemaker only	34	33	16	11	18	11
% employed full-time	36	34	54	52	51	31
% employed part-time	12	15	12	12	12	14
Income (%)						
< $35,000	85	72	44	34	30	24
$35,000+	15	28	54	66	70	76
Percent with private or government medical insurance	57	58	87	74	92	90
Language acculturation index (five-point scale)	1.6	1.7	4.2	3.9	—	—

FERTILITY AND REPRODUCTION

Before examining the number of children women had, there are four other factors related to sexuality and reproduction that deserve attention: age when sexual relations were initiated, the number of sexual partners, age at first child, and use of birth control pills. Although discourses and ideologies shape the truth for political ends, their truth claims are still subject to examination. The discourse on Latina reproduction suggests that Latinas and white women would differ significantly in these fertility-related behaviors.

Figure 4.1 presents information on the age when the women sampled in Orange County in the early 1990s initiated sexual intercourse. Latina immigrants were somewhat less likely than U.S.-born women, both Latinas and whites, to begin engaging in sexual intercourse before age 18. On average, white women (mean = 18.1 years) began sexual relations about a year younger than all Latinas surveyed (mean = 19.0), a statistically significant difference.[5] The difference is statistically

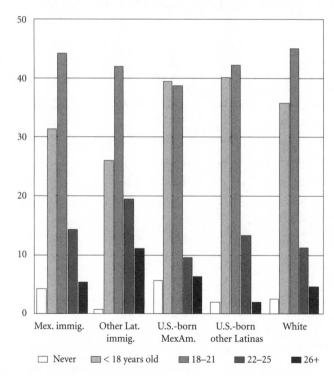

Figure 4.1. Age at first sexual intercourse for women in early 1990s survey only (in percentages).
SOURCE: CRLGS Orange Country 2006 Study.

insignificant when U.S.-born Latinas (mean age = 17.9) are compared with white women,[6] but it is significant when Latina immigrants (mean age = 19.5) are compared with white women.[7] Latina immigrants were about a year and a half older than whites in Orange County when they initiated sexual intercourse.

Latinas and white women also varied on the number of reported sexual partners (Figure 4.2). Latina immigrants were more likely to report having had no more than two sexual partners.[8] White women were more likely than Latinas to report having had five or more sexual partners. Latinas in general (mean = 2.5) and white women (mean = 6.3) differed significantly in the mean number of reported sexual partners.[9] Once again, U.S.-born Latinas

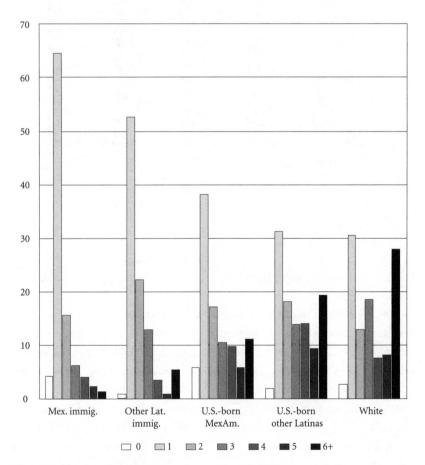

Figure 4.2. Number of sexual partners of women in early 1990s survey only (in percentages).
SOURCE: CRLGS Orange Country 2006 Study.

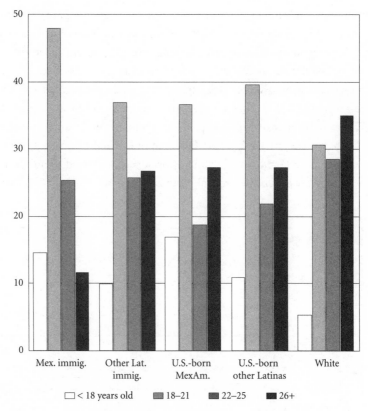

Figure 4.3. Age of women at the birth of their first child in early 1990s survey only (in percentages).
SOURCE: CRLGS Orange County 2006 Study.

(mean = 4.3) did not differ significantly from white women,[10] but Latina immigrants (mean = 1.8) did.[11]

There were also significant differences in the age when women had their first child (Figure 4.3). Few white women, relative to Mexican immigrants and U.S.-born women of Mexican descent, had their first child before age 18. Whites were more likely than Latinas to have their first child after age 25. The mean age at which white women had their first child (24.3) was significantly greater than that for Latinas generally (21.6),[12] U.S.-born Latinas (21.9),[13] and Latina immigrants (21.4).[14] In contrast to a stereotype of rampant fertility among Latinas, all the women sampled waited, on average, until they were over 20 years old to have their first child.

Finally, a majority of all the women in the early 1990s study had used birth control pills at some point in their lives: Mexican immigrants (64.5 percent), other Latin American immigrants (62.3 percent), U.S.-born Mexican-origin women (72.2 percent), other U.S.-born Latinas (75.3 percent), and white women (85.4 percent). The large proportions of Latinas who were willing to use birth control pills indicated that Latinas were concerned with family planning and the control of fertility, contrary to the popular rhetoric surrounding Latina fertility. Although two-thirds of Latinas generally had used birth control pills, they were still significantly less likely to have done so than white women, most of whom had used the pill.[15] However, the difference between U.S.-born Latinas and white women was not significant.[16]

We turn now to the number of children ever born to Latinas and white women in the early 1990s survey. This variable refers to the number of children a woman had at the moment of the interview, not the total number of children she would have in her lifetime. Table 4.3 presents the number of children by various age categories to indicate the influence of age and to take into account the different age structures and fertility patterns of Latinas and white women. Examining only women up to 44 years of age—the convention in most studies of fertility—may capture a majority of women during their peak years of fertility, but it leaves out more older white women than Latinas. About 59 percent of the white women surveyed in the early 1990s were between 18 and 44 years of age, whereas 83 percent of the Latinas were within that age range.

Table 4.3. Mean number of children ever born (CEB) to Latinas and white women in Orange County by women's age categories for the early 1990s study only

	Latinas			Whites		
Age category	Women (N)	Children (N)	Mean	Women (N)	Children (N)	Mean
18–30-year-olds	376	469	1.25	82	57	0.70*
31–44-year-olds	289	755	2.61	165	244	1.48*
45+-year-olds	137	488	3.56	170	431	2.54*
18–44-year-olds	665	1224	1.84	247	301	1.22*
Women of all ages	802	1712	2.13	417	732	1.76*

*t-test $p = < .001$.

Latinas between 18 and 30 years old had only 1.2 children, while white women in this age group had 0.7 children—a significant difference. Given that both groups were still early in their reproductive years, these numbers would increase in time, but by how much is difficult to predict. For both Latinas and whites, the trend was toward fewer children. With each succeeding age category, the number of children increased. However, the key age category was women 18–44 years of age. Both Latinas and white women in these prime childbearing years are below the 2.0 children per woman required for population replacement and well below the 2.1 children needed for population growth.

Age is only one factor influencing fertility. How does a Latina's immigration history and generation in the United States influence the number of children she has? Table 4.4 presents the number of children born to women in our Orange County study between the ages of 18 and 44 in relation to immigration and generation patterns. Since Mexican-origin women have been the subject of heightened surveillance and the target of much of the discourse on Latina fertility, Table 4.4 provides information on them separately. The table also presents the national data on children ever born to Mexican-origin women provided by Frank Bean and his colleagues.[17] There are a couple of distinct comparative advantages to using these data, which were obtained by pooling individual records of women of childbearing age from the June 1986 and June 1988 Current Population Surveys (CPS). First, the information on the number of children ever born is broken down by generation in the United States, from immigrants to third and later generations. Second, the CPS data are only a few years earlier than the data collected in the early 1990s Orange County study.

What is striking about the information in Table 4.4 is the low number of children among almost all the women. White women in Orange County, with a mean of 1.22 children, had fewer than the 1.27 children for white women nationally. Latinas generally also had fewer than 2.0 children per woman. With 1.93 per woman, Mexican-origin women showed a dramatic decrease from the 4.4 children per woman found in the early 1970s. Mexican immigrants who migrated to the United States as adults (15 years old or older) had the highest number of children per woman (2.31), but their rate was lower than that found among their counterparts nationally. But the number of children born to Mexican immigrants who migrated as children (under 16) fell to 1.55 per woman, only 22 percent higher than white women (although statistically significant).[18] Immigrants from countries other than Mexico had a mean of 1.81 children per woman. When all Latin American immigrants, including Mexicans, were

Table 4.4. Mean numbers of children ever born (CEB) to Latinas of ages 18–44 (early 1990s study only) and Latina/white CEB ratios

		Orange County study		National fertility data provided by Bean et al.[a]	
	N	Children ever born (mean)	Latina/ white CEB ratio	Children ever born (mean)	Latina/ white CEB ratio
All Mexican-origin	514	1.93	1.58	1.81	1.42
First generation					
Child immigrants	88	1.55	1.27	1.55	1.22
Adult immigrants	301	2.31	1.89	2.45	1.93
Second generation	65	1.17	0.96	1.40	1.10
Third-plus generations	60	1.42	1.16	1.71	1.35
White women	247	1.22	1.00	1.27	1.00
Latin American immigrants (not Mexican)	77	1.81	1.48		
U.S.-born Latinas (not Mexican-origin)	73	1.27	1.04		
All Latin American immigrants	466	2.08	1.70		
All U.S.-born Latinas	199	1.28	1.05		
All Latinas	665	1.84	1.51		

[a]Bean, Swicegood, and Berg, "Mexican-Origin Fertility."

examined together, they had 2.08 children per women, a rate that demographically replaces the parents but contributes minimally to growth.

The fertility story was even more dramatic for U.S.-born Latinas. Second-generation Mexican-origin women actually had fewer children per woman (1.17) than white women, although the difference is statistically insignificant.[19] This figure was lower than for second-generation Mexican Americans nationally. Third-plus-generation Mexican-origin women had 1.42 children per woman, which is more than second-generation Mexican-origin women but still only 16 percent more than white women in Orange County, also insignificant.[20] Third-generation Mexican-origin women in Orange County had fewer children on average than their counterparts nationally. When all U.S.-born Latinas sampled in Orange County were examined together, they had a mean of 1.28 children per woman, only 5 percent more than white women in Orange County and almost equal to white women nationally.

Table 4.5. Mean numbers of children ever born to Latinas and white women, ages 18–44, in the 2006 study only

	N	Mean number of children ever born
All Mexican-origin	246	1.79
First generation		
Child immigrants < 15	44	1.07
Adult immigrants 15+	145	2.24
Second generation	41	1.22
Third-plus generations	14	1.14
White women	46	1.63
Latin American immigrants (not Mexican)	19	1.37
U.S.-born Latinas (not Mexican-origin)	8	1.25
All Latin American immigrants	208	1.91
All U.S.-born Latinas	65	1.22
All Latinas	273	1.75

The women in the 2006 study had similar patterns of fertility as women in the earlier study (Table 4.5). Some means were a bit higher than in the early 1990s study, but that is what one might expect, given that the women in the 2006 study were generally older and the immigrants had been in the United States longer. However, all Mexican-origin women, Mexican immigrants who migrated as children, and the U.S.-born second- and third-plus generations all had means of less than 2 children per woman. Only Mexican immigrant women who had migrated as adults (15 or older) had, on average, more than 2 children.

I should note that there is an important limitation when examining fertility across generations using cross-sectional data—for example, census and survey data. Figuring out the first generation is easy; they were born in another country and migrated to the United States. The second generation was born in the United States but had at least one foreign-born parent. The third generation is more difficult in that those who were U.S.-born and had both parents born in the United States also includes all subsequent generations, which is why the category is called the third-plus generation. Often the third-plus generation of Mexican-origin women showed a slight increase in fertility relative to the second generation.[21] The problem is that because the third-plus generation includes individuals of multiple generations, it is difficult to know what is really going on.

Table 4.6. OLS regression with the number of children ever born as the dependent variable for Latinas and white women ages 18 and older in both studies

	Model 1 (early 1990s study)		Model 2 (2006 study)	
	Ba	SE	B	SE
Age	.060	.003***	.046	.005***
Years of schooling	−.079	.012***	−.049	.020*
Married 0. No 1. Yes	.709	.090***	.297	.145*
Latino-White 0. Latina 1. White	−.152	.127	.002	.199
Language acculturation (five-point scale)	−.140	.041**	−.206	.067**
Constant	.706	.171***	.910	.358

SOURCES: Chavez et al., "Undocumented Immigrants in Orange County, California" (early 1990s study); CRLGS Orange County 2006 Study.

NOTE: OLS = ordinary least squares; B = beta; SE = standard error

Summary statistics for Model 1: $N = 1206$; $R^2_{adj} = .327$; SE = 1.44127; $F = < .0001$.

Summary statistics for Model 2: $N = 655$; $R^2_{adj} = .264$; SE = 1.45627; $F = < .0001$.

$*p < .05$; $**p < .01$; $***p < .001$.

Finally, I wondered if the difference in the mean number of children ever born to Latinas and white women would be significant in a multivariate analysis, which controls for the influence of other variables. Table 4.6 presents the findings from an ordinary least squares (OLS) regression using the number of children ever born as the dependent variable. The independent variables include Latina/white (values = 0, 1), married (0 = not married, 1 = married), education (total years), age (total years), and the language acculturation variable (five-point scale). Income was not included because it correlated closely with language acculturation in the early 1990s study. Latinas who scored low on their integration into English-speaking U.S. culture and society also generally had lower incomes. A variable indicating U.S. or foreign birth was also not included since it too correlates highly (.9) with the language acculturation variable.

The data analyzed in the OLS regressions came from the early 1990s study and comparable data from the 2006 study. In Model 1, only the early 1990s data were examined. Age, education, marital status, and language acculturation were significant predictors of fertility. As a woman aged and married or lived with someone, she was more likely to have children. As she became more educated and increasingly acculturated into the larger society as indicated by the language acculturation index, she was likely to have fewer children. Ethnicity, however, was not significant for understanding fertility when controlling for these other variables.

In Model 2, using the 2006 study data, the same pattern occurred. Being Latina or white did not significantly predict the number of children women had. Age and marital status were predictors for more children. Increasing education and language acculturation were significant predictors of fewer children.

What variables help us understand fertility among Latinas when they are examined alone? Table 4.7 shows the results of an analysis with only Latinas in the equation. In Model 3, the number of children Latinas had was significantly influenced by the same variables: age, education, marital status, and language acculturation. However, religion, which was not significant when included in the analysis with both Latinas and white women included (not shown here),

Table 4.7. OLS regression with the number of children ever born as the dependent variable for all Latinas of ages 18 and older in the 2006 Orange County study only

	Model 3 (2006 study)		Model 4 (2006 study)	
	B	SE	B	SE
Age	.051	.007***	.051	.007***
Years of schooling	−.073	.026**	.077	.025**
Married 0. No 1. Yes	.453	.195*	.524	.193**
Religion 0. Catholic 1. Other religious preference	.675	.196**	.597	.194**
Income	.146	.205	.099	.200
Language acculturation (five-point scale)	−.209	.079**		
Generations in U.S. (four-point scale, includes 1.5 generation)			−.191	.071**
Constant	−.363	.554	−.404	.550

SOURCE: CRLGS Orange County 2006 Study.
NOTE: OLS = ordinary least squares; B = beta; SE =standard error
Summary statistics for Model 3: $N = 297$; $R^2_{adj} = .253$; SE = 1.44502; $F = < .0001$.
Summary statistics for Model 4: $N = 299$; $R^2_{adj} = .248$; SE = 1.44263; $F = < .0001$.
*$p < .05$; **$p < .01$; ***$p < .001$.

was statistically significant when Latinas were examined independently. Interestingly, Latinas who claimed they were Catholic were likely to have fewer children than their non-Catholic counterparts, when holding these other variables constant. In Model 4, generations in the United States were used in the analysis rather than language acculturation. This was a four-point variable that included immigrants who migrated at 15 years of age or older (first generation), those who migrated under 15 years of age (1.5 generation), second generation, and third-plus generations. Over generations, Latinas had fewer children, a statistically significant pattern.

LATINAS AS AGENTS OF CHANGE

Dorothy Roberts has observed that welfare reform and policies to regulate fertility are propelled by powerful stereotypes: "Myths are more than made-up stories. They are also firmly held beliefs that represent and attempt to explain what we perceive to be the truth. They can become more credible than reality, holding fast even in the face of airtight statistics and rational argument to the contrary."[22] The taken-for-granted assumption in the discourse on Latina fertility and reproduction is that Latinas are a population with "their pants down" and thus their reproductive behavior poses serious threats to the nation. Latina hyper-fertility threatens the nation's demographic future by adding to population growth and changing its ethnic-racial composition (read: proportionally fewer whites). The children Latinas produce are viewed as forming the basis for a potential takeover or reconquest of U.S territory. Latinas and the children are perceived as destabilizing and bringing imminent destruction to the nation's medical and other social services.

Data on Latina reproductive behavior cannot possibly refute the deeply held beliefs upon which such cataclysmic stories are based. However, the evidence presented here does not support this highly pejorative view of Latina reproduction-related behavior. In comparison with white women, Latinas do not begin sexual activities at a relatively early age nor do they have relatively more sexual partners. They may have their first child a couple of years earlier than the white women in the sample, but on average they are over 20 years old when they do so.[23] Importantly, most Latinas have used birth control pills at some point in their lives. These findings do not provide evidence for reproductive behavior that is out of control.

Moreover, Latinas are not static when it comes to fertility. They, like other women in the United States, Mexico, and the world in general, have experienced rather dramatic declines in fertility. This is confirmed by evidence on the number of children ever born to Latinas in Orange County. Latinas who migrated at a young age had fewer children than older immigrants. U.S-born Latinas, even Mexicans, had fewer children than other Latina immigrants. This pattern, observed in separate studies fifteen years apart, underscores that reproductive behavior can vary among Latinas as their life experiences change.

Multivariate analysis suggests that several factors influence the number of children women have and that these factors are more important than being Latina or white. Age, education, and marital status consistently predicted whether women had more or less children. In addition, Latinas with increasing facility with English, perhaps because it increases sources of knowledge about reproductive control and economic opportunities, had fewer children. Ethnicity was not a statistically significant variable for understanding fertility differences. Among Latinas, religious affiliation was a significant predictor of fertility, with Catholics having fewer children than non-Catholics. In contrast to the discourse on Latina reproduction, Latinas in Orange County were not slaves to tradition, mindlessly adhering to Catholic doctrine.

Since I first began writing about issues of Latina reproduction,[24] decreasing fertility has become more obvious to others. For example, the state of California is reconsidering population projections because of an "unexpectedly large decline in the Latino birthrate."[25] In addition, Philip Martin, an economics professor, has noted Mexico's precipitous drop in birth rates and predicted that there will be a dramatic decline in Mexicans available to work in the United States in the not-too-distant future.[26] Such predictions suggest that a few years after spending billions of dollars to build a fence along the U.S.-Mexico border, there may not be enough Mexicans on hand to come across and fill U.S. labor needs.

In another recent study, Emilio A. Parrado and S. Philip Morgan focused on the number of children ever born to U.S. Hispanic and specifically Mexican-origin grandmothers, mothers, and daughters over time and compared the results to white women's fertility.[27] They used a methodology that allows them to provide a clearer sense of generational change than with standard cross-sectional data (census and survey data) on first, second, and third-plus generations. Parrado and Morgan combined data over multiple years of the U.S. Census and Current Population Surveys on women with completed fertility histories. They found that fertility differentials between Mexican-origin women in the United States and white women were reduced across generations and that fertility fluctuated in relation to changing socioeconomic conditions. They concluded:

Contrary to the idea that Hispanic fertility may be less responsive to improvements in human capital or socioeconomic conditions, either due to a cultural proclivity to high fertility or to blocked opportunities in the U.S., we find a strong negative effect of years of education on the number of CEB [children ever born] among Hispanic women that is actually slighter larger than that found among white women. This is especially the case among the third immigrant generation.[28]

Parrado and Morgan's findings on Latina fertility and reproduction support those provided here.

In the discourse on Latina fertility and reproduction, it is assumed that the extreme decline in birth rates among white women is a positive value against which equally dramatic declines among Latinas inevitably come up short. An unasked question is, at what point do extremely low birth rates become problematic? The implications of falling birth rates were the subject of the *Los Angeles Times* headline that read: "Nation's Birthrate Drops to Its Lowest Level since 1909."[29] The implications have to do with family structure, how communities spend money, how the nation finances retirement, and the pressure for more immigration. A pattern of extreme fertility decline in industrialized nations may not be the most reasonable course. Latina fertility levels may in fact be more reasonable from a societal point of view than the continually decreasing fertility rates among Americans in general and white women in particular. Rather than Latinas being characterized as having "comparatively high" birth rates, white women could be characterized as having "comparatively low" birth rates. Would it be possible to make the following observation: the abnormally *low* fertility rates of white women are leading to demographic changes and increased pressure for immigration?

In the final analysis, the discourse surrounding Latina fertility and reproduction is actually about more than reproduction. It is also about reinforcing a characterization of whites as the legitimate Americans who are being supplanted demographically by less legitimate Latinos. For this reason, the empirical evidence examined here may easily be dismissed by those who prefer perpetuating a discourse that undermines Latino claims of citizenship.

MEDIA SPECTACLES AND THE PRODUCTION OF NEOLIBERAL CITIZEN-SUBJECTS

Part 2

5 ORGAN TRANSPLANTS AND THE PRIVILEGES OF CITIZENSHIP

ONCE CONJURING UP IMAGES OF FRANKENSTEIN-TYPE OPERATIONS, organ transplants are now routine medical treatments. And yet organ transplants are not easy to get. Organs are in short supply, making them a scarce resource, and transplant operations are expensive. These limiting factors result in heart-wrenching images of people, often young children, waiting at death's door for a heart, lung, or kidney transplant.[1] For example, in Romeoville, Illinois, 15-year-old Leonardo Sanchez was dying of end-stage kidney disease. He desperately needed $250,000 to be placed on a waiting list for kidney transplants because he was undocumented and did not have medical insurance.[2] His father was a butcher and earned $300 a week, out of which he sent money to his wife and four children in Mexico. Leonardo's father had brought him to the United States as an undocumented immigrant in 2003 to try to get him the medical attention he required.

Then there was the case of 13-year-old Edgar Gutierrez, who, on January 4, 2005, had a kidney transplant in Atlanta, Georgia. Edgar, too, was an undocumented immigrant from Mexico. Without money or medical insurance, Edgar was able to obtain a transplant thanks to generous donations, especially by a CNN executive and a retired Delta Air Lines pilot, who took pity on his case.[3] Liliana Garcia, age 13, also needed a kidney transplant in Michigan. Liliana was also an undocumented immigrant, and her parents had brought her to the United States because, as her mother said, "What else could I do? I didn't come here to get papers, or to make money. I came here to save my daughter's life. In Mexico, if you don't have money, they'll just let you die. Here she has a chance."[4] Another young person, Diego Alvarez, age 14, was living in Aurora, Illinois, where his family had migrated from Mexico in the fall of 2005. Diego and his family overstayed their tourist visas in the hope of receiving a double-lung transplant for his worsening case of cystic fibrosis. With little money and no medical insurance, the Alvarez family was pinning its hopes on Illinois's new medical insurance program for all children regardless of immigration status, but it would not cover the $1,766 bottle of prescription medication that Diego needed each month.[5]

Not all immigrant children waiting for organ transplants are Mexican. Twenty-year-old Madeeha Faryad, a Pakistani immigrant living in Virginia, had been diagnosed with cardiomyopathy and was in need of a new heart. However, she, too, was undocumented and lacked medical insurance and therefore had been denied placement on the transplant list. She and her family were desperately seeking donations to pay for the transplant.[6] The United States is not the only country facing transplant issues. In Britain, Ese Elizabeth Alabi, age 29 and mother of infant twin boys and a two-year-old son, died after she became ill with dilated cardiomyopathy (an enlarged heart), requiring a heart transplant. Unfortunately, Ese, an immigrant from Nigeria, had been visiting her husband in Britain, and her illness caused her to overstay her visa, making her a lower priority for government-financed medical care.[7]

Adult undocumented immigrants also face obstacles getting organ transplants, because even if they are employed, they often lack medical insurance.[8] For example, Angel, in his early 30s, worked as a waiter in New York and needed a kidney transplant in 2011. His brother was a match and was willing to donate a kidney. Angel was getting dialysis, costing $75,000 a year paid through a government program, but could not find a way to cover the $100,000 kidney transplant that would make dialysis unnecessary. For Angel, the major obstacle turned out to be insufficient funds to cover the post-transplant medical costs.[9]

One of the most renowned transplant cases is that of Jesica Santillan, the subject of an edited book that brought together scholars from various perspectives to focus just on her case.[10] Jesica, at 17 years old, was suffering from a birth defect that had left her heart and lungs unable to function properly. Her only chance was a transplant to replace the defective organs. She underwent surgery at Duke University Medical Center on February 7, 2003.[11] Tragically, the transplanted organs were of a different blood type from Jesica's.[12] Doctors quickly found new organs and transplanted those into the young woman's body, but it was too late—her brain had experienced too much damage. Jesica died on February 22, 2003.[13]

What do all of these cases have in common, beyond the medical dilemmas each patient faced? The patients were all immigrants and unauthorized residents, raising issues of citizenship and the allocation of limited resources such as organs.[14] As one newspaper article commented, transplants for immigrants "illuminate a poignant aspect of the immigration debate that has divided this country. The price of providing health care to undocumented immigrants is estimated to be in the billions. But denying life-saving health care to a child living in our midst seems unthinkable to many in a nation founded by immigrants."[15] For others, allowing immigrants, especially undocumented immigrants, to receive the organs of citizens is also unthinkable.

These cases, and the others like them, are embedded in the politics over immigration. At the center of this politics are differing perceptions of who is an American, as well as ideas about the alleged threats to the United States posed by some immigrants, particularly Mexicans, that were discussed in Chapter 1. Only by examining cases of organ transplants for immigrants in relation to this other story of Latino threat can we begin to make sense of the furor that often accompanies organ transplants for immigrants, not in biomedical terms but in cultural, social, and political terms.[16]

The human body has long been a metaphor for the nation.[17] The word *nation* here refers to the people who share a national identity—for example, those generally referred to as "Americans," members of "U.S. society," or even "we, the people." *Nation* is also commonly used to refer to the country or nation-state, as in "the American nation or the French nation." Immigrants are said to change the "face of the nation," meaning the demographics of the people in the United States.[18] We speak of "the body politic" to refer to concerned citizens. We also speak of the nation's "well-being" or refer to the economy as being "sick," using health metaphors for the body of the nation. Because the nation-as-body is such a taken-for-granted construction, immigrants are easily represented using metaphors of illness, disease, parasites, and plagues that threaten the nation.[19] Immigrants are said to penetrate the body of the nation metaphorically—in much the same way that germs penetrate the human body—and can, if left unchecked, weaken and even kill the nation by destroying its institutions. In this sense, the body's skin is like the nation's borders. Immigrants, if they are to be tamed and their pathological potentials neutralized, need to be absorbed into the body of the nation. Immigrants, over time and over generations, might become part of the national body. But if there are problems with integrative

processes—that is, with assimilation—then we sometimes hear about the nation's inability to "digest" any more immigrants.[20]

Rather than digesting and absorbing immigrants, the nation can also metaphorically expel them from the body of the nation. They are excluded through
categorization ("illegal aliens," "unauthorized," "undocumented"), representation ("invading force," "population threat," "unassimilable"), and policies (limited access to social services, obstacles to regularizing immigration status) that
keep them out of the nation's body, as if their inclusion would constitute "de-
filement."[21] These rejected and abject subjects live in a liminal space where the
boundary between their everyday lives *in* the nation and their lives as *part of* the
nation is maintained as a way of ensuring their control and social regulation.
But the metaphor of the body/nation has its limits. As Judith Butler has noted,
"for inner and outer worlds to remain utterly distinct, the entire surface of the
body would have to achieve an impossible impermeability."[22]

And yet the nation's body is often reduced to the citizen's body by those
advocating less immigration. But what happens when the borders between citizens' bodies and immigrants' bodies become as porous as the nation's political
borders? What issues are raised when it is literally the internal parts of the body,
the organs, that are mobile? Why does transplanting the organs of citizens into
the bodies of immigrants incur such public outrage?

Focusing on one iconic case, that of Jesica Santillan's botched organ transplants, offers insights into the cultural politics of organ transplants. By the time
of her death, and most surely afterward, Jesica came to embody more than the
tragedy of an untimely demise. Her body came to signify a national tragedy,
the nature of which has come to be interpreted in many ways. As an allegory of
contemporary U.S. immigration and medical history, Jesica's story is now a part
of our history.[23] That story can be read at various levels. At the denotive level,
there are the basic elements in the brief overview of the story given above.[24] But
there is a more complex level, that of connotation, where messages about social
and cultural values, narratives, myths, common sense, and ideologies abound,
often in contestation and in competition for primacy. It is at this more meaningful level of connotation that Jesica's story must be read, for it is here that we
find that it is a story within a story.

Jesica and her parents are Mexicans (Figure 5.1). They were living in Mexico,
in 2000, when Jesica's parents decided to bring her to the United States to find
a way to get the organ transplants she needed to live. Apparently, Jesica and
her mother, lacking documents to enter legally, crossed into the United States

Figure 5.1. Jesica Santillan. Courtesy of Mack Mahoney, president, Jesica's Hope Chest Inc. (a foundation for critically ill children).

clandestinely with the aid of a coyote, or smuggler. At the time of her transplant, Jesica may have had a humanitarian visa because of her illness, but her immigration status is unclear.[25] It was her original status as an "illegal alien" that carried great currency in the many iterations of her story before and after her death.

Jesica's story is about a Mexican, about an "illegal immigrant," about a sick and dying girl in need of an organ transplant, about medical malfeasance, and about an unnecessary death. Jesica's experiences, and the public opinion surrounding her case, act as a mirror that reflects the struggles of Americans to reconceptualize what it means to be American in a period of rapid demographic change. In this mirror metaphor, Jesica's story tells us less about Mexican immigrants and more about attitudes among some vocal members of U.S. society. Are organ transplants one of those benefits of citizenship that must be protected from noncitizens? Should persons not in the country legally be allowed to receive organ transplants at all? Should noncitizens receive an organ transplant only after any citizen who needs one? Or, as one headline for an article on Jesica put it, "Organ Donation: Should National Origin Matter?"[26]

The Santillan case forces us to reflect on issues of belonging, of legitimacy, and of the rewards of membership in a community or nation.[27] For it is here that we will observe the biopolitics surrounding citizenship that are so essential to the representations of Jesica Santillan and other immigrant recipients of organs, and that help us to begin to answer a question raised by Paul Farmer: "By what mechanisms, precisely, do social forces ranging from poverty to racism become embodied as individual experience?"[28] How did Jesica's individual experiences come to embody debates over citizens and foreigners, membership in the nation, and threats to the nation? By exploring these questions, the linking of the biological/body with the privileges of citizens takes on new meanings, a new biological citizenship. By *biological citizenship*, I mean that the battle over scarce medical resources can become the grounds for struggles over social membership, and the basis for staking claims to citizenship.[29] With whom does one share scarce medical resources? What are the practices of exclusion, the ways in which some people are deemed less legitimate contenders for such resources? Answering these questions requires that we peel back assumptions about who is imagined as part of the community and thus deserving of social resources.

"Illegal" immigrants, such as Jesica, are typically outside the imagined community of the nation, a status that is underscored by the controversy over organs for immigrants.[30] Jesica's organ transplants bring into focus the often taken-for-granted assumption that there exists, or should exist, a queue for organ transplants and that citizens should have priority for organs donated by co-nationals. As the newsletter *Border Watch* observed shortly after Jesica's death, "This year, at least one more American taxpayer will die waiting for the transplant that Duke University chose to give to a citizen of a foreign nation.... The greater tragedy in the Jesica Santillan story is a system that rewards illegal aliens for entering the United States to access our health care system, thus condemning some of the American taxpayers who pay for that system to premature deaths. Few could deny the sheer unfairness of such a situation."[31] However, according to the United Network for Organ Sharing, transplant centers must provide no more than 5 percent of organ transplants to foreign nationals.[32] In 2002, foreign nationals received 936 of the 22,709 organ transplants, or 4.1 percent.[33] Also, some time ago the federal government discontinued reimbursing hospitals for organ transplants for undocumented immigrants.[34] The impact on access to organs is clear: between 1988 and 2007, nonresident aliens accounted for 3,777 of 414,901 total organ transplant recipients, or less than 1 percent of all transplants. In contrast, organ donors of unknown citizenship or unreported citizenship status accounted for 2.5 percent of all organ donations during that time.[35] The issue is complicated by undocumented immigrants working in jobs that often do not provide private medical insurance and denied participation in insurance programs mandated by the Obama administration's new health care law. Uninsured Americans donate about 5 to 10 percent of organs but receive almost zero percent of organ transplants because they lack insurance to cover the cost of the transplant or the cost of follow-up medical care.[36] The queue exists, and at the back of that queue, as much of public opinion indicates, should be people like Jesica, an undocumented Mexican immigrant.

I argue here that the public opinion that surfaced around Jesica's organ transplants, and transplants for immigrants in similar cases, must be examined within a national discourse that constructs Mexican immigrants, especially undocumented Mexican immigrants, as a threat to the nation. The construction of the "Mexican Immigrant as Threat" occurs not in one statement alone but through repetitive statements in various public discourse contexts (see Chapter 1). As Judith Butler has observed, the signification attached to bodies, such as Jesica's, "must be understood not as a singular or deliberate 'act,' but, rather as the reiterative and citational practice by which discourse produces the effects that it names."[37] Central to the construction of Jesica and "people like her" are a set of essential binary oppositions that work to establish that she is outside the culturally imagined membership of the nation; that is, she is one of "them" rather than one of "us" and thus is undeserving of benefits, such as organs, reserved as a privilege of membership in the "us." The analysis that follows calls attention to the binary oppositions in the cultural construction of Jesica Santillan.

IMMIGRANTS AND ACCESS TO MEDICAL CARE

The construction of Jesica ("the illegal immigrant") as a threat to medical resources for citizens and to the nation in general builds on the more than forty years of alarmist media representations of Mexicans, Mexican Americans, and Latinos in general, as elaborated in Chapter 1. Immigrants such as Jesica become contextualized not as individuals but as signifiers of alarmist rhetoric of excessive population growth and overuse of prenatal care, children's health services, education, and other social and medical services. As I have observed elsewhere,[38] the nation has had a love-hate relationship with immigrants, at once realizing their economic benefit while at the same time fearing their impact on citizen-laborers and society in general. Medical care for immigrants also fluctuates between these two poles, although more toward the restrictive end, at least since the Immigration Reform and Control Act of 1986 (IRCA). The act excluded some categories of legal immigrants from Medicaid during their first five years in the country. But in addition to its restrictive measures, which included employer sanctions, IRCA also included an amnesty program. Also in 1986, Congress barred undocumented immigrants from medical care for any condition except medical emergencies.[39] However, the U.S.-born children of poor, uninsured undocumented immigrants are typically covered by government-financed medical programs, and in some cases so is prenatal care for the mother.[40] In 1996 the Personal Responsibility and Work Opportunity Reconciliation Act (also known as the Welfare Reform Act) restricted state and federal benefits for noncitizen immigrants who were legal permanent residents.[41] It is no wonder that attitudes toward medical care for immigrants have, as Beatrix Hoffman noted, "reflected the nation's erratic immigration policies."[42]

Public debate on medical care for immigrants has been heated, and too voluminous and in too many forums to be surveyed adequately here. A few examples suggest the issues framing access to medical care. The cover of the December 1974 issue of *American Legion* magazine (see Figure 1.1) depicts immigrants pouring across the border and inundating medical, educational, economic, and other social institutions. Such alarmist imagery is matched by equally alarming public discourse. For instance, the Federation for American Immigration Reform (FAIR), a group advocating restrictions on immigration, titled its March 4, 2003, newsletter's featured story "Health Care for Illegal Aliens Draining Tax Funds."[43] Then in February 2004, FAIR asserted, based on its study "The Sinking Lifeboat: Undocumented Immigration and the U.S. Health Care System," that "high rates of immigration are straining the health care system to the breaking point." FAIR director Dan Stein commented, "Our immigration policies are doing incalculable harm to millions of people who are trying to protect their health and the health of their families."[44] The "people harmed," it goes without saying, are natives and citizens, the legitimate and deserving members of society, and not immigrants, who are the implied culprits in Stein's quote. California's congressman from the 46th District, Dana Rohrabacher, echoed these views when expressing his concern that "Americans receive the [medical] care they deserve." In contrast, "every dollar spent on healthcare for illegal immigrants is a dollar less available for your family and mine."[45]

Medical care is often described as a "magnet" for immigrants despite evidence to the contrary.[46] As *Border Alert* noted in response to Jesica Santillan's transplant, "Every year hundreds of foreign nationals die attempting to cross our dangerous southern border illegally. Almost all of them are tempted to try the dangerous crossing by the perceived rewards, or 'magnets,' for illegal aliens on this side of the border. These magnets include employment, free education, birthright citizenship for babies, promises of eventual amnesties, and, of course, superior and free health care." As Figure 5.2 suggests, the reward for illegal entry into the United States is medical care, at the expense of citizen taxpayers.

Michelle Malkin, speaking of Jesica Santillan's transplants as an example of why immigrants are drawn to the United States, draws upon the notion of compassion fatigue: "In a world of scarce resources, compassion must have limits. We cannot afford to be a medical welcome mat to the world."[47] Ironically, although in some cases families may be drawn to the United States for organ transplants, in the vast majority of cases the overwhelming motivation for migration is to work, not to receive medical services.[48]

Figure 5.2. "Politically Correct" cartoon by Jim Huber. Used by permission of the artist.

Uncompensated medical care expenses for uninsured patients is a serious problem faced by hospitals throughout the nation.[49] And immigrants do play a part in this problem, not by choice but by their disadvantaged position in the U.S. labor market. Immigrants, particularly the undocumented, tend to be employed in low-paying jobs that do not provide medical insurance, and they are barred from most government-supported, nonemergency medical services. Without the means to gain access to medical care, which is available by paying in cash or through public or private medical insurance, immigrants find the door closed to most health services.[50] Paul Farmer would call this a form of "structural violence" that pervades the lives of less powerful people, such as uninsured, undocumented immigrants.[51]

Malkin's views on the limits of compassion and Farmer's notion of structural violence must be contextualized. Since the 1970s, the neoliberal doctrine of free markets and minimal government intervention, especially through social support programs, has become pervasive in the world, owing greatly to policies of the United States (Reaganism) and Great Britain (Thatcherism).[52] Governments, according to this doctrine, should work toward liberating the individual to pursue entrepreneurial interests while guaranteeing property rights, free trade, and the integrity of money.[53] Although economic inequalities have increased with neoliberal reforms, the so-called welfare state has taken on a negative connotation under neoliberalism.[54] As a result, "deregulation, privatization, and withdrawal of the state from many areas of social provision have been all too common."[55]

Neoliberalism's hallmark practices of benign neglect and personal responsibility often mean that immigrants must choose between personal health and economic survival in the United States. Moreover, the conditions under which they move to the United States and work are subject to political debate, nativist reactions, surveillance, and personal danger, all factors that are detrimental to their health.[56] A few comments by immigrants exemplify the problems they encounter in relation to medical care.[57]

Marcela was 53 years old, married, and a legal resident who had been in the United States for about seventeen years. Even though she had a major medical problem, Marcela had difficulties getting medical care: "I had a mammogram months ago and they told me that I had to get a biopsy, but I have yet to do it. I don't have the resources, because my spouse has been out of work for six months and we don't have insurance to cover it."

Ester was 30 years old and a legal resident who had been in the United States for about thirteen years. Although she eventually acquired medical insurance, for many years she did not have it. She explained what it was like trying to get medical care without insurance: "It is very difficult to get service if you do not have money in your hand. For example, at the hospitals, if you do not have money in your hand, although you look like you are ready to pass out, if you are dying, they will not give you service. You have to have a deposit of one hundred to thirteen hundred dollars. So that was the problem, if you did not have money and no insurance."

Luzmila, who was 27 years old and single, had been in the United States for about seven years, and was not a permanent legal resident at the time of her interview, described her situation: "I don't have insurance. Not to have insurance is something awful, right? Because here in the United States medical care is very expensive. And you know that for many people, what we earn is barely enough to eat and live. So when we have these types of illnesses, we don't go to the doctor, because of a lack of money. Insurance would help a great deal because then they would attend to you and you would not have to pay."

Lola was 27 and married, had been in the United States for about ten years, and was a legal permanent resident at the time of her interview. Without insurance, she often faced making a decision between her health care and that of her children: "Sometimes people don't have money for exams. Because these exams are expensive, right? Sometimes they have many children, and their money is not enough for everyone to have medical care."

As these women's observations suggest, they were fully aware of the constraints a lack of medical insurance imposed on their lives. Add an undocumented immigration status to a lack of medical insurance, and the result is that immigrants living and working in the United States are at the mercy of neoliberalism's "culture of indifference."[58] Their reluctance to seek medical care in spite of their need for it suggests that an underuse of medical services may be more of a problem than public discourse would have it. Indeed, two recent studies highlight the degree to which popular perceptions of immigrants' use of medical services are out of sync with empirical evidence. The first study examined the use of emergency room services across the country and found that most emergency room patients had private insurance or Medicaid. They used emergency rooms because they found them convenient, especially because those facilities were open after work hours. The uninsured may have found the emergency room to be the provider of last resort, but they tended to use medical care less.[59]

The second study suggested that immigrants might not receive an inordinate share of the nation's medical resources after all. The study examined nationwide data to compare 1998 health care expenditures of immigrants residing in the United States with the expenditures of U.S.-born persons.[60] Expenditures included those for emergency room visits, office visits, hospital-based outpatient visits, inpatient visits, and prescription drugs. The study found that per capita expenditures for immigrants were 55 percent lower than those for U.S.-born persons. Similarly, medical expenditures attributed to uninsured and publicly insured immigrants amounted to about half the amount attributed to the U.S.-born under similar conditions. Immigrant children had 74 percent lower expenditures than the U.S.-born children. Only in one area, emergency room expenditures, did immigrant children exceed the expenditures for U.S.-born children, which the authors attributed to the difficulty immigrants had in accessing routine and ongoing medical care for their children. The study also examined expenditures by ethnicity and found that per capita expenditures for Hispanic immigrants ($962) were about half (51 percent) of those for U.S.-born Hispanics ($1,870) and were the lowest in comparison with U.S.-born and immigrant whites ($3,117 and $1,747, respectively), blacks ($2,524 and $1,030, respectively), and Asian / Pacific Islanders ($1,460 and $1,324, respectively). Another study found that undocumented Latino immigrants, in particular, used medical services less than U.S.-born Latinos.[61] Nevertheless, despite such seemingly contradictory empirical evidence, popularly held beliefs about excessive use of medical services by immigrants continue to pervade the discourse surrounding organ transplants.

Jesica Santillan's story also was framed by the rapid growth in the immigrant population in North Carolina since the late 1980s.[62] Between 1990 and 2000, the number of foreign-born in North Carolina increased from 115,077 to 430,000, representing a 274 percent change.[63] North Carolina ranked number one in terms of the percent of change in a state's foreign-born population, 1990 to 2000.[64] About 40 percent of the foreign-born in North Carolina were born in Mexico, and 53 percent were of Latin American origin.[65] The Latino population in North Carolina is less likely than other groups to have medical insurance, and their health issues are "consistent with the fact that they are a very young, mainly recently-arrived immigrant population with more males than females."[66] With a median age of 24 in 2000, Latinos in North Carolina were much younger than the median age of 35 for the state's total population.[67] North Carolina, then, as one of the "new" destinations for Mexican immigrants in the post-1990s period, suddenly found itself in a situation with which it had little experience.

A *Washington Post* headline in 2000, the year Jesica and her family moved to North Carolina, observed: "Hispanic Immigration Boom Rattles South: Rapid Influx to Some Areas Raises Tensions."[68] The article focused on North Carolina and the economic demand for entry-level workers in an economy, including especially poultry production, that had just 2 percent unemployment at the time. Immigrants, particularly from Mexico, responded to the labor demand. Rather than the stereotypical black/white construction of ethnic relations, North Carolina suddenly had to learn to live with Mexican, other Latin American, and Asian immigrants. The article quoted several North Carolinians on the subject. "In the South, we're in the situation where what is basically a biracial community that was dealing with issues of prejudice has now become a multiracial community," a researcher at a Chapel Hill think tank commented. A resident of Siler City, forty miles west of Raleigh, complained of the "Little Mexico" the city was becoming: "I don't want to say anything against anybody, but, hey, they just came in and took over." Another resident noted, "And these new people are not white Anglo-Saxons, which makes it harder, because after all, this is still the south." An article in the *New York Times* a year later, titled "Pockets of Protest Are Rising against Immigration," noted that protests in North Carolina stemmed from rapid demographic changes related to immigration, especially from Mexico.[69]

Consequently, conditions were ripe for alarmist views of immigration to become associated with Jesica Santillan's presence in North Carolina and with her organ transplants. The furor over her transplants was swept up in the decades-long maelstrom of anti-Mexican immigration rhetoric. In essence, Mexican immigration, as a central focus of the Latino Threat Narrative, is associated with narratives of threat, danger, invasion, and depletion of social services, including medical services. These grand narratives are readily available for applying to local people and events, such as Jesica Santillan and her organ transplants in North Carolina.

DESERVING/UNDESERVING MEMBERS OF SOCIETY

A Google search of the Internet results in a rich array of public opinion on the Santillan case. These views can be separated into two broad categories. One category contains reactions of outrage over the medical incompetence that led to Jesica receiving organs of a different blood type, which resulted in her death. The second category of public reaction revolves around her having received donated organs for a transplant in the first place. It is this second category of reactions that I am concerned with here and that I examine below.

Although before the transplants Jesica was portrayed in positive terms, as an "angel" in dire medical straits who required an organ transplant to avoid an early death, this characterization soon changed.[70] The first hint that Jesica's organ transplant would become a political touchstone in the debate over immigration appeared shortly after her first transplant operation, just two days before she died. On February 20, 2003, Michelle Malkin published an article titled "America: Medical Welcome Mat to the World" on VDARE.com, a website supported by the Center for American Unity. In addition to writing columns such as this one, Malkin has, according to Amazon.com, appeared on Fox News as a commentator, on talk radio shows, and on C-SPAN's *Washington Journal*, *The McLaughlin Group*, ABC's *20/20*, and MSNBC. Malkin is also the author of the book *Invasion: How America Still Welcomes Terrorists, Criminals, and Other Foreign Menaces to Our Shores*. For Malkin, Jesica became an example of the undeserving "illegal" immigrants coming to America to take from the deserving citizens. In the online article, she questioned the appropriateness of Jesica's receiving an organ transplant on the grounds of Jesica's immigration status and the cost to the health care system for providing follow-up care. Although Jesica's mother's insurance and a charity fund specifically for Jesica paid for her operation—making her case atypical compared with that of uninsured undocumented immigrants—the article questioned who would be responsible for expensive long-term care after the operation. Emphasizing the burden placed on hospitals, even closures, caused by providing unreimbursed medical care for undocumented immigrants, Malkin raised the question, "Will any federal immigration authority have the guts to enforce the law and send her and her family back home to Mexico?"

At the core of Malkin's case against Jesica's organ transplant was the issue of legitimate potential organ recipients, U.S. citizens, who might not have received organs because Jesica had. "According to national figures," Malkin wrote in the online article, "16 patients die in the U.S. each day while waiting for a potentially life-saving transplant operation. How many American patients currently on the national organ waiting list were denied access to healthy hearts and lungs as a result of Santillan's two transplant surgeries? Who will tell their stories?" Malkin's article was cited in later articles concerning the Jesica Santillan case.[71]

CITIZENS/FOREIGNERS; LEGITIMATE/ILLEGITIMATE

On March 6, 2003, Joe Kovacs published an article on *WorldNetDaily* that elaborated on the core issues in Malkin's article, focusing on Jesica's immigration status and U.S. citizens who must wait for organs. The article bore the headline "Coming to America: Transplants for Illegals Igniting U.S. Firestorm; Case of Smuggled Mexican Teen-ager Prompting Public to Cry 'Citizens First.'" The article focused on the story of Lauren Averitt, a young woman waiting anxiously for a lung transplant, and her story converged with Jesica's at many points. Both were in desperate need of organ transplants. They shared the same blood type. And they had North Carolina in common; Lauren had been born there, and Jesica died there. However, Jesica had been born in Mexico, not the United States. As the article noted, "What's different about Lauren, though, is that no one smuggled her across the border to get her on a waiting list for new organs. She was born here in the United States in Wilmington, N.C., and now lives in South Carolina."

The article emphasized that Jesica received her transplant before Lauren, which subverted what should have been the natural order of things, citizens first, foreigners last: "The significance of such geographical disparity has sparked a firestorm of controversy across the continent, with many Americans venting outrage at how illegal aliens like Jesica are able to leap ahead of the many thousands of U.S. citizens patiently waiting and praying for their own personal miracle." In the article, Kovacs not so subtly drew upon the binaries of citizen/foreigner, legal/illegal, and deserving/undeserving to make his points. Through such binary constructions, Lauren and Jesica came to embody polarized icons in the debate over immigration.

A final example underscores the citizen / illegal alien dichotomy. On May 31, 2003, Peter Brimelow weighed in on the Santillan controversy in an article appearing on VDARE.com. A well-known restrictionist in the immigration debate following the publication of his book *Alien Nation*, Brimelow made his position clear in the title of this article: "That Santillan Saga: Lies, Damned Lies, Immigration Enthusiasts and Neosocialist Health Bureaucrats." The main point of the article was summed up this way: "The truth, of course, is that privileged access, paid for by Americans, was the subtext of the entire Santillan Saga. More than 75,000 Americans are on the federal transplant waiting list. Only 24,000 organs are available each year. Each year, while on the waiting list, more than 5,300 people die. So why give any organs at all to someone who is in the U.S. illegally?" Brimelow further argued that the barriers to medical care experienced by Latinos were self-created: "Doesn't the 'Latino community' face these 'barriers' because they've chosen to immigrate to an English-speaking country—to a significant extent, in violation of that country's laws?" What was not clear was whether Brimelow would have a problem with an illegal alien from an English-speaking country receiving an organ transplant. Did he object to undocumented immigrants in general or to the entire "Latino community," which he generalized as all immigrant and all Spanish-speaking?

Another website put it more bluntly. The top of its homepage read: "Keep American organs in Americans!" under which was an image of a beating heart. Under that was another heading that read: "Where are *YOUR* organs going?" followed by text stating, "To let an American die so some foreign national illegally in the country, or some convict behind bars can get the organ or organs needed to live, it is nothing more than an act of TREASON!"[72] The same website had examples of "former donor" cards, specifically stating that because organ donations were not guaranteed to go to U.S. citizens only, the card's bearer had decided not to donate them (Figure 5.3).[73]

Some residents of North Carolina also appeared to view Jesica and her transplants from the vantage point of citizens versus foreigners. One 65-year-old woman was quoted in the *Raleigh News and Observer* as reconsidering being an organ donor after hearing that Jesica and her family paid a smuggler to get them into the country. She said she would "prefer that her organs go only to U.S. citizens": "I definitely do not want them to go to an illegal alien. I don't think they should be able to come in here and take our hospital and our medicine and turn around and sue us." Notice the "they" in contrast to "us" and "our" in the woman's quote. Another local resident quoted in the article similarly asked, "Why were organs given to someone who is here illegally?"[74]

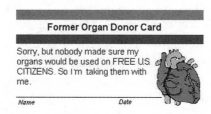

Figure 5.3. Anti-immigrant card for "former organ donors," available at http://www.geocities.com/americanorgans.

THE CULTURAL SIGNIFICANCE OF JESICA SANTILLAN

One of the perhaps unavoidable consequences of the publicity surrounding Jesica Santillan's organ transplants and death was that her life was reduced to that of icon, a virtual identity, as she became "the illegal Mexican alien" subject in the ongoing debate over immigration in American public discourse. As the case became a sounding board for views on current immigration patterns, the debate dissolved into a number of structural oppositions, or essential binaries:

Belonging	Not-belonging
Us	Them
Inside the nation	Outside the nation
English speaker	Non–English speaker
Citizen	Noncitizen
Native	Foreigner
Legal immigrant	Illegal immigrant
Deserving	Undeserving
Giver/contributor	Taker/consumer
Organ donor	Organ recipient
Transplant	No transplant
Life	Death

Difference is constructed through such binary oppositions. Importantly, the terms in these binaries are not equal but exist in a power relationship such that one term is dominant and the other subordinate, one positive and one negative, one normal and one pathological.[75] These binaries helped construct Jesica and other immigrants in her position as unacceptable members of society. Once constructed through such essentializing binaries, difference was readily represented as a threat to Americans who die waiting for organs taken by people like Jesica (now metonymically representing a class of people, "illegal aliens") and as a threat to the health care system that their presence undermines. Jesica became a symbol of society's Others, who, as Michel Foucault notes, "for a given culture, [are] at once interior and foreign, therefore to be excluded (so as to exorcise their interior danger)."[76]

Jesica Santillan's organ transplants occurred within the context of the often vitriolic debate over Mexican immigration. Her medical condition and need for organs to save her life became mired in discussions of her very presence in this country. She was portrayed as a threat to citizens who perhaps died because she received organs. Although Jesica's medical condition made her a strong candidate for consideration as a humanitarian transnational citizen deserving of compassion and U.S. medical intervention, her nationality and immigration status made her an illegitimate donor recipient in the eyes of many. She became a symbol of the threats to the nation posed by Mexican immigration, and her story raised all-too-familiar questions: Why is she here? How do citizens suffer because she is here? Who pays for her health care? Such questions underscored the difficulty of imagining Jesica as one of "us," which was perhaps exacerbated by the fact that Jesica and her family were essentially voiceless in the entire affair.[77] Jesica and her family were typically spoken for (in particular by Mack Mahoney, who became Jesica's benefactor) and about (in the press by reporters, pundits, medical practitioners, and a concerned public).

What is lost, or obscured, in this construction of Jesica Santillan as the prototypical "illegal alien," noncitizen, undeserving of citizen organs? Binaries are important for understanding one-dimensional identity constructions, but they do not reflect the complexity of lives "on the ground." The ambiguity and nuance of actual lives get lost in the construction of types in a social drama such as that surrounding Jesica. For one thing, Latinos vary as to where they were born, national background, education level, gender, and many other aspects of their lives, and thus they are not reducible to simple citizen/noncitizen, insider/outsider binaries. Undocumented immigrants often find ways to become legal residents. Their children, if born in the United States, are citizens. Jesica herself was not the popularly imagined prototypical "illegal immigrant seeking medical care" in that her mother had medical insurance, and to help meet her medical expenses, a local citizen (Mack Mahoney) had set up a fund, to which many other local residents contributed, blurring the sharp division between citizens and immigrants.

Moreover, the citizen/noncitizen focus must be broadened to include issues of biopolitics and biopower.[78] I use these terms to refer to how subjects, as members of a population, intersect with issues of economy, national policy, and power, as suggested by Michel Foucault and later elaborated on by Paul Rabinow and Nikolas Rose.[79] *Biopower* refers to control over life, and, according to Foucault, occurs at two levels: the level of the body, through discipline and surveillance, and the level of populations, through regulation, control, and welfare.[80]

Public discourse that accuses immigrants of draining medical resources and posing a threat to the very life of citizens by taking organs serves as a practice that disciplines immigrants, who may be reluctant to seek health care. Medical providers are also disciplined in that they are compelled to impose limitations on services, such as the United Network for Organ Sharing (UNOS) policy that no more than 5 percent of organs can go to "foreigners," which includes undocumented immigrants. These limitations are applied even though evidence suggests that immigrants may provide more organs than they receive. For example, commenting in a 2003 newspaper article, a spokeswoman for UNOS noted, "As a percentage, every year, U.S. citizens receive more organs than they donate."[81] She went on to say that, in 2001, U.S. citizens received 96.2 percent of transplants in the country, but only 94.8 percent of organ donors were citizens. The rest of the organs were donated by immigrants of various types. In North Carolina, where the Jesica Santillan drama played out, Latinos were among the most likely group to donate a family member's organs. About 78 percent of Latinos had done so during the first six months of 2002, whereas only 62 percent of other groups had.[82]

An important outcome of the high-decibel contestations over who deserves life and who deserves death is to insure that, in contrast to commonly held perceptions, immigrants are a net plus in the organ exchange market. That is, immigrant biovalue is high because they have, building on Kaushik Sunder Rajan's work, "surplus health" when it comes to organs.[83] By *biovalue*, I mean the value of the body as a commodity. As Rose and Novas have noted, "as politics begins to take on more 'vital' qualities, and as life itself becomes invested with both social meaning and capital, the vitality of each and every one of us becomes a potential source of *biovalue*."[84] By *surplus health*, I mean the potential for citizens to acquire from immigrants healthy organs for potential transplants in excess of those provided to immigrants. This leads to two interrelated observations. Organ transplants are embedded in biopower's strategies for the governing of life, and struggles over who to let die and who to help live are mired in discourses of citizenship and belonging.

The net flow of organs described above could be considered a "gift," in the sense of Marcel Mauss's famous discussion.[85] Gifts have been considered essential to notions of social reciprocity, the glue that holds societies together. However, the biopolitics of organ transplants and citizenship are such that the immigrants' gifts of organs are unrecognized and do not contribute, in a substantial way, to ameliorating the controversial nature of the exchange. This mystification of the net plus in exchange value, from immigrants to citizens, is not limited to organ transplants but pervades the anti-immigration discourse. For example, undocumented immigrants are now said to provide a subsidy of as much as $7 billion a year to the U.S. Social Security system and $1.5 billion in Medicare taxes.[86] However, such gifts on the part of undocumented immigrants have done little to assuage the proponents of anti-immigrant measures. That biopolitics is about governing and disciplining populations, in this case immigrants, helps us understand why immigrant "gifts" are not generally recognized as such and seemingly do not easily translate, for some, into mutual feelings of social solidarity. Ignoring such gifts does have possible negative implications, as one medical ethicist has observed: "Will this biased portrayal [of undocumented immigrants and organ transplants], coupled with a general lack of access to organs, lead to fewer individuals donating a resource that is already in high demand and low supply? Moreover, how can we justify allowing illegal immigrants to donate, but not receive, organs?"[87]

The biopolitics of organ transplants serves another function. It effectively shifts attention away from serious discussion of the ethical issues related to medical care for uninsured, undocumented immigrants.[88] For instance, Jesica's case reflects how the rights and privileges of citizenship can be narrowly defined. However, what about human rights and medical care?[89] Are there rights to lifesaving medical care that exist outside of citizenship as defined in a narrow legalistic sense, rights that exist in a shared humanity?[90] Agamben has pointed to this conflict in citizens' rights versus human rights: "In the system of the nation-state, the so-called sacred and inalienable rights of man show themselves to lack every protection and reality at the moment in which they can no longer take the form of rights belonging to citizens of the state."[91] Unfortunately, alarmist discourse constructs Jesica, a Mexican immigrant with medical needs, through binaries so simplistic that little space exists for broader considerations of human rights. Indeed, such considerations are anathema to many. Biological citizenship, as examined here, means that some members of society (immigrants such as Jesica) are less valued than others (citizens).[92] The division of the population into unequal parts combines with notions of race and racial differences to justify seemingly rational policies that quite literally make a difference between life and death.

6 THE MINUTEMAN PROJECT'S SPECTACLE OF SURVEILLANCE ON THE ARIZONA-MEXICO BORDER

ON APRIL 1, 2005, volunteers began arriving along the Arizona-Mexico border, converging on Tombstone, the site of the historic Wild West shootout at the OK Corral between Wyatt Earp's men and a gang of roughneck cowboys.[1] These modern-day volunteers came in search of another confrontation, another example of cowboy justice, only this time the scofflaws were "illegal" immigrants. The volunteers came to be part of the Minuteman Project, a name with immediate appeal because it evoked the patriotic volunteers who fought against British rule of the American colonies. The Minuteman Project's ostensible goal was to monitor the Arizona-Mexico border in the hopes of locating clandestine border crossers. However, this surveillance operation also had a larger objective: to produce a spectacle that would garner public media attention and influence federal immigration policies.

The Minuteman Project's start date of April 1, also known as April Fool's Day in the United States, provided the appropriate symbolic beginning to the Minuteman Project's spectacle in the desert and its effort to "trick" the press into becoming unwitting co-conspirators in the group's desire to shape public policy. By giving the media an event to cover, the group managed to have its message about a need for greater border surveillance broadcast to millions of people.

The Minuteman Project's spectacle in the Arizona desert must be viewed in relation to decades of the Latino Threat Narrative, which was elaborated in Chapter 1. The U.S.-Mexico border has been a key location in this discourse. It is the site at which surveillance is concentrated to control legal and unauthorized immigration. It is where the "battle" takes place in a "war on illegal immigration."

Over the last few decades, the U.S.-Mexico border has been likened to a "war zone," with increasing levels of militarization and with, at various times, the National Guard and military personnel conducting surveillance.[2] The politics over border control has, since the early 1980s, led to ever greater expenditures on border surveillance and enforcement, with, as some would argue, relatively little impact.[3] It must be underscored that anti-immigrant discourse may not have caused the increased border militarization to occur. However, the discourse of invasion, loss of U.S. sovereignty, and representation of Mexican immigrants as the "enemy" surely contributed to an atmosphere that helped justify increased militarization of the border as a way of "doing something" about these perceived threats to the nation's security and the American way of life.[4]

The Minuteman Project's enlistment of citizens to conduct surveillance along the border is a logical consequence of the decades-long maelstrom of rhetoric associating Mexican immigration with invasions and reconquests. However, the difference between the metaphor of a war zone and the actual practice of increased militarization along the U.S.-Mexico border raises a number of issues, including those of human rights.[5] At the very least is the issue of the incongruity between military personnel trained for war and the job of the Border Patrol, which more often than not involves servicing unarmed civilians seeking work or to reunite with their family. The idea of untrained civilian border guards or militia, such as the Minutemen, expands these concerns exponentially.

THE SPECTACLE IN THE DESERT

Jim Gilchrist founded the Minuteman Project in October 2004. A few months later, in early 2005, Gilchrist put a call out for citizens to come to the Arizona-Mexico border to monitor and report "illegal" immigrants.[6] Although a resident of California, Gilchrist's motivation for his call to action in Arizona was his belief that the George W. Bush administration and the U.S. Congress had failed to provide the funds necessary to secure the borders against "millions of illegal migrants" flowing into the United States from Mexico, a powerful theme in the post-9/11 political debate over security.[7] According to the group's website, the reason for creating the Minuteman Project was "to bring national awareness to the decades-long careless disregard of effective U.S. immigration law enforcement" and "to protest the refusal of the Congress and the President to protect our borders from illegal immigrants who have not had criminal background checks by, and through, the U.S. Embassy in their home country, thereby creating an imminent danger to all Americans, and creating the dilution of U.S. citizens' voting rights by foreign nationals."[8] Note the focus on rights and privileges of citizenship, which, from the Minuteman Project's perspective, were losing their value as a result of immigration. The concerns of the Minuteman Project were therefore much broader than illegal border crossers.

The Minuteman Project used iconic symbols to wrap their cause in patriotism and nationalist fervor and to spur people to action.[9] National symbols such as the bald eagle, Uncle Sam, the Minuteman icon of the Revolutionary War, and the American flag were, and continue to be, ubiquitous on its website, in its publications, and on its posters, T-shirts, and other products. In this way, the group's members imbued themselves with the revolutionary-like zeal of those defending citizens' rights because of the government's failure to do so. For example, the back of a shirt worn by some Minuteman volunteers read: "Minuteman Project, Arizona Border, April 2005: Americans doing the job government won't do." The words "Team America" were centered on a white field in the shape of a map of the United States, with the rest of the shirt in shades of green in a military-style camouflage pattern (Figure 6.1). Many of the images exuded a masculine presence, such as Uncle Sam's stern disposition in one of the posters (Figure 6.2) and the Minuteman's upright vigilant posture in

Figure 6.1. Minuteman Project T-shirt. Reprinted by permission of Jim Gilchrist.

Figure 6.2. Minuteman Project poster advertising the Arizona events, originally available from http://www.teamamericapac.org.

the organization's logo.[10] Nationalistic fervor was enhanced by such slogans as "Defending our borders," which contributed to the representation of the Minutemen as legitimate defenders of a nation in crisis. The narrative enacted here was of citizens, especially males, coming to the defense of the nation's borders, which were under siege by invading force that the nation's own government was unwilling or unable to control. It was a patriotic discourse meant to spur patriotic Americans into action against two enemies, the noncitizen border crossers and the U.S. federal government.

Jim Gilchrist chose Arizona because in 2005 that was the area where a disproportionate number of undocumented migrants crossed. Of the 1.1 million unauthorized border crossers apprehended in 2004, one-fifth were caught in a single Arizona county (Cochise County).[11] Such statistics are, as Jean and John Comaroff put it, part of the "alchemy of numbers" that helps construct the rhetoric of fear discussed in Chapter 1.[12] Although such statistics can be used to signify "invasion" and "threat," they do not illuminate the political economy that creates a demand in the U.S. labor market for immigrant labor.[13] Statistics are useful, however, to motivate the enlistment of Minutemen. For example, Mike McGarry, the Minuteman Project's media liaison, commented in April 2005: "We have something in the neighborhood of three million people from all over the world breaking into the country. And we have an out-of-control— by any definition could be termed an invasion."[14] McGarry underscored the notion of criminality when he invoked the "breaking into the country" image, thus portraying the actions of citizen groups, such as the Minuteman Project, as reestablishing the rule of law.

Gilchrist had the following goals for the Minuteman Project's Arizona spectacle: (a) draw attention to "illegal immigration" and the lack of border security; (b) reduce the number of apprehensions along the border where the group monitored; and (c) influence the U.S. Congress to put a ten-year moratorium on illegal immigration and cap the number of legal immigrants at 200,000 per year.[15] Although monitoring the U.S.-Mexico border was Gilchrist's immediate objective, the larger goal was to use the citizen patrols on the border to draw attention to his larger aim of influencing public opinion and federal immigration policy.

The government's immediate reaction to the Minuteman Project, before it actually began its operations, was not favorable. President Bush took a strong position: "I'm against vigilantes in the United States of America. I'm for enforcing law in a rational way. It's why we've got the Border Patrol, and they ought to be in charge of enforcing the border."[16] At the time Bush made this statement, he was meeting with Mexico's president, Vicente Fox, with whom he had discussed immigration reform early in 2001, during his first administration and before the 9/11 attacks.[17] The organizers of the Minuteman Project were outraged by Bush's use of the term "vigilantes," which carries a negative connotation, identifying a group of individuals who operate outside the law, or "rational" law enforcement, by taking action into their own hands. Gilchrist continually stressed that the Minuteman Project was a nonviolent protest along the lines of Martin Luther King's.[18] However, one of the main concerns of the Minuteman Project's organizers in the days leading up to April 1 was the possibility of violence, given that many of the volunteers would carry guns. Moreover, one of the organizers, Chris Simcox, had been convicted on federal weapons charges, and the white supremacist group Aryan Nations was recruiting Minuteman volunteers.[19] In addition to Bush's condemnation of the Minuteman Project, Joe Garza, spokesman for the Border Patrol's Tucson sector, dismissed the Minuteman Project's impact, stating that his agency was not planning to change any operations as a result of the Minutemen's activities.[20]

Despite such official reservations about the Minuteman Project, Jim Gilchrist proclaimed success a few days before the Minuteman Project volunteers even began arriving in Arizona: "I struck the mother lode. It has already accomplished what we want to accomplish: nationwide awareness. And we haven't even started the project yet."[21] Gilchrist's emphasis on nationwide awareness underscored the public-spectacle nature of the Minuteman Project and its goal of disciplining the federal government.

It is easy to see why Gilchrist was claiming success before the group began operations. On March 30, 2005, two days before the official start date, the Bush administration announced that more than 500 additional Border Patrol agents would be deployed along the Arizona-Mexico border, bringing the total to about 2,900, along with additional aircraft. In addition, top Homeland Security officials would be arriving in Tucson to add to the visible display of the administration's efforts to enforce the border.[22] Government officials claimed there was no connection between the Minutemen's activities and this new deployment of resources to the Arizona border.[23] However, a spokesman for the Minuteman Project, Bill Bennett, pointed to these deployments as a sign of success: "President Bush called the Minuteman Project a bunch of vigilantes—but if it's the case that this [federal crackdown] did start because of the Minuteman Project, then the project is a success. I find it very interesting that this is all coinciding."[24]

APRIL 2005 ON THE ARIZONA-MEXICO BORDER

Before the official start of operations on April 1, Minuteman Project organizers expected 1,300 volunteers.[25] By April 2, however, only about 200 volunteers had shown up and were stationed in seven outposts along a twenty-three-mile stretch of border.[26] One newspaper described the Minutemen's activities this way: "In four member teams, they rode out caravan-style for several miles along red-dirt roads flanked by rocks and prickly brush. They fanned out hundreds of yards apart along a skimpy barbed wire fence at the Mexico border, eager to catch men and women trying to sneak into the United States."[27]

Like many spectacles, this one had costumes. The Minutemen volunteers came equipped with military-style camouflage clothing, binoculars, bulletproof vests, aircraft, walkie-talkies, and even guns, since it is legal to carry firearms in Arizona (Figure 6.3).[28] The Minuteman Project's spectacle in Arizona had all the trappings of a quasi-military campaign, which was not surprising, given that many of the volunteers had served in the military in places such as Vietnam and Iraq.[29] Jim Gilchrist, the founder of the Minuteman Project, was himself wounded in Vietnam.[30]

The volunteers' motivations for coming echoed the discourse on Mexican immigration discussed in Chapter 2. "We have an illegal invasion of our

Figure 6.3. Minuteman Project volunteer, April 2005. Photo by Robert King. Reprinted by permission of Zuma Press.

country going on now that is affecting our schools, our healthcare system and our society in general," one volunteer commented. "No society can sustain this."[31] Speaking about immigration, a volunteer said, "It's destroying America."[32] Another noted, "I'd like to see my brother get a wheel chair lift rather than an illegal alien get a free education. I just think you've got to take care of your own."[33] And yet another predicted, "I think all of this will put the federal government on notice as to where we stand as citizens."[34] Such comments clearly delineated simple dichotomies, such as us/them, invaded/invaders, victims/destroyers, legitimate/ illegal members of society, and citizens/noncitizens, all of which defined both citizens and those characterized in a position of "illegality."[35]

In addition to these motivations, there must have been the appeal of performing a contemporary version of an Old West narrative of cowboys versus the Mexicans, or Texas Rangers versus the Mexicans, or simply border vigilantes. In the post–U.S.-Mexican war period, a military campaign arose to pacify the Mexican-origin population in the border states of California, Texas, New Mexico, Arizona, and Nevada. Some of these activities were sanctioned, such as those of the Texas Rangers, whose long history began in 1823, when Stephen F. Austin hired a few men to protect Anglo settlers in the Mexican territory of

Texas.[36] After Texas declared its independence from Mexico, a "Corp of Rangers" helped guard against uprisings of Tejanos (Texans of Mexican descent) and Mexican incursions into the Texas side of the Rio Grande.[37] In 1874 the Texas Legislature organized the Texas Rangers to fight Mexican bandits, Indians, and outlaws (Figure 6.4). Less formal but just as effective were the border vigilantes who meted out justice, Wild West style, and whose actions one scholar has likened to ethnic cleansing.[38] The practices of these times became part of the legend of the Old West, romanticized in a wide range of cultural productions: comic books, novels, plays, music, movies, and television. The Texas Rangers, in particular, have been immortalized in folklore and the media, including television's *The Lone Ranger* and many movies (Figure 6.5).

Like the Texas Rangers and border vigilantes of old, the Minuteman Project was holding out the opportunity to roam the West in search of Mexican scofflaws. Participants could not only engage in the thrill of the hunt but also send a symbolic message to Washington by taking the law into their own hands. It was this complex set of images and planned activities around the pursuit of Mexicans that undoubtedly informed President Bush's comment about

Figure 6.4. Las Norias Bandit Raid: Texas Rangers with dead Mexican bandits, October 8, 1915. The Robert Runyon Photograph Collection, RYB00096, Center for American History, The University of Texas at Austin.

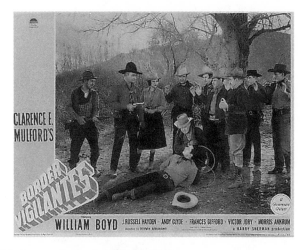

Figure 6.5. Movie poster for *Border Vigilantes* (1941).

"vigilantism" by the Minuteman Project in Arizona. As a Texan, Bush was familiar with the Texas Rangers' history and the concerns of Texas's Mexican American population about such activities. Even such criticism of the Minuteman Project's border surveillance activities in Arizona reflected an image of Wild West vigilantes (see Figure 6.6).

Figure 6.6. Minutemen portrayed as Wild West cowboys. Courtesy of Walt Staton, Arizona Independent Media Center.

Figure 6.7. Minuteman volunteer in Arizona. Photo by Michael Brandy. Reprinted by permission of *Deseret Morning News.*

In early April, Minutemen volunteers, with their guns and other parapher-nalia, arrived in Arizona ready to "hunt the Mexicans." As the message on the T-shirt in Figure 6.7 indicates ("Some people are alive simply because it's illegal to kill them"), the cowboy mentality was alive and well among the Minutemen volunteers.

MEDIA CIRCUS

Although the number of Minuteman volunteers was less than anticipated, the media turned up in full force. In fact, as the *Los Angeles Times* observed: "The number of media members here Friday to cover the volunteer border patrols nearly outnumbered the Minutemen. Reporters from around the world descended on Tombstone, population 4,800. Along with journalists came some filmmakers working on documentaries about the U.S.-Mexico bor-der."[39] Ironically, Chris Simcox, editor of the *Tombstone Tumbleweed* and one of the organizers of the Minuteman Project, seemed to blame the media for manufacturing the event: "The media has created this frenzy and this monster. They are looking for Bigfoot, the Loch Ness monster, the vigilante."[40] How-ever, Jim Gilchrist was more candid: "We have already accomplished our goal a hundredfold in getting the media out here and getting the message out."[41] As Gilchrist's comment indicates, the Minuteman Project's goal of creating a media spectacle was clearly elevated above other objectives originally elaborated for the project. Indeed, the other goals seemed to have been forgotten, perhaps in light of the fewer than expected volunteers. Or perhaps his statement laid bare the point being made here, that media attention was Gilchrist's only real objective in staging this spectacle.

On April 3 the media reported on still larger increases in surveillance power along the Arizona-Mexico border. The Department of Homeland Security had upped the ante by assigning more than 700 additional Border Patrol agents to the area.[42] The U.S. Senate also approved an amendment to hire 2,000 Border Patrol agents, a direct affront to President Bush's 2006 budget, which called for only an additional 216 new agents.[43] Both the new deployments of agents and new hiring goals came just as Minutemen were beginning to monitor the border.

By April 5 there appeared to be fewer clandestine border crossers in the areas monitored by the Minuteman Project. Chris Simcox was quick to claim another success: "We've shut down the whole sector. That's success."[44] However, the reduced number of clandestine border crossers was also influenced by other factors, not the least of which was the Mexican police force Grupo Beta, which was patrolling the Mexican side of the border and warning would-be migrants of the Minutemen's presence.[45] Two weeks into the project, the Border Patrol had apprehended about the same number of clandestine border crossers as during the same period the year before.[46] However, such considerations did not deter Jim Gilchrist from bragging: "None of this would have happened if it wasn't for the Minuteman action. This thing was a dog and pony show designed to bring in the media and get the message out and it worked."[47]

Although the Minuteman Project was planned to be a month-long monitoring exercise, Gilchrist claimed victory and formally ended the project's border monitoring on Wednesday, April 20, 2005.[48] Border monitoring was to continue, however, under the guise of an organization named Civil Homeland Defense, headed by Chris Simcox. The Minuteman Project also spawned other related projects along the U.S.-Mexico border in Texas, New Mexico, California, and far from the border in Idaho and Michigan.[49] The fallout from the Minuteman Project also had other ramifications. On April 19, California governor Arnold Schwarzenegger caused quite a political furor when he announced that closing the borders was a good idea: "Close the borders in California and all across, between Mexico and the United States . . . because I think it is just unfair to have all these people coming across." He added that border enforcement was lax.[50] In mid-August the governors of New Mexico and Texas went even further, declaring their respective counties along the U.S.-Mexico border to be "disaster areas," thus freeing up government funds to spend in the region.[51] Although the Minuteman Project's April offensive ended prematurely, it helped turn the public debate on immigration reform decidedly toward increased border enforcement, eclipsing guest worker programs, legalization programs, and other issues.

Jim Gilchrist managed to turn his fifteen minutes of fame into an extended spotlight on "illegal aliens" and the U.S.-Mexico border by running as the American Independent Party's candidate for U.S. Congress in Orange County, California. The Forty-eighth Congressional District was solidly Republican, but Gilchrist managed to use his one-issue campaign to stir up politics. His campaign attracted media attention and a war chest of about $500,000, both of which helped him win third place in the November 29, 2005, primary election, with 15 percent of the vote.[52] Gilchrist still came in third in the final primary vote on December 6, 2005, but he increased his share of the electorate to 25 percent.[53] In the course of the campaign, the favored candidate and eventual winner, John Campbell, had to insist that he, too, was tough on immigration. Two votes that Campbell had cast as a member of the California legislature became favorite Gilchrist targets.[54] One vote allowed undocumented students who had grown up in California to pay in-state tuition at public colleges and universities rather than the more costly tuition charged students from foreign countries. The other vote concerned Mexican consulate cards and their use as valid identification in California. By the time of the final election, Campbell had repudiated these votes and joined Gilchrist in opposing a guest worker program and other moderate immigration reforms.[55] Immediately following his defeat at the polls, Jim Gilchrist assured his followers of his intentions to continue to seek elected office and to focus attention on illegal immigration.[56] In other words, he would continue to use the spectacle of surveillance to garner media attention.

THE SPECTACLE REVISITED

Renato Rosaldo has observed: "The U.S.-Mexico border has become theater, and border theater has become social violence. Actual violence has become inseparable from symbolic ritual on the border—crossings, invasions, lines of defense, high-tech surveillance, and more."[57] To this list, I would add the Minuteman Project. The border theater that occurred in Arizona was indeed a symbolic ritual of surveillance. The group's April 2005 offensive to monitor the

Arizona-Mexico border engaged in practices of both spectacle and surveillance to achieve its goals, especially the larger objective of targeting public opinion and the federal government's immigration policies. The Minuteman Project's border surveillance is viewed here as a practice of power that seeks to define the juridical border between "citizens" and "Others," that is, "illegal aliens."[58]

Michel Foucault's concepts of "spectacle" and "surveillance" provide a useful theoretical and analytical framework for assessing the Minuteman Project and its goals. In *Discipline and Punish*, the spectacle is isomorphic with the scaffold, the public execution of prisoners in eighteenth-century France.[59] The spectacle was a public performance that enacted upon the body of the prisoner the power of the sovereign and thus clarified the distinction between the sovereign and those he governed: "[The spectacle's] aim is not so much to reestablish a balance as to bring into play, as its extreme point, the dissymmetry between the subject who has dared to violate the law and the all-powerful sovereign who displays his strength."[60] A key to the spectacle of public torture was "above all, the importance of a ritual that was to deploy its pomp in public."[61]

These two aspects of the spectacle, that it demarcates power positions and does so in a public way, were central to the activities of the Minuteman Project on the U.S. border in Arizona. In this case, the public performance was one that emphasized the power and privileges of citizenship, controlled by the democratic state now standing in place of the sovereign. The subjects in this spectacle were the "illegal aliens" who dared to violate the law and, in doing so, put the privileges of citizenship into question, at least for the Minuteman organizers and participants.

But we must not forget that, for Foucault, surveillance represented a move away from fully public executions as a means of discipline. Foucault used the Panopticon, the model of the "modern" prison in which each prisoner found himself or herself the object of the centralized and constant gaze of the guards, as a metaphor for the power of surveillance. Surveillance became a totalizing practice that worked on the very bodies of prisoners, who internalized the demands of power. In this way surveillance instilled discipline in subjects and produced docile bodies.

Rather than placing these two practices in opposition, I view the Minuteman Project's border monitoring as a combination of both spectacle and surveillance. In short, the Minuteman Project used surveillance to produce a spectacle on the Arizona-Mexico border. Finding clandestine border crossers became part of the show, or what one might describe as a media circus. In the final analysis, the success of the Minuteman Project was not in numbers of border crossers found and detained but in the attention the project received and the disciplining it achieved, that is, its ability to force governmental reaction aligned with its cause.

The Minutemen's monitoring may not have provided a great deterrent to clandestine border crossers in the long run. First of all, the demand for immigrant labor continues to act as a magnet for Mexicans and others. This demand results from a complex set of interacting factors, none of which are carefully examined in the Minuteman Project's public discourse. For example, rarely if ever discussed are the effects of low fertility rates and an aging U.S. population, especially during periods of economic expansion; middle- and upper-class Americans' desire for cheap commodities, food, and services; economic pressures related to globalization and low-wage production in developing countries; or the economic benefits provided by immigrants, not the least of which is their consumption of U.S. goods, a benefit expressed on the cover of *BusinessWeek*'s July, 18, 2005, issue: "Embracing Illegals: Companies Are Getting Hooked on the Buying Power of 11 Million Undocumented Immigrants." Simply increasing surveillance along the U.S.-Mexico border does little to address these salient factors that create a demand for the type of labor supplied by undocumented migrants. Consequently, it is likely that the Minuteman Project's monitoring of a small area along the U.S.-Mexico border simply resulted in potential unauthorized border crossers moving elsewhere, seeking less guarded areas.

Without a doubt, however, the spectacle of surveillance was very effective in reaching the target audience, the public. The Minuteman Project's April "offensive" on the Arizona-Mexico border was a media success, or as one newspaper put it: "Sifting hoopla from hard facts can be tricky, but the Minuteman Project has succeeded in its key goal—shifting the nation's eyes to illegal immigration."[62] Not only did the media turn out in full force, but stories on the Minuteman Project saturated newspapers nationwide.

As Figure 6.8 indicates, newspaper stories on the Minuteman Project went from a few score a month in February to almost six hundred in April. Although there was a precipitous drop in the number of citations in the months after April, the number did not fall to pre-March levels the rest of the year. There continued to be an interest in the group's activities for months after the April spectacle, rising sharply again in December with coverage of Jim Gilchrist's run for Congress. In addition, in December the U.S. House of Representatives passed its immigration reform bill, HR 4437, to which Minuteman Project representatives, mostly Jim Gilchrist, provided responses in newspaper stories.

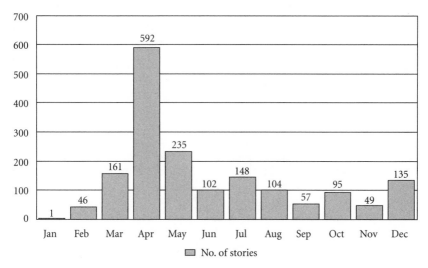

Figure 6.8. Monthly numbers of newspaper stories about the Minuteman Project in 2005.
SOURCE: America's Newspapers Online Database.

In 2006 the Minuteman Project continued to garner media attention, typically around localized mini-spectacles of surveillance. For example, Minuteman volunteers in local chapters throughout the country staged protests at
day laborer sites and at businesses they believed hired undocumented workers,
which drew some media attention. On May 5, Minuteman volunteers filled a
handful of cars, small trucks, and minivans for a cross-country trip to Washington, D.C., as a way of protesting the lack of border enforcement and to provide a counterdemonstration to the massive immigrant marches occurring at
that time (see Chapter 7).[63] Most notably, perhaps, the Minuteman Project established itself as a voice in the public debate over immigration, a voice reporters would now routinely seek out for responses to immigration-related stories.
As Figure 6.9 indicates, the Minuteman Project maintained an important level
of media coverage in the early months of 2006. In particular, as the immigrant
marches took place in April and May, the Minuteman Project's media presence
also increased as reporters sought out organization members for comments
reflecting the "other side" of the story.

Because of media attention, the Minuteman Project has become a nationally recognized anti-immigration group. Jim Gilchrist and Jerome Corsi's book
Minutemen: The Battle to Secure America's Borders, published in 2006, continues the quest to get out the group's anti-immigration message. The Minuteman Project also maintains its website, with up-to-the-minute commentary on

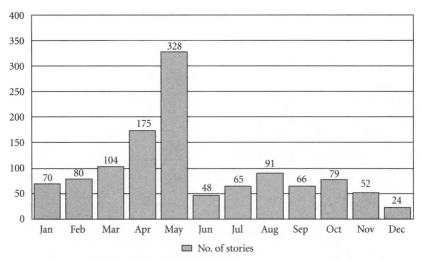

Figure 6.9. Monthly numbers of newspaper stories about the Minuteman Project in 2006. SOURCE: America's Newspapers Online Database.

immigration-related events and pointed criticism of government officials who appear to favor a guest worker program or a path to citizenship for undocumented immigrants.

Widespread public recognition, however, can bring both fame and infamy, support and derision. The Minuteman Project has become a symbol in its own right. Rather than the immigration issue it means to highlight, the organization itself has become the subject of political cartoons, public commentary, and counterprotests and even the source of characters in television shows. For example, Minuteman Project–type characters were featured on an episode of the television drama *The West Wing*. Through such representations, public culture engages contemporary topics such as immigration. For example, the comic strip *La Cucaracha* makes fun of the tendency to blame immigrants for all of society's problems, even personal problems (Figure 6.10). A second example ridicules the hypocrisy of condemning undocumented migration while at the same time the U.S. economy, and an urban and suburban middle-class lifestyle, has become dependent on immigrant labor (Figure 6.11). Another cartoon targets the government's lack of desire to develop a rational immigration policy, while at the same time representing the Minuteman as silly and juvenile, thus undermining the Minuteman Project's surveillance strategy as the solution (Figure 6.12). In each of these examples, the Minutemen become the subject, the symbol, used as the means to comment on immigration issues.

Figure 6.10. *La Cucaracha* cartoon pokes fun at the Minuteman Project. La Cucaracha © 2005 Lalo Alcaraz. Distributed by Universal Press Syndicate. Reprinted with permission. All rights reserved.

Figure 6.11. Two Minutemen argue over who to detain in this John Branch cartoon. Reprinted by permission of John Branch / San Antonio Express-News.

Figure 6.12. In this cartoon by Mike Keefe, Uncle Sam discusses with a Minuteman the difficulty of figuring out who to detain. Courtesy of Mike Keefe / The Denver Post. Permission granted by Cagle Cartoons.

Finally, there have been humorous attempts to cash in on the Minuteman Project. For example, Minuteman Salsa appeared on the market, despite salsa's being a cross-border intrusion into U.S. cuisine (Figure 6.13). Such irony, however, seems lost in the promotional text for the salsa:

America's Patriotic Salsa

Minuteman Salsa is proud to be America's 100% US-born and bred Southwestern salsa.

You don't support illegal immigration. Buy Minuteman Salsa and keep foreign-made salsa from slipping across the border into your pantry.

A portion of the proceeds of every sale of Minuteman Salsa will benefit the courageous men and women of the Minuteman Project, guarding America's borders.

Deport Bad Taste, Buy Minuteman Salsa™[64]

FINAL THOUGHTS

From the perspective of critical cultural analysis, the spectacle in the desert lends itself to several interpretations. The Minuteman Project grew out of a sense of frustration with new global realities that reduce the power of national

Figure 6.13. Minuteman Salsa.

borders to delimit the nation-state as an autonomous territory. Anthropologists have been arguing that these flows reflect the unmoored or deterritorialized nature of contemporary post–nation-state realities that make national borders permeable in many ways.[65] Indeed, the world is now on the move as capital, culture, people, and information flow across once-formidable national borders at an increasingly rapid pace.[66] The local response to such transnational flows can be positive, including a sense of identification with newcomers and the development of transnational identities that transcend national borders.[67] Or transnational flows can lead to a renewed nationalism, which, as Manuel Castells notes, is "always affirmed against the alien."[68]

The Minutemen are an example of this latter response. The organizers and sympathizers of the Minuteman Project viewed its activities as a stand against the destruction of the nation-state, symbolized by the inability of the state to control the flow of unauthorized border crosses. For the Minutemen, the breakdown of the border, as they perceived it, was an empirical assertion that the border was, for all practical purposes, a legal fiction.[69] Their dramatics were an attempt to reaffirm the contours of the nation-state, which from their perspective were in danger of being "lost." Through their actions, the Minutemen hoped to restore a clearly defined border around the nation-state's territory. The spectacle of surveillance on the Arizona-Mexico border drew the line, as it were, along the entire U.S.-Mexico border.

The Minuteman Project engaged in a performance that inscribed citizenship and the nation in a way similar to that which anthropologists have shown for gender.[70] Through the dramatics of their "hunt" for noncitizen "prey," the Minutemen enacted a rite of policing noncitizens, an act of symbolic power and violence that defined their own citizen-subject status. At the same time, the spectacle in the desert was a nation-defining performance. Unauthorized border crossers, those "space invaders," were kept in their own national territory.[71] For a couple of weeks in a small area along the two-thousand-mile U.S.-Mexico border, the danger to the nation posed by people out of place was averted, at least in some people's minds. The Minutemen's monitoring of the border was a corporal spectacle, and for many the Minutemen came to embody the citizen who exerts power to preserve the privileges and purity of citizenship and the integrity of the nation-state.

POSTSCRIPT

In March 2007 the Minuteman Project's board of directors removed Jim Gilchrist from his leadership position for alleged accounting irregularities.[72] Turmoil ensued, with more staunchly anti-immigration advocate Barbara Coe taking over the group's reins. Looking back, Gilchrist's ousting was one of many problems leading to fracturing over the Minuteman Project's practices and immigration message, and its eventual loss of importance and membership. But from the beginning there were problems with competing border groups, such as Glen Spencer's American Border Patrol.[73] New splinter groups also soon formed as leaders clashed over goals and ideologies. Chris Simcox broke with the Minuteman Project early on to form the Minuteman Civil Defense Corps. Since 2006, more groups have formed with aggressive stances toward border surveillance and more rabidly anti-immigration positions than that of Jim Gilchrist, who would come to lament the number of "kooks" and "right-wingers" attracted to the Minuteman cause:

> Some in other groups wanted to go down with rifles, hunting gear and fixed bayonets, and let's defend America. Your ultra right wingers. As right wing as my adversaries on the left may make me appear, I'm really a moderate kind of guy, wide open for free speech, anti-violence, and let the reasonable mind judge the issue. I'm for the respectable repatriation of the millions of illegal aliens in the country. But I am not for beating them on the street corners or intimidating the heck out of them or for reducing them to the status of, you might say, cold fear. . . . That apparently has been a dividing line between me and others who are on the ultra-right wing of this issue, who essentially are nothing but a bunch of skinheads.[74]

The number of hard-line nativist groups that have splintered off from the Minuteman Project include the Minuteman American Defense, the Federal Immigration Reform and Enforcement (FIRE) Coalition, the Minuteman Civil Defense Corps (MCDC), the San Diego Minutemen, and many more. The Southern Poverty Law Center, which tracks nativist and hate group activities, found a disturbing increase in nativist extremist groups between 2007 (144 groups) and 2009 (309 groups).[75] However, the shine of the border vigilante movement began to lose its luster after a horrific murder by Shawna Forde and her accomplices.

Shawna Forde was a member of the Minuteman American Defense organization, which she founded and directed. She was also a Tea Party regular, but we will come to the significance of that below. On May 30, 2009, in Arivaca, Arizona, Shawna and two men—Jason Bush, a white supremacist, and Albert Gaxiola, a convicted drug dealer—invaded the home of Raul "Junior" Flores. Shawna believed Raul was a drug dealer who had cash stashed in his home, money she could use to fund her border vigilante organization. Catching Raul, his wife, Gina Gonzales, and their nine-year-old daughter, Brisenia, asleep, the intruders claimed to be law enforcement officers. After entering, Shawna and her accomplices shot Raul, who died at the scene, and Gina, who pretended to be dead. Then the most chilling scene unfolded. As Gina described it, the shooter emptied his gun shooting her and Raul. She could hear her daughter crying and begging, "Please don't shoot me, please don't shoot me." The gunman calmly reloaded and then shot Brisenia in the head.[76] Shawna Forde and Jason Bush were sentenced to death and Albert Gaxiola to life in prison for their roles in the murders of Raul and Brisenia and the attempted murder of Gina.[77]

As the reality of vigilante justice became clear, Minuteman-style groups began to dwindle, down to about fifty-three such groups in 2011.[78] The media also lost interest in the Minutemen, with only twenty-nine newspaper stories nationwide during the five months between January and May of 2012. As Jim Gilchrist noted: "No longer will you have a Minuteman organization going to the border with thousands of people."[79] As enthusiasm for the Minutemen waned, its followers found a new outlet for their views in the emerging Tea Party movement. In a spectacle reminiscent of the Minutemen, more than six hundred anti-immigrant activists gathered on the U.S.-Mexico border in Cochise County, Arizona, for a Tea Party Nation rally in August 2011.[80] On land owned by Glenn Spencer, leader of the American Border Patrol, Tea Party candidates for the U.S. Senate and House of Representatives spoke to the crowd, as did Maricopa County sheriff Joe Arpaio. Arizona state senator Russell Pearce was also there, telling the assembled Tea Party enthusiasts: "We have an invasion going on that's going to destroy this Republic."[81] According to one account, more than a hundred leaders of Minuteman-style groups have joined local chapters of the Tea Party.[82]

7 THE IMMIGRANT MARCHES OF 2006 AND THE STRUGGLE FOR INCLUSION

ON MAY 1, 2006, I joined about ten thousand immigrants and their supporters as they marched through downtown Santa Ana, California.[1] I was struck by how orderly the marchers were and how the march arrived at a plaza right on time for the scheduled noon rally. In the crowd were men, women, and children, most wearing white shirts and carrying signs or U.S. flags. They marched both against the proposed House of Representatives bill HR 4437, which would have made felons of all undocumented immigrants, and they marched for inclusion into U.S. society as respected members. In other words, the march was a political statement, a taking over of the village square, to claim recognition as social and cultural citizens and to show support for legislation that would allow them to eventually become legal residents and citizens of the United States.

Despite the marchers' calm and peaceful deportment, their claims for citizenship were represented as the objects of a media spectacle. Representations can be extremely polemical, for, as Aihwa Ong has noted, "struggles over representation are the ideological work of citizen-making."[2] The immigrants marching for inclusion in U.S. society and recognition of their social and economic contributions to society may have had a positive response to their message from some members of the larger society. However, other, less positive responses were mobilized by anti-immigration organizations, in particular, and subsequently by state policies that have focused on border enforcement and increased surveillance rather than opening up new avenues for citizenship, cultural or legal. For example, a few months after the marches, on October 26, 2006, President George W. Bush signed into law the Secure Fence Act of 2006 (HR 6061), authorizing the Department of Homeland Security to construct approximately seven hundred miles of fencing along the U.S.-Mexico border.[3] How could the immigrants' messages of inclusion have become the fodder for anti-immigrant rhetoric and restrictive immigration policies?

To begin to answer this question, we need to focus on symbols and images that became lightning rods in the public discourse that erupted during and after the immigrant marches of 2006. National symbols are part of the visual lexicon in a discourse on immigration and citizenship and, as such, can be interpreted as symbols of both unity and division.[4] As David Kertzer has observed, political symbols have a palpable quality, serving as profound and concrete metaphors for ideas and concepts.[5] A flag, for example, "is not simply a decorated cloth, but the embodiment of a nation; indeed, the nation is defined as such by the flag as the flag is defined by the nation."[6] Symbols of a nation define an individual's sense of self; they visually represent personal and group identities.[7] Kertzer argues that national political symbols polarize the world, categorizing people as either with us or against us.[8] Moreover, because these oppositions are ideologically patterned and filled with so much emotion, they push people to take action.[9]

Not surprisingly, therefore, the meaning of national flags waved during the marches and the language used to sing the national anthem became the objects of controversy. The use and meaning of these symbols became contested ground for both the immigrant marchers and those who resented the marchers' claims to cultural and social citizenship. The immigrant marchers were endangered by the Latino Threat Narrative's representation of their lives and by proposed government policies that would make their lives even more difficult. For the marchers, waving the U.S. flag became a demonstration of their desire for inclusion in U.S. society and a denial of the basic tenets of the Latino Threat Narrative that characterize them as un-American. For others, particularly anti-immigration groups, the Mexican flag, the U.S. flag in the hands of undocumented immigrants, and the Spanish version of the national anthem became symbols of the perceived dilution of the rights and privileges of citizenship because of the immigrants' presence.

A brief historical overview sets the stage for the events that transpired and the battles over symbols and meanings that ensued as immigrants and their supporters marched throughout the nation in the spring of 2006. In addition to the dreaded HR 4437, the marches came a year after the Minuteman Project staged its own spectacle of border surveillance in Arizona. Although the Minutemen are examined in Chapter 6, suffice it to say here that these immigration-related media spectacles do not exist in isolation; they exist within shared cultural, social, and historical contexts and thus can, and often do, speak to each other across time and space.

A CALL FOR ACTION

The immigrant marches were not one event but many. One of the first events by a supporter of immigrants' rights to gain national recognition occurred on Tuesday, February 27, 2006. Cardinal Roger M. Mahony of the large Archdiocese of Los Angeles called upon Catholics to spend Lent fasting and praying for humane immigration reform.[10] At the same time, Cardinal Mahony criticized the Minuteman Project's border surveillance program as "a misguided reaction to national security concerns."[11] In response to the House of Representatives' restrictive immigration bill, Cardinal Mahony indicated that he would instruct priests to defy any law that required them to ask immigrants for legal documents before providing assistance. As Mahony said, "the whole concept of punishing people who serve immigrants is un-American. If you take this to its logical, ludicrous extreme, every single person who comes up to receive Holy Communion, you have to ask them to show papers. It becomes absurd and the church is not about to get into that."[12]

Cardinal Mahony's call for action expressed a rejection of the state's reliance on legal status as the ultimate definition of a citizen. Instead, Cardinal Mahony argued that "all of us are immigrant people," thus asserting shared universal citizenship. Of course, the vision of a shared humanity is religiously based in this case. "This is part of our heritage of God's care and concerns for all peoples," the cardinal said. "At no point . . . is God asking us to build walls or borders."[13] This biblically based vision of a universal citizenship was underscored by Auxiliary Bishop Rutillo J. del Riego of the Diocese of San Bernardino, who said, "This is not about politics from our point of view, this is about how we treat other human beings."[14] Such pronouncements take citizenship out of the domain of the nation-state and into an imagined universal community as the basis for belonging. For these religious leaders, treating all people with respect is a moral imperative, a position they explicitly took in opposition the rhetoric of the anti-immigrant groups.

In March, immigrants and their supporters organized a number of events. One of the first events to capture the media's attention occurred on Saturday, March 4, when a dozen immigrant day laborers began a cross-country run to call attention to the discrimination and exploitation of immigrant workers.[15]

In this case, the Minuteman Project's public spectacle of surveillance on the U.S.-Mexico border was a motivating factor for, if not the cause of, the day laborers' own attempt at media attention. One of the organizers, Carlos Mares, an immigrant from Mexico, criticized the Minuteman Project for its activities. However, the principal message of the cross-country run, according to Mares, was aimed at the U.S. Congress: "We're trying to show the federal government they should recognize the contributions of immigrants, especially day laborers. We demand fair legislation, not just for Latin American workers but also for workers from Africa, Asia and all over the world."[16] The day laborers used the media spectacle, a form of political activity, to claim economic citizenship, an assertion based on their economic contributions to U.S. society.

Although massive immigrant demonstrations caught national media attention beginning the weekend of March 25, there was actually a large march in Chicago on March 10. Initial estimates were that about 100,000 immigrants and their supporters filled the streets of downtown Chicago, but later estimates put the number as high as 300,000.[17] Despite its size, the Chicago march and rally flew under the national radar, not receiving coverage in such national newspapers as the *Los Angeles Times* or the *New York Times* in the days immediately following the event. The lack of prominence in the national media was perhaps due to the unexpected success of the march. Not even the organizers expected such a large turnout, which exceeded predictions by as much as ten times.[18] Opposition to HR 4437, which among its many provisions called for a seven-hundred-mile fence along the U.S.-Mexico border and would make felons of undocumented immigrants, served as the catalyst for the march. As one organizer said about the bill, "It's wrong. These people work here. They pay taxes. They are Americans."[19] Such claims for citizenship were echoed by Chicago's mayor Richard Daley: "Those who are undocumented, we are not going to make criminals out of them. Everyone in America is an immigrant."[20] Daley's views represented an understanding of citizenship based on similarity of experience in, and thus belonging to, the community. Such universalist views were also expressed in one marcher's call for civil rights for immigrants: "It's not just about undocumented workers, it's about human beings and basic rights."[21]

The Chicago demonstration held important lessons for the organizers of upcoming immigrant marches.[22] A key element of the Chicago immigrant march and rally was the role played by a Spanish-language radio in mobilizing participants.[23] In the days leading up to the event, Rafael Pulido, a popular Spanish-language radio show personality, criticized the House of Representatives' immigration bill and urged his listeners to attend the march and rally.[24] Pulido also urged the marchers to wear white as a symbol of peace and to carry U.S. flags as a symbol of patriotism. Spanish-language media—and among students, the Internet—would prove to be effective mobilizing strategies in the spectacular immigrant marches that soon followed. The display of American flags was also a lesson not lost on the organizers of subsequent marches.[25]

On Friday, March 24, hundreds of mostly Latino students in Southern California staged walkouts at Garfield, Roosevelt, and Montebello high schools and disrupted classes at other high schools to protest HR 4437.[26] Students engaging in the walkouts were perhaps emboldened by Cardinal Mahony's public show of support for immigrant rights as well as the recent public demonstrations by day laborers in Los Angeles and activists in Chicago. Some students were also influenced by *Walkout*, an HBO television movie of the Latino student protests for educational equality that took place in the 1960s at Garfield and other East Los Angeles high schools.[27] *Walkout* aired one week before the students began their demonstrations.

Students voiced their reasons for marching and emphasized the contributions of immigrants. One Latina freshman commented: "Without immigrants this country wouldn't be anything. This protest is not about rebellion. We're not criminals. We're in this country to work." Another Latino student, age 14, said, "This economy is based on immigrants," and stated that he would like to give all immigrants the opportunity to become naturalized citizens like his parents.[28] Both students rejected the notion that to come to the United States without papers was a felonious act; rather, to work was a contribution to society and the basis for claims to citizenship.[29] In contrast to the Chicago demonstration a week earlier, many students carried Mexican flags or green balloons, reflecting one of the dominant colors of the Mexican flag (Figure 7.1). Although U.S. flags could also be seen among the student protestors, there was an immediate and visceral response to the Mexican flags on radio talk shows and later among television pundits such as Lou Dobbs, to whom we will return.

Events began to occur rapidly at this point. On Saturday, March 25, about 500,000 people marched in downtown Los Angeles for immigrant rights.[30] A photograph of the event (Figure 7.2) captures the sheer volume of people, making this one of the largest public spectacles ever witnessed in Los Angeles. Media representations such as this photo led to negative responses by anti-immigrant groups, concerned that such huge numbers of people indicated a mass invasion of immigrants. Other protests occurred in Phoenix and as far

Figure 7.1. Student demonstrators in downtown Los Angeles, March 24, 2006, were captured in "City Hall Protest," by Spencer Weiner, *Los Angeles Times,* March 28, 2006. Copyright 2006 Los Angeles Times. Reprinted with permission.

Figure 7.2. "Convergence at City Hall," by Gina Ferrazi, *Los Angeles Times*, March 25, 2006. Copyright 2006, Los Angeles Times. Reprinted with permission.

away as Charlotte, North Carolina.[31] Once again, the House of Representatives' proposal to criminalize undocumented immigration was a motivating factor for the march. In contrast to the student demonstrators the previous day, these marchers prominently displayed the American flag.

On Sunday, March 26, about 3,500 people marched through downtown Los Angeles in support of the United Farm Workers and to demonstrate against the House of Representatives' punitive immigration bill.[32] Then on Monday, March 27, students again walked out of classes, only this time the walkouts were more widespread. Urged on by word of mouth and the power of the Internet, especially myspace.com, nearly forty thousand students in Los Angeles, Riverside, San Bernardino, and Ventura counties walked out of classes to demonstrate their opposition to the proposed legislation.[33] Thousands of people, including schoolchildren from Oakland, marched in downtown San Francisco for immigrants' rights.[34] Similar protests occurred in Fresno, California; Yakima, Washington; Washington, D.C.; Phoenix, Arizona; Detroit, Michigan; Columbus, Ohio; Houston, Texas; Woodbridge, Virginia; Norwood, Massachusetts; and Longmont, Colorado.[35] Student walkouts continued in the Los Angeles area for the next couple of days, finally subsiding after police began to aggressively enforce truancy laws.[36] Many students again waved Mexican flags in their demonstrations.

FLAGS AS SYMBOLS OF INCLUSION AND EXCLUSION

The controversy surrounding Mexican flags erupted in full force at about this time. Although Mexican flags were prominent in the student demonstrations, they were a minority of the flags in the larger immigrant marches and rallies, where the U.S. flag vastly outnumbered all other flags. The large number of U.S. flags at the immigrant marches was due in part to the urging of Spanish-language radio DJs. As DJ Eddie "Piolin" Sotelo said, "If we want to live here, we want to demonstrate that we love this country and we love the American flag."[37]

Students, many of whom were U.S.-born citizens, more often waved Mexican flags, which for some indicated a renewed pride in their heritage rather than a symbol of disloyalty to the United States. As one eighteen-year-old said, "It's my pride. It's my roots. I want to express it and show to other people where I come from, what Mexico has done for the United States." A sixteen-year-old student who carried both an American and a Mexican flag when marching stressed that this action did not signal disloyalty to the United States:

"St. Patrick's Day just passed. Just because they wave an Irish flag doesn't mean that they care about Ireland more than they do the U.S."[38]

However, negative response to the Mexican flag did focus on issues of loyalty and nationalism. Representative Henry Bonilla (R-Texas), speaking on NBC's *Meet the Press*, commented: "When you come here and wave a Mexican flag in our face in a country that's giving a lot of these people an opportunity that they've never had before, I think a lot of Americans are insulted."[39] Joseph Turner, founder of Save Our State, a group advocating restrictions on immigration, said: "This isn't Mexico. This is America. . . . What [annoys me] most is the arrogance that they are going to fly a foreign flag on my soil."[40] A message to subscribers of the Federation for American Immigration Reform's e-newsletter dated April 13, 2006, ran the headline "Illegal Aliens March . . . Tell Them America Won't Surrender" under a photograph of a Mexican flag flying above a U.S. flag upside down that was allegedly raised by students at Montebello High School in Whittier, California. Notice that all the marchers were labeled "illegal aliens," thus questioning the citizenship of even U.S.-born Latino students, legal immigrants, and other U.S. citizens who participated in the demonstrations. Lou Dobbs, who has made immigration one of the top issues on his CNN television show, also did not appreciate the Mexican flags: "I don't think we should have any flag flying in this country except the flag of the United States. And let me tell you something else, since we're talking about double standards. . . . I don't think there should be a St. Patrick's Day. I don't care who you are. I think we ought to be celebrating what is common about this country, what we enjoy as similarities as people."[41]

A political cartoon by Mike Shelton exemplifies how the flag controversy was interpreted (Figure 7.3). In the cartoon, Mexicans are freely crossing an unguarded U.S.-Mexico border and running toward a U.S. city in the background. At the border is a box of U.S. flags with a sign that says "Take one." The Mexicans are all carrying Mexican flags; as they cross the border, they look quizzically at the box of U.S. flags, none of which is taken. The cartoon reflects the idea that only Mexican flags appeared at the immigrant marches, when in reality they were prominent only in the student demonstrations. U.S. flags were the overwhelming majority of flags at the large immigrant marches. Many more examples could be given, but the die was cast. The issue of flags as simultaneously symbols of inclusion and exclusion would become as much a part of the discourse surrounding the marches for immigrants' rights as the marches themselves.

Figure 7.3. Cartoon reflecting the flag controversy, by Mike Shelton. Copyright March 29, 2006. Reprinted by permission of the Orange County Register.

MORE IMMIGRANT MARCHES AND
VOLATILE CONTROVERSIES

Scattered demonstrations continued into April, such as one in Costa Mesa, California, on Saturday, April 1. Speaking against the proposed immigration legislation, an Anaheim city councilman, who had attended the march, supported the immigrants' claims for inclusion: "For me, this is an American issue. Immigrants are the fabric of the United States. These people work here. They pay taxes here. Their children go to school here."[42] On Sunday, April 9, about 350,000 to 500,000 marched in downtown Dallas, 50,000 in San Diego, and still others in geographically diverse cities across the country, such as Fort Worth, Miami, St. Paul, Birmingham, Des Moines, St. Louis, Salem, and Boise.[43] An even larger national demonstration was called for Monday, April 10.[44] Organizers hoped to mobilize two million people to participate in more than 140 demonstrations in dozens of cities.[45]

At this point, the symbolism of flags was a dominant concern of the demonstration organizers. Juan Carlos Ruiz, the coordinator of the National Capital Immigrant Coalition, said that in Washington, D.C.,

> you're going to see a sea of people wearing white shirts and white blouses and carrying the American flag, honoring this country because this is the country we want to belong to. That doesn't mean we are renouncing the love we have for our countries. All that shows is that we want to be here, we are committed and pledge to the values and the symbols of this country, and the flag is one of them.[46]

In Los Angeles, Cardinal Mahony urged protestors to put away flags from other countries, saying, "Do not use them because they do not help us get the legislation we need."[47] Photographs of the April 10 marches across the country do, indeed, indicate the predominant presence of American flags and white shirts (Figure 7.4).

Marchers carrying American flags echoed the organizers' views. Said one fellow who had come to the U.S. illegally and worked picking crops, "Our roots are Mexican, and we don't want to lose that, but at the same time I feel more American." A woman who was a pastry chef said, "We love our country, we love

Figure 7.4. Demonstration in Columbia, South Carolina, April 10, 2006. Photograph by Gerry Melendez. Reprinted by permission of The State (Columbia, S.C.).

Americans." Another marcher said, "A lot of us here broke the law to get here. That doesn't mean we don't love America."[48] Once again, what these examples suggest is that the demonstrators viewed their actions as a plea for inclusion in U.S. society. They recognized that their current lives were intertwined with U.S. life, even though they expressed affection for, and even connections with, life back in their country of origin.

For the immigrant marchers, carrying the U.S. flag was an expression of belonging and a visible, concrete symbol of their desire for inclusion. Their actions are examples of what Levitt and Schiller refer to as "ways of belonging"— "practices that signal or enact an identity which demonstrates a conscious connection to a particular group." As the authors explain, "These actions are not symbolic but concrete, visible actions that mark belonging such as wearing a Christian cross or Jewish star, flying a flag, or choosing a particular cuisine. Ways of belonging combine action and an awareness of the kind of identity that action signifies."[49] Although legal status and nativist attitudes may make inclusion of immigrants into society problematic, the marchers, with their U.S. flags in full display, were making a statement about their sense of belonging and their social and cultural citizenship.

Building on these themes, Andres Oppenheimer, a columnist in the *Orange County Register*, interpreted the new political activism of immigrants as a reflection of a new form of citizenship, the emergence of "transnational citizens."[50] This had occurred, he argued, because of the ease of communication and travel between countries, dual-citizenship possibilities, and a perception among immigrants that undocumented immigrants help, rather than hurt, the U.S. economy. "I don't see the new 'Latino power' as a strident separatist movement," Oppenheimer wrote. "More likely, it will be a subdued mixture of U.S.-born Hispanics and transnational citizens who will be largely invisible most of the time, but will take to the streets if they feel threatened."[51]

The Minuteman Project provides an example of alarmist reactions to the immigrant marches. Posted on the organization's website on March 27 were the headline "Illegal Alien Armies March on U.S. Cities" and the subheading "Jim Gilchrist and America's Minutemen Remain Unmoved by the Anarchist Demands of Illegal Alien Mobs in Their Defiance to American Rule of Law."[52] The message was clear: the nation was under attack by invading "armies" of "anarchists" and "illegal alien mobs" who cared little about the rule of law, thus reinforcing the organization's representation of them as criminals. In the body of the text, Jim Gilchrist reaffirmed the message that the country was at "war," facing an "insurrection," and on the brink of a "democratic disaster of epic proportions." Perhaps it is best to let Gilchrist's words speak for themselves:

America is experiencing a democratic disaster of epic proportion.

These armies of bused-in demonstrators who have converged on Los Angeles, most of whom are in the U.S. illegally, are demanding citizen rights, privileges, and benefits, and threatening that if their demands are not met, then the ultimatum is anarchy.

If federal and local governments buckle under the pressure exerted upon them by throngs of illegal alien bullies and their anarchist sympathizers, who have no legal standing and who flaunt the flag of another nation, it is classic insurrection.

Now we are occupied by an army of some 30 million non-citizens, illegal alien invaders who perversely place demands on U.S. citizens. If these demands are not met, will anarchy and insurrection follow? Are we on the cusp of a national disorder not seen since the Civil War? Do we succumb to weak-kneed cowardice in the face of blatant threats against the rule of law? Or, do we stand boldly against the demons of disorder and intimidation that will certainly strip all Americans of their Bill of Rights and their rights to the enjoyment of life, liberty, property and the protection afforded by the rule of law?[53]

Five days later, the Minuteman Project posted another article on its website, in which it clarified even further its view of the threat posed by the marchers the previous weekend.[54] Following the headline—"America on Notice: Occupying Army Demands More from Their Captives!"—was the subhead "Is the New Rule of Law, 'The Biggest Thugs with the Biggest Clubs?'" What had been described as an immigrant invasion had now escalated into a war in which captives had been taken. But the invading army were no longer just anarchists with no respect for the law. Now the immigrants and their supporters were "thugs" with "clubs," suggesting an unruly mob striking out at other, defenseless members of society, but also creating the image of people who were in a precivilized, less socially evolved state. Reading the content on the Minuteman Project website, one would not guess that the marches had been overwhelmingly peaceful and that the organizers had worked with local governments on guidelines and parade routes to ensure the safety of participants and nonparticipants alike.

In the text of the article, one could observe the concern with issues of citizenship and how the immigrants' claims for citizenship had been delegitimized:

On March 25th 2006 the United Armies of Illegal Aliens marched on Los Angeles being welcomed with opened arms from Mayor Antonio Villaraigosa. The message went forth that the invaders demand all U.S. citizenship rights and privileges without pledging allegiance to the Red White and Blue, however many did pledge allegiance to the Red, White and Green. . . .

The illegal armies across the United State have unified to lay claim on not only the South West United States but also to enslave the American tax payer by forcing good hearted Americans to foot the bill. The bill is now due. The education system is being destroyed by anti-American teachings that encourage the destruction of the constitution. The health system is crumbling under the pressure of the weight of millions of illegal aliens who refuse to assimilate into America unlike the tens of millions of legal immigrants who happily joined the American spirit and celebrated the American culture.

Through a rapid barrage of alarmist rhetoric, the Minuteman Project's representations of the demonstrations undercut the marchers' claims of social and cultural citizenship. The marchers' loyalty to the nation was questioned because of their alleged "allegiance" to the Mexican flag. The immigrants' "demand" for "citizen rights, privileges and benefits" was also derided as improper behavior. "Laying claim" to the Southwest and "enslaving" other Americans were also threatening behaviors attributed to the marchers and their sympathizers. Rather than viewing the marches as an act of democratic political action, and thus a reflection of learning to act as members of U.S. political culture, the marchers were said to "refuse to assimilate." And finally, citizenship for all Americans was threatened by marchers and their supporters, who were out to destroy the U.S. Constitution.

Before the controversy over the March rallies could die down, hundreds of thousands of immigrants and their supporters again marched and rallied across the nation on Monday, April 10. Rallies were held in many states, and Washington, D.C., and Los Angeles had perhaps the largest rallies, with about 500,000 marchers in each city. But large rallies were also held in Phoenix, Houston, Omaha, Boston, Atlanta, and many other cities.

"We Are America" was a common slogan on the signs carried by the marchers, who once again voiced their concern about the proposed legislation that would make it a felony to be in the United States without immigration documents. Marchers asserted desires for belonging and having cultural citizenship in the nation where they lived and worked.[55] American flags were prominently on display in marches across the country, and in Washington, D.C., rally

Figure 7.5. Philadelphia march, April 10, 2006. Photograph by Matt Rourke. Reprinted by permission of AP / Wide World News.

organizers led participants in reciting the Pledge of Allegiance. Although most of the marchers were Latino, there were participants from many backgrounds. Reports included marchers originally from Ethiopia, Peru, El Salvador, Mexico, and many other countries.[56] Asian Americans were also participants in Los Angeles, Philadelphia, and other cities (Figure 7.5).

What was surprising was that large numbers of protestors came out on a Monday, a workday.[57] Since most of the marchers were working-class immigrants, their presence meant that they were giving up income to attend the rallies. One Salvadoran immigrant housecleaner at the Washington, D.C., rally said she would have to work a double shift so that she could attend the rally. "I'm here working for a future for my baby," she said as she held her twenty-one-month-old daughter, who carried a small American flag and wore a T-shirt that read, "I am not a criminal."[58] Another marcher said, "I'm legal. But if I try to help someone who has no papers, I'm a criminal [according to HR 4437]. For years, I was very quiet—only work and pay taxes. Now it's necessary to protest."[59] In many cities where rallies were held, business slowed or came to a standstill as workers demonstrated their concerns over immigration reform. As one bricklayer from Guatemala said, "The foreman said everybody has to show up today, but we came [to the march] anyway. We have to march. There won't be any brickwork there today."[60]

The rallies began to have an impact in many ways. The Republicans in the House of Representatives started to back away from the most extreme measure in HR 4437, making it a felony to be in the country without proper documentation.[61] Republicans even tried to shift the blame to the Democrats, saying that the Democrats had not cooperated in removing the provision from the bill. The immigrant marches also spawned counterdemonstrations, although the latter tended to be much smaller in numbers, often just a handful of people. One counterdemonstrator, a twenty-two-year-old woman in Washington, D.C., carried a sign that read, "Keep walking, just 1,800 miles until you're home." She refused to accept the demonstrators' claims of cultural citizenship, because, as she said, "I think that when illegal immigrants come here and expect to have entitlements given them just as U.S. citizens that it's totally preposterous."[62] Finally, for some observers, the marches may have reinforced their opinion that the U.S.-Mexico border required greater surveillance. Many others, however, supported a more comprehensive approach to immigration reform despite the ongoing marches. In a *Los Angeles Times* / Bloomberg poll taken at the time of the marches, 63 percent of Americans indicated that they supported tougher enforcement and a guest worker program, while only 30 percent supported tougher enforcement alone. Sixty-six percent supported allowing undocumented immigrants who had been living and working in the United States for a number of years, with no criminal record, to start a path to citizenship.[63]

The streets were barely cleared before planning began on a nationwide rally for May 1, the traditional day to celebrate labor. This rally was billed as "A Day without an Immigrant," and organizers asked workers to take a day off from work as a way of showing how important immigrants are for the economy, and students to take a day off from school.[64] This suggestion split supporters and detractors alike. Los Angeles Mayor Antonio Villaraigosa asked students to stay in school, and President Bush and Los Angeles's Cardinal Roger Mahony asked workers not to boycott work.[65] Los Angeles disk jockey Renan "El Cucuy" Almendarez Coello, who was so influential in rousing his listeners to participate in earlier marches, was also unsure of this work-boycott strategy. As he said, "We are hard workers. We came to the United States to work. We should work Monday. Work dignifies us."[66]

Despite these reservations, on May 1 hundreds of thousands, perhaps even a million or more, immigrants and their supporters marched again in cities throughout the country, half a million in Los Angeles and 400,000 in Chicago being among the largest demonstrations.[67] Although the boycott's goal of a general work stoppage did not materialize, many businesses, especially res- taurants, trucking, markets, and other services, were heavily impacted by the loss of workers who attended the marches and rallies.[68] Most marchers were Latinos but immigrants from many countries joined in, including those of Pol- ish, African, Asian, and Irish descent.[69] U.S. flags again predominated, as did white shirts signifying peace, in what were widely hailed as peaceful and joy- ous marches (Figures 7.6 and 7.7).[70] One photograph (Figure 7.7) in particular captured the extent to which immigrant marchers took the symbolism of the American flag to heart. It shows an immense American flag requiring many people to hold it up as they walked along the parade route. The flag appears to hover above the marchers, who appear to embrace the message of desiring to belong to the nation of "Old Glory."

Editorials in the *Los Angeles Times* and the *New York Times* focused on the contradictions between the rhetoric of anti-immigrant groups, pundits, and politicians on the one hand, and the deportment of the marchers on the other. As the *Los Angeles Times* put it:

Figure 7.6. Santa Ana, California, May 1, 2006. Photo by author.

Figure 7.7. The Los Angeles march on May 1 is documented in this photo, "Old Glory, New Arrivals," by Mark Boster, May 2, 2006, *Los Angeles Times.* Copyright 2006, Los Angeles Times. Reprinted with permission.

Instead of being dominated by aggressive anarchists bent on "reconquista" [reconquest] and violent confrontation, even Monday's first march in Los Angeles . . . was yet another passionate and upbeat party. . . . L.A.'s invisible workforce emerged not in a spirit of anger or defiance but with pride and exuberance. It was all so, well, American. The scale and tenor of the demonstrations have had the salutary and corrective benefit of marginalizing those who conflate Latino immigration with crime, a lack of patriotism, a security threat or any other ill under the sun. Six months ago, opponents of reform drove the political debate. No more. . . . The singular triumph of this spring's protests is that they have indelibly attached a human face to a debate dominated by dehumanizing words such as "illegals" and "aliens." And that face brings a message resonant across 230 years: "We want to be one of you."[71]

The *New York Times* sounded a similar tune:

The worst among our citizens and politicians are eager to depict illegal immigrants as criminals, potential terrorists and alien invaders. But what we saw yesterday, in huge, peaceful rallies in Los Angeles, Las Vegas, Chicago, Denver, New York, Atlanta, and other cities, were regular people: the same types of assimilation-minded moms, dads and children we wistfully romanticize on holidays devoted to, say, St. Patrick and Columbus. . . . These immigrants, weary of silent servitude, are speaking up and asking for something simple: a chance to work to become citizens, with all the obligations and opportunities that go with it. . . . It is not only the border-obsessed Minutemen who should be shamed by yesterday's joyous outpouring. Lawmakers who have stymied comprehensive immigration reform with stalemated name-calling and cold electoral calculation should listen up. A silent, shadow population is speaking with one voice. The message, aimed at Washington but something the whole country should hear, is clear: We are America. We want to join you.[72]

Despite such exuberant praise for the marchers and their objectives, there were, of course, less effusive responses. Patrick Buchanan viewed the marches as evidence of Mexico's conspiracy to reconquer the U.S. Southwest.[73] Minuteman Jim Gilchrist continued to refer to the marchers as a "mob": "When the rule of law is dictated by a mob of illegal aliens taking to the streets, especially under a foreign flag, then that means the nation is not governed by a rule of law—it is a mobocracy."[74] Gilchrist and others who favor more restrictive immigration policies were not convinced by the marchers' claims to social and cultural citizenship, as well as their desire for a political solution that would provide a path to legal citizenship. The political cartoon shown in Figure 7.8 captures the way that the marchers' "demands" for rights was also represented as an affront to the nation's citizens. Note that the lone flag in the cartoon is Mexican.

CONTROVERSY OVER A SPANISH VERSION OF THE NATIONAL ANTHEM

A few days before the May 1 demonstrations, a new controversy erupted over the promotion of a Spanish version of the national anthem, "The Star-Spangled Banner." The public uproar over the national anthem turned into another media spectacle that almost eclipsed the immigrant marches themselves. On April 28, "Nuestro Himno" (Our Anthem)—a Spanish version of "The Star-Spangled Banner" sung by a number of Latin pop stars—hit the airwaves.[75] Adam Kidron, a British music producer and head of the record label Urban Box Office, came up with the idea as an "ode" to millions of immigrants seeking a better life.[76] The singers voiced their positive intentions. Geo Doleo, of the pop group Voz a Voz, commented, "We feel like we're part of one voice. We're here finding the dream. It's a way of saying we're not bad people. We're here to do good things."[77]

Singing the song in Spanish allowed the values and ideals that the song conveys to be transmitted to those who had not yet learned English. However,

Figure 7.8. Cartoon of Uncle Sam and marchers, by Mike Shelton. Copyright May 2, 2006. Reprinted by permission of the Orange County Register.

national symbols are often viewed as quasi-sacred.[78] Changes to both the language and the lyrics of the anthem were red flags to those who viewed any changes to national symbols as heresy. Then again, Spanish itself was a contentious issue, raising concerns over assimilation so prevalent in the Latino Threat Narrative. The English version and a translation of the Spanish version follow.

The Star-Spangled Banner
(First verse)
O, say, can you see, by the dawn's early light,
What so proudly we hail'd at the twilight's last gleaming?
Whose broad stripes and bright stars, thro' the perilous fight,
O'er the ramparts we watch'd, were so gallantly streaming?
And the rockets' red glare, the bombs bursting in air,
Gave proof thro' the night that our flag was still there.
O, say, does that star-spangled banner yet wave
O'er the land of the free and the home of the brave?

Our Anthem[79]

Verse 1

Oh, say, can you see, by the dawn's early light,

What so proudly we hail as night falls?

Its stars and stripes floated yesterday

In the fierce combat, the sign of victory

The flame of battle, in step with liberty.

Throughout the night it was said, "It is being defended."

Chorus:

Oh, say! Does it still show its beautiful stars

Over the land of the free, the sacred flag?

Verse 2

Its stars and stripes, liberty, we are the same.

We're brothers, it's our anthem.

In the fierce combat, the sign of victory,

The flame of battle, in step with liberty.

Throughout the night it was said, "It is being defended."

Chorus:

"Oh, say! Does it still show its beautiful stars?

Over the land of the free, the sacred flag?"

Negative reaction came swiftly. Radio talk-show hosts and listeners, as well as television and Internet pundits, criticized the singing of the national anthem in Spanish.[80] A sampling of responses suggests the concerns raised by the song. George Key, the great-grandson of Francis Scott Key, who wrote the poem that provided the words for the song, called the Spanish version "despicable."[81] Conservative columnist Michelle Malkin dubbed it "The Illegal Alien Anthem."[82] Even Latinos were worried about the reaction. Benigno "Benny" Layton, a bandleader in Texas who had recorded a conjunto version of "The Star-Spangled Banner" as an instrumental, commented, "I'm a second generation American. I love my country, and I love my [Mexican musical] heritage, and I try to keep it alive. But some things are sacred that you don't do. And translating the national anthem is one of them."[83] President Bush added to the criticism when he said, "I think the national anthem ought to be sung in English. And I think people who want to be a citizen of this country ought to learn English, and they ought to learn to sing the national anthem in English."[84] English and Spanish are themselves symbols here, the former representing U.S. national unity and the latter symbolizing a threat to that unity.

However, the issues raised by the Spanish version of the national anthem are not so black-and-white. Francis Scott Key penned various versions of his poem, and the 1931 law that made "The Star-Spangled Banner" the national anthem does not specify the exact words, nor is there an official instrumental arrangement.[85] There have been many renditions of "The Star-Spangled Banner," from country to gospel, from rap to Jimi Hendrix's famous rock-guitar version. Even the anthem in a non-English language is not new. In the 1800s there were German, Latin, and Yiddish versions, and the U.S. Bureau of Education printed a Spanish version in 1919.[86] At the time President Bush said that the anthem should be sung only in English, there were four Spanish versions on the State Department's website.[87] There were even reports of candidate George W. Bush singing the anthem in Spanish at campaign functions in Texas, as well as at Hispanic festivals and parties after he assumed the presidency.[88]

The increasingly partisan and divisive public discourse on immigration undoubtedly influenced President Bush's stance on the national anthem, especially at a time when he was still holding out the possibility of comprehensive immigration reform legislation. He could ill afford to appear weak on controlling Spanish-speaking immigrants. The controversy over the Spanish version of the anthem, however, undermined the immigrant marchers' claims to cultural citizenship by questioning their reverence for national icons and their continued use of Spanish rather than English, an alleged sign of their lack of desire, or inability, to assimilate.

The Spanish version of the national anthem was not the only song finding its way into the public debate over immigration. In a case of dueling songs, "So Long, Texas—Hello, Mexico! (The Illegal Immigration Song)," which surfaced in September, was a satirical critique of Mexican immigrants and the immigrant marches.[89] Sung in a sonorous Texas country style, this humorous song played on anti-Mexican immigration sentiments by poking fun at the marchers' claims for cultural citizenship. The song alludes to the Mexican reconquest of Texas. First, there is the observation that the Lone Star State should be called Texico. The merging of the words "Texas" and "Mexico" in this way symbolizes the steady transformation of the state's demography until the people of Mexico overtake the people of Texas. Then there is the "tide [that] keeps rollin' across the line"; "tide" is a metaphor for the uncontrolled flow of migrants and "line" refers to the U.S.-Mexico border. As a result, the singer says, he will go to

Mexico and act like Mexicans in Texas: only take the clothes on his back, drive a "rattletrap" car, and "demand equal rights, though I'm here illegally." In a direct reference to the immigrant marches, the singer says, "I'll demand equal rights . . . protest in the streets . . . sing English words to their national anthem . . . [and] fly the Lone Star flag and Old Glory in Mexico." The song also relates the "abuses" felt or imagined to have been committed by Mexicans in Texas: having government forms printed in their own language, getting free medical care and free education for their children, and suchlike.

By making fun of the marchers and their claims to citizenship, the song challenges their legitimacy to make such claims. Moreover, the representations of the immigrants who are the subject of the song builds upon negative stereotypes that undermine any claims to citizenship. The personal characteristics the singer assumes in the course of the song—the traits often ascribed to Mexican immigrants—are those of a poor person with no possessions, driving without a driver's license and with no automobile insurance, having no occupational skills or means of employment, and receiving free medical care and education. The politics of fertility and reproduction are also clearly alluded to: the singer says he has many children, which is one of the things he is good at, the other thing being playing guitar. He also seeks the attention of women in Mexico, referring to the alleged desires of male Mexican immigrants for U.S. women. Mexican migration, in other words, continues unchecked across the border, until that old cowboy no longer feels that his home state is his. It has been lost, taken and reconquered by both the unchecked flow and the high fertility of the immigrants.

FINAL OBSERVATIONS

The spectacle of immigrants and their supporters marching and rallying across the United States raised the nation's consciousness about the severity of congressional immigration proposals. America also learned a bit more about the immigrants in their midst, those faceless folks who do much of the work cast aside by the educated and well-off among the citizenry. Suddenly those who lived shadowed lives were demonstrating in the open, in reckless disregard of the practices of surveillance and laws of deportation governing their lives. The least powerful in society, regarded as subalterns, were speaking by the millions in a unified voice against policies the lawmakers were proposing. At the same time, the marchers were asserting their right to be treated with respect and dignity, as economic, social, and cultural citizens. The marches forced immigrants, especially the undocumented, into the imagined community of the nation in a brash new way. In the process, the marches reminded us of the civil rights marches of an earlier time and of the grand American tradition of immigrants and their children learning to participate in the political life of the nation.

By challenging the government and the Minutemen's spectacle in the Arizona desert of exactly a year earlier, the immigrant marches forced us to think about what unifies us as a nation, what it means to be an American, and the emotional investment we have in quasi-sacred national symbols such as flags and anthems. The marches laid bare the dilemma of citizenship in the context of a hyperemphasis on the rule of law as a defining requisite for citizenship. For opponents of immigration, the violation of the nation's immigration laws undercut any claims for citizenship or even providing a path to citizenship. The immigrant marchers, however, by claiming "We are not criminals," were asserting their claims to citizenship on other grounds.

At this point one must ask, what type of citizen-subjects were the immigrant marchers claiming to be? In one sense, their claims for economic, social, and cultural citizenship stood in opposition to their media-constructed lives, in which unauthorized status is equated with criminality and negative characteristics such as migrancy and use of social services are emphasized. The immigrant marchers highlighted their economic contributions to the U.S. economy and their desire for social and legal integration. In another sense, however, the immigrant marchers represented themselves as neoliberal citizens, thus positioning themselves as the new "model" citizens.[90] What do I mean by "neoliberal citizens"?

Neoliberalism is more than just a set of policies; as Vincent Lyon-Callo has observed, "it is a set of ideas and ways of imagining the world."[91] A key aspect of this imagined world is the assumption of personal responsibility as the key to individual freedom and economic competitiveness. Under U.S. neoliberalism, immigrants are "free" to participate in the labor market. Even undocumented immigrants find only token, or symbolic, resistance to their employment.[92] However, living under the regime of neoliberalism also constitutes one as a neoliberal subject. Biopower and government control of populations become meaningful for understanding the neoliberal citizen-subject as expressed by the immigrant marchers. Biopower includes modes of subjectification, through which individuals are constructed as subjects "who work on themselves in the name of individual or collective life or health."[93]

According to Aihwa Ong, immigrants internalize values and self-govern their behavior and very being so that they can optimize their choices to make themselves efficient and competitive in volatile market conditions. Immigrants internalize what is required of them as a result of their lives being circumscribed by a multitude of regulations regarding immigration, detention, deportation, access to social services, medical care, driver's licenses, Social Security cards, bank accounts, work authorization, and many other micropractices of control. They work on themselves, in what Ong calls self-engineering, to try to stay healthy so they don't need medical care, to acquire marketable skills, to start small businesses, and to perform at optimal productivity.[94]

During the marches, immigrants reassured the public of their internalized self-monitoring and their self-engineering; they emphasized their embodiment of the type of workers required in today's competitive labor market. They presented themselves as neoliberal citizens, asserting their positive economic contributions to society despite a lack of government support and often vociferous anti-immigrant sentiment.

8 DREAMERS AND ANCHOR BABIES

SPECTACLES OF EXCLUSION NOT ONLY TARGET adult immigrants; their children also encounter public situations in which their citizenship is questioned. For example, in March of 2012 a basketball team from a high school in Texas that is 96 percent Latino played a team from a mostly white high school. After the game, the mostly white high school's fans expressed their joy at winning the game by chanting "U-S-A." It appeared to the mostly Latino high school students that they were being treated as foreigners. As the school's representative commented on Fox News, "the implication [of the chant] is they are not American citizens."[1]

In a similar incident, also in March of 2012, Kansas State's basketball team played Southern Mississippi. Kansas State won, but not before Angel Rodriguez, the team's guard, was subjected to Southern Mississippi's band chanting "Where's your green card?" It did not matter that Rodriguez is Puerto Rican and thus a U.S. citizen. As a Latino, his citizenship is now part of a discourse about legitimacy and belonging.[2]

The rhetorical shift in the Latino Threat Narrative from immigrant reproduction to their children (Chapters 3 and 4) makes seemingly commonsense immigration reform proposals difficult to discuss without raising heated political debate. What should society do with the children of undocumented immigrants? Two issues have become part of the public discourse. First of all, there are those undocumented immigrants who came as children (the 1.5 generation—see Chapter 2). Should they receive some form of relief, for example a possible path to citizenship? Then there are the U.S.-born children of undocumented immigrants. Their presence, for some, poses a constitutional crisis of sorts. Should the Fourteenth Amendment be relegated to the dustbin of history, so that these children would not automatically be allowed to become U.S. citizens at birth?

I take up first the plight of undocumented young people brought to the United States as children, during their formative years. Despite being raised in the United States, as insiders, anti-immigration advocates characterize them as undeserving outsiders, thereby undermining any debate over possible immigration reform that would allow them to change their status. The outcome of this stalemate has been that these young people live in perpetual limbo, waiting for the larger society either to deport them or to recognize them as legitimate members of their communities, as people who can contribute to the economic, social, and cultural life of the nation. In fact, many of these young people believe they do contribute to society, and thus there has emerged a social movement around national- and state-level immigration reforms often referred to as the DREAM Act (Development, Relief, and Education for Alien Minors Act). This movement has led to public demonstrations in support of various DREAM Act proposals. Although the political fervor that resulted in the huge mega-marches discussed in the last chapter has not been sustained since the Immigrant Spring of 2006, the DREAM Act proponents have been actively staging public spectacles such as marching, holding mock graduation ceremonies, and engaging politicians in order to promote their cause. The DREAMers, as they call themselves, have even "come out of the shadows" to reveal their presence to government authorities, thus opening themselves up to possible deportation.

UNDOCUMENTED CHILDREN OF IMMIGRANTS

The literature refers to the 1.5 generation as those who migrated at a young age (typically under 15 or 16 years old) in recognition of the fact that most or all of their schooling and much of their cultural and social development occur in the host country.[3] According to the Pew Hispanic Center's research, there were 1.5 million undocumented children under age 18 living in the United States in 2008.[4] As many as 65,000 undocumented young people graduate from U.S. high schools each year.[5] Although there are many similarities between the unauthorized 1.5 generation and the second-generation children of immigrants, there is an important difference between them, that is, their relationship to citizenship status.[6] Some of the 1.5 generation experienced a condition of illegality because of their unauthorized entry into the United States, or they may have entered with permission—tourist or student visas—but then overstayed visa end dates.

Because moving from an illegal status to becoming a Legal Permanent Resident has become much more difficult as a result of changes in U.S. immigration law, most notably the 1996 Illegal Immigration Reform and Immigrant Responsibility Act, many 1.5-generation adults continue to live in the United States without proper documentation from the federal government.[7]

The undocumented 1.5 generation experience a condition of "illegality" that, as Susan B. Coutin has observed, means that "individuals can be physically present but legally absent, existing in a space outside of society, a space of 'non-existence,' a space that is not actually 'elsewhere' or beyond borders but that is rather a hidden dimension of social reality."[8] I would add that for many of these young people, being illegally present is not to be "outside of society" but to be allowed to participate in some aspects of society—schooling, for example—but not allowed to work and or participate in other socially important ways in society. It is in this way that for undocumented children of immigrants, being "illegal" affects their subjective understandings of the world and their identities, as Rocío's, Juan's, and Carlos's cases (introduced in Chapter 2) exemplify.[9]

Scholars such as Judith Butler and Sarah Willen have pointed to the effects of living as abject subjects.[10] The definition of *abject* comes to us from the Latin "to cast away" or "to throw away" and is used to describe those with the lowest, most contemptible, and most wretched social status.[11] According to Butler, "The 'abject' designates that which has been expelled from the body, discharged as excrement, literally rendered 'Other.' This appears as an expulsion of alien elements, but the alien is effectively established through this expulsion."[12] Various intersections of race, gender, sexuality, nationality, migrancy, and any number of other categories can demarcate the abject in society. For our purposes here, it is the body of the nation from which undocumented children of immigrants are expelled. Although they live *in* the nation, they are often not perceived or legally fully rendered as part *of* the nation.[13] Theirs is a life in legal and social limbo.

Because undocumented children grow up steeped in U.S. culture, their illegality poses fundamental dilemmas. They must often make critical life decisions within the constraints imposed by their status. Lupe was brought to the United States at age 8 and was 21 years old when I interviewed her. Lupe explained the anxiety she felt trying to decide if going to college was a possibility for her:

> You become depressed, you become very depressed. You work so hard and now what? You start questioning yourself. Is it worth it? Was it worth it? And

what now? You have two options. Either you take the college route because education is education, and I'm learning and I like what I'm learning, and I'm going to continue to learn. Or you take the other route, where you just say, that's it. I'm just going to start working. It wasn't worth it. My mom or my dad, or my neighbor, was right. Why am I still going to school if I am not going to be able to continue with my education? So two paths, you have to decide which one to take.

Lupe's comments reflect the depth of her anguish at her abject status and uncertain future. Ultimately, she decided to attend the University of California. Many young undocumented students like Lupe try to continue their education, knowing that being undocumented will ultimately mean they cannot put their education to work without risking any hope of becoming a legal resident. For many others, their immigration status is a formidable obstacle to higher education and income. As Figure 8.1 shows, only about one in five of the undocumented 1.5-generation Latinos in our survey of the greater Los Angeles area had thirteen or more years of schooling, meaning they had at least one year of college.[14] That is less than half of the 1.5-generation Latinos who were legal

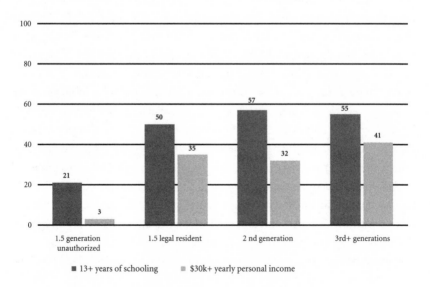

Figure 8.1. Years of schooling and personal income among Latinos by generation and immigration status in the greater Los Angeles Area (in percentages).
SOURCE: IIMMLA Study.

residents and later generations of Latinos born in the United States who went on to college. Not surprisingly, very few of the undocumented 1.5-generation Latinos earned $30,000 or more a year, especially when compared to legal resident and citizen Latinos. Looked at another way, 1.5-generation Latinos who were legal residents were over eleven times more likely to be in the higher income category than undocumented 1.5-generation Latinos. For young undocumented immigrants, legal status is crucial for social and economic mobility.

Recognizing that something must be done with the eleven million undocumented, the U.S. Congress has debated immigration reform, with little consensus. With general comprehensive reform difficult, many in Congress have focused on the narrower DREAM Act. The DREAM Act, however, has been in Congress in some form since it was first introduced in the Senate in 2001, and it has still not passed.[15] Each time the DREAM Act comes up for a vote in Congress, the DREAMers' hopes are raised, only to be deflated.[16] There have been some victories, nonetheless, at the state level. On July 25, 2011, California governor Jerry Brown signed into law the California Dream Act, which allows undocumented college students to apply for privately funded financial aid.[17] Along with California, the states of Texas, Illinois, Nebraska, New Mexico, New York, Utah, Washington, Kansas, Connecticut, and Maryland have passed their own versions of the DREAM Act, or laws that allow undocumented students to attend public colleges and universities and pay in-state tuition rather than the more costly out-of-state or foreign-student tuition.[18] However, Arizona, Georgia, South Carolina, and Indiana do not allow undocumented students to gain state residency for tuition purposes, and Maryland and Kansas have repealed their laws granting in-state tuition to these students. State laws on access to higher education continue the nation's schizophrenic policies toward undocumented children. Even states sympathetic to the plight of undocumented students do not have the power to resolve the issue of a path to citizenship.

Rather than passively accept this state of affairs, undocumented students across the country have formed a number of organizations, such as the Immigrant Youth Justice League, the Dream Act Coalition, and others, with the goal of promoting federal legislation that would provide them with a way to legalize their status. Their efforts have focused on the federal DREAM Act. Under the DREAM Act, most students of good moral character who came to the United States before they were sixteen years old and had at least five years' United States residence before the date of the bill's enactment would qualify for conditional permanent resident status if they met any of three criteria: (1) graduated from a two-year college or a vocational college or studied for at least two years toward a bachelor's or higher degree; (2) served in the U.S. armed forces for at least two years; or (3) performed at least 910 hours of volunteer community service. Undocumented youth would not qualify for this relief if they had committed crimes, were a security risk, or were inadmissible or removable on certain other grounds. About 2.15 million youth are potential beneficiaries of the DREAM Act.[19]

The DREAMers also advocate for laws at the state level to allow them to attend colleges and universities, to receive financial aid, and to pursue other avenues to social integration. They have also effectively developed Internet advocacy with groups such as the Undocumented Youth Action and Resource Network (www.dreamactivist.org) and the National Immigrant Youth Alliance (theniqa.org) that regularly post information on impending deportations, legislative proposals on immigration, and other related issues. One DREAM activist posted a list of seventy-one DREAM Act–related organizations nationwide as of July 2010 (see Figure 8.2). This included thirty-four student organizations, eighteen state-based immigrant rights organizations, eleven policy organizations, and eight online-based organizations.[20] It is perhaps obvious, but academics often talk about the importance of a sense of belonging and attachment

Figure 8.2. Map of DREAM Act–related organizations as of July 2010. Although there are more sites than are visible owing to overlaps in location, what is clear is the national scope of DREAM Act activism. Map compiled by Marisol Ramos for DreamActivist.org.

to home when discussing immigrants. Such extensive activism on the part of undocumented youth testifies to a sense of belonging in the United States and a desire for recognition in the nation they call home.

DREAM Act activists have used key symbols in spectacles to promote their cause. Most notably, they use the image of students in graduation robes and mortarboards to draw attention to their plight as college students without legal immigration status (see Figure 8.3).

DREAMers reproduce these symbols on T-shirts, posters, and websites. They also don robes and mortarboards in mock graduations held at the end of the academic year. While many are local, there is also a large annual graduation held in Washington, D.C., organized by the National Immigrant Youth Alliance. At these events, students raise banners that state their frustrations, such as "I graduated, Now What?" and "It is not my fault my parents brought me here 4 a better future."[21] DREAM activists also stage local demonstrations, often resulting in the arrest of the activists. This is an incredibly courageous act, in that by "coming out" DREAMers leave the relative safety of living in the shadows. The slogan the DREAMers use to represent this change in behavior is "Undocumented and Unafraid" (see Figure 8.4). By publicly exposing themselves in this way, undocumented students risk deportation by immigration officials who now have their identification information. But for DREAM activists, living in legal limbo is no longer tenable and so they stage these drastic spectacles for inclusion despite the possibility of deportation. Jose Antonio Vargas poignantly relates his decision to come out of the shadows:

> Like many others, I kept my legal status a secret, passing myself off as a U.S. citizen—right down to cultivating a homegrown accent. I went to college and became a journalist, earning a staff job at the *Washington Post*. But the

Figure 8.3. Dream Act activists regularly use this symbol of graduates as part of their campaign to change the law.

Figure 8.4. March 10, 2010, Coming Out of the Shadows Week, Chicago. Photograph by Miguel Gutierrez Jr.

deception weighed on me. When I eventually decided to admit the truth, I chose to come out publicly—very publicly—in the form of an essay for the *New York Times* last June. Several immigration lawyers counseled against doing this. ("It's legal suicide," warned one.) Broadcasting my status to millions seemed tantamount to an invitation to the immigration cops: Here I am. Come pick me up.[22]

Without a resolution, undocumented youth raised in this country often feel unwanted, as if society is willing to just throw their lives away. Catarina's case shows how living an abject life has affected her thinking about higher education and identity. Catarina, who was 21 years old at the time I interviewed her, had come to the United States when she was 8. Her father had arrived before Catarina and acquired legal permanent residency through the legalization program of the 1986 Immigration Reform and Control Act. Catarina's mother joined her husband, who was working as a gardener in Santa Ana, California. Much of his family had preceded him there and were able to provide the new arrivals with a great deal of help and support. Catarina's mother, although undocumented, worked as a housekeeper. When she became pregnant, she returned to Mexico to deliver Catarina because delivery was cheaper there and she was not yet used to life in Santa Ana. Because of her family's fateful decision, Catarina was not born in the United States and was not a citizen when she entered the United States. Catarina's undocumented status has plagued her pursuit of education and has affected her sense of identity.

Catarina had a 4.0 GPA in high school but knew she could not attend the University of California because at that time undocumented students had to pay tuition at the much higher foreign-student rate. Consequently, she went to a community college and later transferred to the University of California, Irvine, where I met her. By this time, California law had changed as a result of AB 540, which meant that students like Catarina could attend the university and pay in-state tuition, with the proviso that they could not receive financial aid. Catarina said that when she heard that AB 540 had passed, "I cried, I cried. I was with my dad in my living room. My sister follows a lot of the legal stuff and we had helped sign stuff to send to Governor Davis. We were involved, I was involved in student government in my community college, and it was like finally something, justice."

At the time of the interview, Catarina was finishing her senior year at the university and, with a 3.9 GPA, intended to apply to graduate school. Her father had acquired U.S. citizenship and had sponsored his wife and children for legal residence, which Catarina was now in the process of obtaining.

Catarina identifies herself as Mexican. She does so because she is an immigrant and not a Chicano or Mexican American, which she associates with being U.S.-born. But she also recognizes that society has pushed her toward emphasizing "Mexican" as an identity. Catarina's experiences as an undocumented immigrant have influenced her identity. Because she has not had the rights and privileges that come with being U.S.-born and a citizen, Catarina says that she does not "think like a Mexican American." In her words:

> Having the barriers that I had, or not having all the opportunities that I see that a lot of the students have, and they might not be taking advantage of them for different reasons—I know I'm no one to criticize their decisions, but I think that's what really makes me consider myself a Mexican. I am an immigrant, immigrant Mexican. . . . You know you are not [American] because society keeps telling you that you're not. You don't have the opportunities that a Mexican American has, because you don't have the social security. So you have to make the decision: "I don't fit in here. They don't want me in here.

Then I fit there, with Mexicans." . . . I think if you have obstacles to integrating, one, they don't want you to integrate. Obviously, they have the obstacles for you not to integrate, so you get to the point where, "You know what? I don't want to integrate. Whether you will eventually want me to integrate for any reason, I am no longer willing to integrate."

Despite her frustration with the obstacles she has faced, Catarina desires U.S. citizenship because of the opportunities and rights it imparts. As she put it, "You need it [citizenship] in order to move on. If I am going to work hard, why not get the benefits?" Catarina also realizes that even though she identifies as Mexican, she is also American in many ways and that living in the United States for most of her life has shaped her sense of self and made her life different from what it would have been if she had stayed in Mexico. Concerning what it means to be American, she said:

It can mean different things. It can mean being acculturated into American culture. It can mean having loyalty for America. For example, after September 11, I felt American. And it's amazing, because regardless of political inequalities, I think of my life and what would it have been if I had not been here. And here I am. There are obstacles, but it's better. It's better here even with the inequalities. I guess it's human nature. We just want something better.

In his 2011 State of the Union address, President Obama highlighted the plight of undocumented students:

Today, there are hundreds of thousands of students excelling in our schools who are not American citizens. Some are the children of undocumented workers, who had nothing to do with the actions of their parents. They grew up as Americans and pledge allegiance to our flag, and yet they live every day with the threat of deportation. Let's stop expelling talented, responsible young people who could be staffing our research labs or starting a new business, who could be further enriching this nation.[23]

It is important to note that the threat of deportation for undocumented immigrants, including the DREAMers, has actually increased under President Obama's administration. For example, in 2009, 387,790 people were deported, a 5 percent increase over 2008, the last year under George W. Bush's administration.[24] The pace of deportations, and their impact on families, has not slowed. In the three years preceding May 2012, the Department of Homeland Security deported 1.1 million people.[25] However, in a dramatic change in policy in August 2011, the Obama administration ordered review of all deportation cases in order to focus on criminals. Those not convicted of a crime could have their deportations suspended, albeit not canceled.[26] This policy change raised the hopes of many, including the DREAMers. As one 21-year-old undocumented student who was brought to the United States as a boy and whose mother is facing deportation put it: "It makes me happy and hopeful. I hope they go through my mother's case, stop her deportation, and, if possible, get her a work permit."[27] However, after seven months of reviewing deportation cases, between November 2011 and May 2012 Department of Homeland Security officials had closed fewer than 2 percent of the cases.[28] Not only has the review been slow but suspended deportation means deportation is still a possibility in the future, and this policy change did not provide work permits. Not surprisingly, about half of those offered suspensions declined, preferring to take their chances in court, where they hoped to win not only a suspension of deportation but legal permanent residence, which would allow them to work legally. Then, on June 15, 2012, President Obama announced an even more dramatic change in policy toward DREAMers. Obama decided to allow some undocumented immigrants who came as children to apply for two-year renewable deferrals on deportation and to apply for work permits.[29] As a "temporary stop-gap measure," this new policy does not provide permanent relief from deportation (and those who come forward will be giving the government information on their whereabouts). In short, the Obama administration's policies do not provide DREAMers or other undocumented immigrants with a path to citizenship, which is something only Congress can do.

The views of the 2012 Republican presidential candidate, Mitt Romney, on the DREAM Act capture the main arguments against it by those who equate it with amnesty for illegal aliens. Romney attacked Governor Rick Perry and the Texas DREAM Act for allowing undocumented students to pay in-state tuition, which, along with a path to citizenship, would be a "magnet" luring even more undocumented immigrants to the United States. Instead, Romney favored making life more difficult through tougher enforcement policies, in that way pushing these young people, and all undocumented immigrants, to "self-deport."[30] As Romney said, "For those who come here illegally, the idea of giving them in-state tuition credits or other special benefits I find to be contrary to the idea of a nation of law."[31] Romney also said that he would veto the DREAM Act if he were president:

I absolutely believe that those who come here illegally should not be given fa-
voritism or a special route to becoming permanent residents or citizens that's
not given to those people who have stayed in line legally. . . . I have indicated
I would veto the DREAM Act if provisions included in that act to say that
people who are here illegally, if they go to school here long enough, get a degree here that they can become permanent residents. I think that is a mistake.
I think we have to follow the law and insist those who come illegally, ultimately return home, apply and get in line with everyone else.[32]

One DREAM Act activist responded to the idea that young people like her
should "self-deport," that they were simply responding to "magnets" such as jobs
and social services attracting immigrants and were undeserving of being recognized as part of the nation. At a demonstration in Mesa, Arizona, she said,
"I am an undocumented youth and I want to be in this country just like any
other person that has grown up here."[33] Her views are similar to others in the
1.5 generation, for whom "home" is the United States. For example, the vast majority (86 percent) of the undocumented 1.5 generation in our survey of the adult
children of immigrants in the greater Los Angeles area (IIMMLA) said that the
United States feels most like home to them, not the country of their birth.

In sum, undocumented 1.5-generation young people live in a legal limbo.
They are guaranteed some legal protections and even rights, especially the right
to primary- and secondary-level education. And yet they remain socially stigmatized because of their status as "illegal immigrants" and subject to the vaga-
ries of deportation policies and practices.

How do the U.S.-born, citizen children of undocumented immigrants fare
in relation to the Latino threat narrative? They are increasingly stigmatized in
public discourse as "anchor babies," which is a term used to question their very
worthiness as citizens.

ANCHOR BABIES

An issue related to Latina reproduction that has become part of the heated
debate over immigration is citizenship for children born to undocumented
immigrants in the United States. In 2008, there were about four million U.S.-
born/U.S.-citizen children of undocumented immigrants.[34] Public debate has
increasingly focused on these U.S.-born children and whether they deserve to be
citizens of the United States. How did this issue become such an important part
of the immigration debate? After all, these are American citizens, not illegal im-

migrants. Using Internet blogs, TV, radio, and other media, proponents of more restrictive immigration policies characterized these citizens as different from other citizens. To accomplish this, a new term (or subject position, à la Michel Foucault) was introduced into public discourse, the "anchor baby," a metaphorical term that is meant to capture the alleged strategy among undocumented immigrants of having a baby who will legally be a U.S. citizen and eventually be able to apply for his or her family's legal residence through the preferences for family reunification. Unlike other citizens, anchor babies are characterized as undeserving citizens because they are part of a devious plot cooked up by their undocumented parents to circumvent the laws of the United States.

Based on the principle of *jus soli*, U.S. citizenship is automatically conferred on any baby born in the United States. As Section 1 of the Fourteenth Amendment to the U.S. Constitution states:

> All persons born or naturalized in the United States, and subject to the jurisdiction thereof, are citizens of the United States and of the State wherein they reside. No State shall make or enforce any law which shall abridge the privileges or immunities of citizens of the United States; nor shall any State deprive any person of life, liberty, or property, without due process of law; nor deny to any person within its jurisdiction the equal protection of the laws.[35]

The word *nation* is derived from the Latin *nascere*, "to be born." This born-into-nation idea, *jus soli* (the right to territory), is the basis for the United States conferring birthright citizenship to those born inside its borders. The principle of *jus soli* is inclusive in that it allows anyone to become a member of the community of citizens simply through birth; citizenship is thus a birthright. The other related principle, *jus sanguinis*, is much narrower in that it defines citizenship through "blood." Having a father or mother (this varies from country to country) who is a citizen confers citizenship on the child. The United States allows citizenship by both *jus soli* and *jus sanguinis* as well as through a process of naturalization, that is, through legal steps to move from a legal permanent resident status to citizenship.

Although this may sound straightforward, public debate has focused on denying birthright citizenship to the children of undocumented immigrants. Changing this principle would entail changing the U.S. Constitution, but that has not deterred public debate on TV, radio talk shows, and websites. The popularization of the term "anchor baby" has justified and legitimized attempts to redefine the meaning of citizenship through repealing the Fourteenth

Amendment to the Constitution or amending it to remove birthright citizenship for children born to undocumented immigrants. Either change to the Fourteenth Amendment would create a class of individuals who, though born in the United States, would not be citizens.

The term "anchor baby" seems to have first appeared in an article in the *Los Angeles Times Magazine* in 1987. In an article profiling their research on troubled Southeast Asian teens by Kenji Ima and Jeanne Nidorf, two San Diego State University professors, the *Times* stated: "They [Southeast Asian teens] are 'anchor children,' saddled with the extra burden of having to attain a financial foothold in America to sponsor family members who remain in Vietnam."[36]

It is interesting that during the course of my own research in the 1980s, which I published in *Shadowed Lives*, I also used the anchor metaphor. I spoke of the many social and cultural linkages to U.S. society that I found among undocumented families and their children's desire, no matter their citizenship status, to stay in the United States. I noted that "this perception of their children's attitudes helps anchor parents in the United States," a finding that helped me explain why undocumented immigrants might stay longer in the United States than they had originally intended.[37] In the overwhelming majority of cases, it is this sense of anchoring that, in my experience, is related to the migration process experienced by undocumented immigrants. But this anchoring effect is completely different from that proposed for "anchor babies."

The "anchor baby" metaphor has a more ominous connotation in public discourse. Beginning in the 1990s, Michelle Malkin, a conservative pundit regularly seen on Fox News and a contributor to Internet blogs, was one of the earliest popularizers of the term "anchor baby." In a 2003 article in *Jewish World Review*, she linked birthright citizenship to undocumented immigration and to post-9/11 fears of terrorism: "Clearly, the custom of granting automatic citizenship at birth to children of tourists, and temporary workers . . . and to countless 'anchor babies' delivered by illegal aliens on American soil, undermines the integrity of citizenship—not to mention national security. . . . The citizenship clause has evolved into a magnet for alien law breakers and a shield for terrorist infiltrators and enemy combatants."[38] Malkin again wrote about anchor babies in her blog entry for June 13, 2004:

> During my book tour across the country for Invasion, this issue [of anchor babies] came up time and again. In the Southwest, everyone has a story of heavily pregnant women crossing the Mexican border to deliver their "anchor

babies." At East Coast hospitals, tales of South Korean "obstetric tourists" abound. (An estimated 5,000 South Korean anchor babies are born in the US every year.) And, of course, there's a terrorism angle.[39]

Michelle Malkin was born on October 20, 1970, in Philadelphia to Filipino parents who were in the United States on student visas. Ironically, this would make Malkin an anchor baby and ineligible for citizenship under her own proposed changes to the Fourteenth Amendment and the restriction of birthright citizenship to only children of citizens or legal residents.

Lou Dobbs used his CNN television program to help make "anchor babies" a household word. Dobbs emphasized the threat posed by anchor babies because they are part of a plot by their parents to gain U.S. citizenship. As Dobbs explained in April of 2006: "Tonight the fight is on in Congress over so-called anchor babies. Some 200,000 anchor babies are born to illegal aliens in this country each year. These babies instantly become U.S. citizens and illegal alien parents of anchor babies can become citizens as well with the sponsorship of those babies as they grow up. Many in Congress in increasing numbers now say those birthright protections simply have to end."[40]

On July 27, 2010, on Fox News, Senator Lindsey Graham provided one of the most egregious arguments for questioning whether so-called anchor babies were deserving of citizenship: "People come here to have babies. They come here to drop a child. It's called drop and leave. To have a child in America, they cross the border, they go to the emergency room, they have a child, and that child's automatically an American citizen. That shouldn't be the case. That attracts people for all the wrong reasons."[41] Graham used an animal metaphor when characterizing undocumented mothers as coming "to drop" a child. In English, we speak of animals—cats, horses, cows, etc.—as dropping their litter, foal, calf, etc. Humans give birth. In Spanish, it is said women "give light" (*dar la luz*) to the baby by bringing it into the world. By using an animal metaphor, Graham both dismissed the women's humanity and underscored their threat to the United States by having babies that are part of a conspiracy to circumvent the nation's immigration laws.[42] Popular expressions of Graham's sentiment include the image shown in Figure 8.5, featuring the words "SQUAT & DROP Should Not Make Anyone an American" above a drawing of a heavily pregnant woman and the classic Mexican man sleeping next to a cactus. In the background is a barbed wire fence representing the U.S.-Mexico border. The man and woman are pictured in front of the fence, that is, in the United States. Not

Figure 8.5. Anchor baby cartoon being sold on clothing, tote bags, and other items available at www.printfection.com.

only has this image circulated on the Internet, but it is sold on T-shirts, tank tops, and other clothing.

A major problem with characterizing "anchor babies" as part of a nefarious plot is that most undocumented migrants come to work in the United States.[43] While some people may cross the border to deliver babies, for most undocumented immigrants having a child in the United States is a secondary effect of immigration, the result of forming a family in the United States or bringing a spouse to join someone already here. Many undocumented immigrants who migrate with the short-term goal of work and then return to their country of origin may fear apprehension if they deliver their babies in hospitals, or they may not even be aware of the advantages of having a U.S.-born child, as was the case with Catarina's family, discussed previously. Furthermore, those who promote the idea of an anchor baby conspiracy have apparently not taken account of the obstacles to sponsorship introduced by the 1996 immigration law. A U.S. citizen must be at least twenty-one years old in order to assist his or her parents in obtaining legal residence, and the process could take many more years from that point. The financial burden of sponsoring a relative is also a hurdle. Sponsors must have incomes well above the legal poverty level and must sign a guarantee of responsibility for any and all costs the person or persons they sponsor might incur, as a guarantee that the sponsored persons do not use publicly funded medical and other social programs. It is a heavy financial burden for low-income citizens to bear.

And yet, despite these factors limiting the usefulness of having a U.S.-citizen child, the anchor baby concept has effectively characterized these young people as undeserving citizens, which has spawned a call to change the nation's citizenship laws.

CHALLENGES TO THE FOURTEENTH AMENDMENT
AND BIRTHRIGHT CITIZENSHIP

The Fourteenth Amendment to the United States Constitution makes citizenship through birth the law of the land. To a certain degree, the amendment codified common law and practices concerning birthright citizenship in the United States up to that time, at least for "free white people." Probably because of the taken-for-granted assumptions borrowed from English common law (birth on the sovereign's territory meant one was a natural-born subject), the original U.S. Constitution only mentions "natural born citizens" to indicate that those born on U.S. territory are citizens and therefore able to be president. As Jennifer L. Hochschild and John H. Mellonkopf have noted, "in settler societies like the United States, *jus soli* was useful in integrating immigrants of diverse origins into a new nation."[44]

The idea that birthright citizenship applied to those born on U.S. territory was discussed in a 1829 treatise on the U.S. Constitution by William Rawle, who wrote that "every person born within the United States, its territories or districts, whether the parents are citizens or aliens, is a natural born citizen in the sense of the Constitution, and entitled to all the rights and privileges appertaining to that capacity."[45] Similarly, in an 1830 case to settle the disposition of the estate of a man born in New York in 1776, the U.S. Supreme Court found that since the man was born when the Americans had jurisdiction over the city, he was a U.S. citizen. The court held: "Nothing is better settled at the common law than the doctrine that the children even of aliens born in a country while the parents are resident there under the protection of the government and owing a temporary allegiance thereto are subjects by birth."[46]

While the principle of citizenship through birth, *jus soli*, was common law and practice in the early republic, it was not applied to babies born to non-whites. After the Civil War, the Fourteenth Amendment made citizenship through birth the law of the land in order to guarantee citizenship to African Americans, who had routinely been excluded from citizenship even though they were born on U.S. soil. Nonetheless, birthright citizenship was not yet settled. U.S.-born Asians were still routinely denied citizenship. In 1898, however, in *United States v. Wong Kim Ark*, the U.S. Supreme Court decided that Asians born in the United States are also U.S. citizens, regardless of their parents' citizenship status (as nonwhites, their Asian-born parents could not be citizens at that time).[47]

The issue of birthright citizenship was a nonissue until 1985, when two Yale professors, Peter H. Schuck and Rogers M. Smith, published *Citizenship without Consent: Illegal Aliens in the American Polity*, in which they questioned granting birthright citizenship to the children of undocumented immigrants. They argued that the United States should move away from its principle of inclusion through birthright citizenship, *jus soli*, and replace it with citizenship by consent. The consent principle would make citizenship subject to consent, or agreement, of the nation, and, if so allowed, by the consent of those seeking citizenship upon reaching the age of legal majority. Of course, the consent principle holds out the possibility that U.S.-born children denied birthright citizenship might also be denied the opportunity of citizenship at a later age because of the nation/state's lack of consent. Then there is the problem of the ambiguous status of U.S.-born noncitizens, which is discussed further below. Schuck and Smith also argue that the Fourteenth Amendment's clause "subject to the jurisdiction thereof" applies only to legal immigrants and not to unauthorized immigrants. This argument does not view undocumented immigrants as being under the jurisdiction of the nation's laws as "people," yet they are not free to break state or national laws, and they are entitled to most of the same constitutional protections as other "people" in the nation. The citizenship-through-consent argument also goes against the precedent set in the *Wong Kim Ark* case mentioned previously and raises the possibility that the consent principle might also be applied to U.S.-born minorities who are out of favor or stigmatized as a threat to the nation at a particular historical moment. In short, when might the principle of consent for citizenship become a principle of exclusion?

Congressional challenges to automatic birthright citizenship for the U.S.-born children of undocumented immigrants began in the early 1990s. In June 1995, a House task force chaired by Representative Elton Gallegly (Republican from Simi Valley, California) recommended an amendment to the U.S. Constitution to end automatic citizenship for U.S.-born children whose parents are undocumented immigrants.[48] Representative Gallegly was an early proponent of this policy.[49] At about the same time, Representative Brian Bilbray of San Diego proposed a measure that "fine-tunes" the Fourteenth Amendment, thus avoiding a battle over amending the Constitution. Representative Bilbray's measure would have changed the Fourteenth Amendment to specify that children born in the United States must have parents who are U.S. citizens or legal residents in order to receive citizenship. Bilbray argued that restricting birthright citizenship in the face of increased immigration "is overwhelmingly popular with the average citizen. Academia can talk about it all they want, but the American people do not like what we are doing now and they want it changed. . . . The naysayers are always trying to find a reason not to do the common sense thing. The first time you see a pregnant woman running across the freeway trying to get into America, you realize this thing has gotten way out of hand."[50]

At the time, Congress was considering a major overhaul of the nation's immigration laws, which would eventually become the 1996 immigration law. Although there were some—such as then–presidential candidates Pete Wilson (governor of California) and Patrick Buchanan, as well as Newt Gingrich (Republican speaker of the House)—who wanted either a constitutional amendment or a statute to deny citizenship to the children of undocumented immigrants, the 1996 immigration law did not include birthright citizenship as an issue, owing to its controversial nature. Senator Alan Simpson (R-Wyoming), who sponsored the Senate's immigration bill, was concerned. As he said, "There are people coming here for the sole purpose of giving birth to a U.S. citizen, to take that child back to their country and know that 21 years later that child will petition and bring in the mother, the father—under our preference system, the entire family."[51] Rather than deny birthright citizenship, the 1996 immigration law made it much more difficult to sponsor relatives, requiring sponsors to have relatively high income levels and to assume any costs sponsored immigrants might incur if they use government-supported social or medical services, as mentioned previously.

Since 1995, several similar measures to deny U.S. citizenship to children born to undocumented immigrants have been considered in the U.S. Congress, including the U.S. Citizen Reform Act of 2005 and the Birthright Citizenship Act of 2007. In 2011, Representative Steve King (R-Iowa) introduced the Birthright Citizenship Act of 2011 in the House of Representatives, and four Republican Senators, David Vitter (Louisiana), Jerry Moran (Kansas), Mike Lee (Utah), and Rand Paul (Kentucky), introduced a similar resolution to amend the Fourteenth Amendment to the Constitution.

When introducing the Birthright Citizenship Act of 2011, Representative King argued that birthright citizenship is a magnet for immigrants: "The current practice of extending U.S. citizenship to hundreds of thousands of 'Anchor Babies' every year arises from the misapplication of the Constitution's citizenship clause and creates an incentive for illegal aliens to cross our borders. . . . Passage of this bill will ensure that immigration law breakers are not rewarded, will close the door to future waves of extended family chain migration, and will help to bring an end to the global 'birth tourism' industry."[52] Ending birthright citizenship for the children of undocumented immigrants, according to Representative King, is a way of "doing something" about immigration rather than more directly passing immigration reform legislation. However, Representative King did not provide any empirical evidence that citizenship was actually a major magnet for undocumented immigrants or that massive return migration to the immigrant parents' country of origin would occur after the bill's passage. Nor is there evidence for the claim that changing the Fourteenth Amendment's citizenship clause would "fix" an unclearly defined immigration "problem."

Representative King added to the spectacle of the debate over the Fourteenth Amendment by carrying into Congress copies of his bill piled high on his shoulder (see Figure 8.6). His stern face and dramatic pose—balancing on his shoulder what looks like thousands of pieces of paper—brings to mind the ancient god Atlas, who carried the weight of the world on his back. Interestingly, the bill was only one page long, so Representative King was carrying quite a few copies.

The Birthright Citizenship Act of 2011 offers a change to the definition of "under the jurisdiction thereof" in reference to qualifying for citizenship.[53] A child born in the United States would acquire birthright citizenship if one of his or her parents is: a citizen or national of the United States; an alien lawfully admitted for permanent residence in the United States whose residence is the United States; or an alien performing active service in the armed forces. In other words, babies with two parents who are undocumented immigrants, or who cannot prove they satisfy at least one of the three provisions, would not acquire birthright citizenship. The bill ends there. It does not clarify with what status, rights, and responsibilities the children who are U.S.-born noncitizens would be endowed. Nor does it clarify how they would be identified, nor any actions or nonactions to be taken by government authorities toward these newborns. While the law would produce a new category of people, U.S.-born noncitizens, it does not consider the legal and social implications, intended or unintended, of the law.

Figure 8.6. Representative Steve King (R-Iowa) carrying copies of the Birthright Citizenship Act of 2011, which he introduced on the first day of the 2011 Congress.

The politics over birthright citizenship is also being played out in the states. Politicians in at least fourteen states are promoting laws to curtail citizenship rights for children of undocumented immigrants.[54] State-issued birth certificates would exclude babies born to undocumented parents. Such laws would usher in a two-tiered system of birth certificates, with one tier for those whose parents could prove they were legitimate citizens or legal immigrants, and another for those born to undocumented parents, indicating their illegitimate and second-class status. Lawmakers claim that such drastic measures are necessary because undocumented immigration is "nothing less than an invasion" and "a malady of epic proportions."[55]

In Arizona, State Senator Russell Pearce made birthright citizenship one of his key issues, claiming that determining citizenship is a right that belongs to the states and not to the federal government.[56] For Pearce, citizenship is also a moral issue: "You can't break into the country and then expect to be rewarded. It's immoral. It's illegal."[57] Pearce expressed these views in political advertisements that featured several Mexican-looking women surrounded by children, sitting in a desert environment, with the words "Ending Birthright Citizenship" emblazoned along the bottom of the image along with his name (Figure 8.7). The implication appears to be that Mexican mothers are coming to the United States, bringing their children, and will probably have more children born in the United States who will be U.S. citizens. Or perhaps the women are already here (we don't really know that this photograph was taken during a border crossing; it could be in a park or a similar setting in the United States) and some or all of their children are already U.S. citizens. Either way, the threat of Latina fertility and the production of future, undeserving citizens comes through loud and clear. In an interesting political twist, Senator Pearce, architect of Arizona's tough immigration law, lost his bid for reelection on November 8, 2011.[58]

After almost thirty years of public debate over birthright citizenship and anchor babies, the fifth edition of the *American Heritage Dictionary*, which

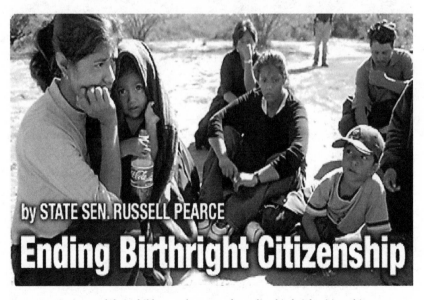

Figure 8.7. Latinas and their children as the reason for ending birthright citizenship.

appeared on November 1, 2011, included the word *anchor baby* with the following definition: "a child born to a noncitizen mother in a country that grants automatic citizenship to children born on its soil, especially such a child born to parents seeking to secure eventual citizenship for themselves and often other members of their family."[59] However, the dictionary's inclusion of *anchor baby* as if the term existed objectively and not as a pejorative, politically constructed concept, soon ran intro trouble. In response, The American Heritage Dictionary now provides a revised definition on its website: "Anchor baby, *n. Offensive.* Used as a disparaging term for a child born to a noncitizen mother in a country that grants automatic citizenship to children born on its soil, especially when the child's birthplace is thought to have been chosen in order to improve the mother's or other relatives' chances of securing eventual citizenship."[60] In its own way, the *American Heritage Dictionary* provides an illustration of how concepts and definitions change over time, although in this case the change occurred in a matter of months.

Surprisingly, Lou Dobbs, who perhaps as much as anyone helped turn the anchor baby issue into a media spectacle, is against changing the Fourteenth Amendment: "The idea that anchor babies somehow require changing the 14th amendment, I part ways with the Senators on that because I believe the 14th amendment, particularly in its due process and equal protection clauses, is so important. It lays the foundation for the entire Bill of Rights being applied to the states."[61] Mr. Dobbs would instead prefer legislative action for dealing with anchor babies.

A THOUGHT EXPERIMENT ON AN IMAGINED HISTORY

Given the furor over so-called anchor babies, you would think the nation had never been here before. History is important not only so we do not repeat past errors but also because history is invoked in the arguments for eliminating birthright citizenship. For example, when he introduced his bill to amend the Fourteenth Amendment to the Constitution, Representative Steve King said, "We need to address anchor babies. This isn't what our founding fathers intended."[62] But was it not exactly what many if not all of our founding fathers intended? Let's not forget one of the key articles in the Declaration of Independence: "He [King George] has endeavoured to prevent the population of these States; for that purpose obstructing the Laws for Naturalization of Foreigners; refusing to pass others to encourage their migrations hither." We fought the War of Independence at least in part for immigration. Moreover, birthright citizenship was U.S. common law long before the Fourteenth Amendment, as explained earlier. And if the founding fathers did not want to integrate the children of immigrants (at least white ones), how do we explain Andrew Jackson? His parents were immigrants from Ireland, and little Andrew was born on U.S. soil in 1767. Andrew not only anchored his parents to American soil, he became the seventh president of the United States.

Anti-immigrant sentiments have waxed and waned throughout our history. In the late 1800s and early 1900s, immigrants from Italy, Greece, Poland, Lithuania, Russia, Hungary, and other southern and eastern European countries were thought by many to be inferior to already established Americans. Many wondered if these foreigners could ever assimilate and become upstanding members of society. These views often extended to the U.S.-born children of these immigrants. Consider the following quotation by Francis A. Walker, superintendent of the census of 1870 and 1889, concerning the children of southern and eastern European immigrants:

> Although born among us, our general instinctive feeling testifies that they are not wholly of us. So separate has been their social life, due alike to their clannishness and to our reserve; so strong have been the ties of race and blood and religion with them; so acute has been the jealousy of their spiritual teachers to our institutions—that we think of them, and speak of them, as foreigners.[63]

Walker was among many who feared these "strange" new immigrants and believed their children could never assimilate. What if, given the level of anti-immigrant sentiment at the time, the country had chosen to deny birthright citizenship to the children of immigrants as part of the major restrictions introduced by the 1924 immigration law? What would have happened? We sometimes engage in thought experiments in the social sciences, and imagining an answer to these questions shows their absurdity, from today's perspective. For example, let's take an institution of national significance—the U.S. Supreme Court. Had our hypothetical elimination of birthright citizenship occurred, some of today's justices might not be citizens. Antonin G. Scalia's father was born in Italy, as was Samuel A. Alito's father. Ruth Bader Ginsburg's father was born in Russia. All three helped anchor their immigrant families into American society, despite the earlier anti-immigrant fears of their continued foreignness. Sonia Sotomayor's parents were born in Puerto Rico and were therefore citizens, but in our hypothetical rollback of birthright citizenship, who knows how Puerto Ricans would have fared? Clearly, today's fears may become tomorrow's source of amusement. The children, grandchildren, and great-grandchildren of the great wave of immigrants in the late 1800s and early 1900s are now integrated into every facet of American life, including at the highest levels.

MAKING CITIZENS ILLEGAL

According to a national poll taken in June of 2011, 61 percent of Americans opposed granting citizenship to the U.S.-born children of "illegal aliens," which is not surprising given the acrimonious public debate over anchor babies.[64] But the prospect of denying birthright citizenship raises profound issues. In *Homo Sacer*, Giorgio Agamben asks, "Who and what is German? And also, therefore, who and what is not German?"[65] He asks this question because of what he views as the slippage between the rights of man (basic human rights) and the rights of citizens. The problem is that the rights and privileges of citizens are not fixed and absolute in today's world. In particular, the rights of persons born into a particular nation may no longer be as permanent and inalienable as was once thought. As people leave one nation and take up life in another, what rights of citizenship follow them? When their children are born in the new nation, to what rights of citizenship are they entitled?

The movement of people across political borders challenges the born-into-nation concept. Stateless people and denationalized people, such as refugees, Agamben argues, break down the continuity between birth and nation. They must rely not on the rights of citizenship but on prior rights associated with being human and on international agreements regarding human rights. Another way in which the nativity and nationality link may be challenged is through laws that take away birthright citizenship, which the people of Ireland recently voted to do for the children of African immigrants and which some members of the U.S. Congress have proposed.[66] Such policies denationalize a people and thus reduce their rights of citizenship to rights that are more fundamental and, ultimately, less secure. Who really protects the human rights of noncitizens? Denationalized members of a society, those denied birthright citizenship as well as delegitimized citizens, may be subject to whatever policies are deemed necessary by the state, including detention, forced removal from the country, or, in the case of the Jews of Germany, the ultimate removal, or "final solution."

A more subtle way to challenge citizenship claims is through discourse that calls into question a group's loyalty to the nation, that casts them as a threat to the nation, that challenges the legitimacy of their claims to membership in the nation. This is precisely what occurs in the debate over birthright citizenship.

The children of undocumented Latinas are portrayed as illegitimate members of society, as nothing more than anchor babies, reducing their very existence and purpose in life to the biopolitics of immigration. According to this view, theirs is a crass attempt to play the system in order to acquire citizenship for their scheming and conniving parents who are themselves illegitimate and undeserving members of society.

Although the idea of anchor babies sounds the alarm for some, even more troubling would be the legal construction of a group of U.S.-born, nationality-less outcasts, as abject subjects. Denying birthright citizenship to those who would almost certainly continue to live among us would render them the most liminal and miserable subjects in the nation. Even 1.5-generation undocumented immigrants, those who have been raised in the United States since they were young children and who often feel despair over the obstacles they face, would be displaced by this new class of nationless and thus even more abject residents.

Perhaps the most serious possible negative outcome of actually changing the Fourteenth Amendment would be the construction of a whole new group of Americans: those who were born in the United States but are not citizens. Why is this a problem? First of all, proposed changes to the Fourteenth Amendment are short on details, especially as to the status of noncitizen U.S.-born children. Would their lives be like those of undocumented immigrants, that is, might they have some legal rights and protections, such as the right to go to school and protections for fair labor standards and practices? Perhaps more important, would U.S.-born noncitizens be deportable? Unless special provisions are written into any changes to the Fourteenth Amendment, U.S.-born noncitizens could be deportable, just like their undocumented parents. Even legal immigrants are deportable if they commit one of the many offenses that allow their legal status to be revoked. Changing the Fourteenth Amendment would, in essence, create a class of U.S.-born noncitizens whose lives would be just as insecure as those of undocumented immigrants. But if they were to be subject to deportation, as are undocumented and even legal residents, where would U.S.-born noncitizens be deported to? To their parents' country of origin? And if deported, what would happen if these U.S.-born noncitizens returned to the country of their birth, the United States, as unauthorized entrants? Would they be undocumented immigrants who are at the same time U.S.-born? What would it mean to have U.S.-born residents and undocumented immigrants living in essentially the same condition of illegality? At a minimum, the definition of the condition of illegality would have to take on an expanded meaning to include the U.S.-born residents caught in this newly constructed circumstance.

In addition, states would be free to pass laws that include or exclude them, as they do legal and undocumented immigrants now. U.S.-born noncitizens would not be protected by the Fourteenth Amendment's prohibition that "no State shall make or enforce any law which shall abridge the privileges or immunities of citizens of the United States." But a major problem with implementing laws for U.S.-born noncitizens would then be distinguishing citizens from noncitizens. Laws in states such as Arizona and Alabama that allow police to detain and question anyone they "suspect" of being an "illegal alien," which the U.S. Supreme Court has allowed to continue, if only temporarily, raise the issue of racial profiling.[67] The catchphrase of popular resistance in those states has become "Do I look illegal to you?" In a post–Fourteenth Amendment America, the new challenge might be, "Do I look like a U.S.-born noncitizen to you?" Surveillance regimes of Foucauldian proportions would have to emerge to answer these questions of identity and status.

Also problematic is the lack of empirical support for the belief that denying these children citizenship will result in their leaving with their parents for their parents' country of origin. While some might, it is more plausible that they will do as the 1.5-generation undocumented immigrants discussed previously have done and continue to reside in the United States, the nation of their birth, despite their status. Thus we would have thousands, potentially millions over time, of U.S.-born noncitizen residents.

Would U.S.-born noncitizens be citizens-in-waiting? We would hope there would be provisions for a path to citizenship for these U.S.-born noncitizens. But what if they cannot satisfy whatever new requirements are created for them to gain citizenship? Or what if they are deemed unworthy and deportable for some reason? Additionally, could they be citizens-in-waiting in perpetuity, or would there be an age or time limit after which, if citizenship has not been attained, they would attain a new status with a different set of rights or lack thereof? These ambiguities create possibilities for adding new layers to lives in social and legal limbo, which would only add to the problems of belonging and social stigma.

Finally, what would happen to the children of U.S.-born noncitizens? Since their parents would not be citizens, the next generation would also be denied citizenship by birth. Thus, a lack of citizenship status could continue over generations. What we would then have in America is a caste, a category from which certain people cannot escape. Social stigma is often ascribed to castes as abject persons lacking full membership in society. Is this not exactly the situation for which the Fourteenth Amendment was needed in the first place?

EPILOGUE

THE LATINO THREAT NARRATIVE characterizes Latinos as unable or unwilling to integrate into the social and cultural life of the United States. Allegedly, they do not learn English, and they seal themselves off from the larger society, reproducing cultural beliefs and behaviors antithetical to a modern life, such as pathologically high fertility levels that reduce the demographic presence of white Americans. Latinos are represented as an unchanging people, standing outside the currents of history, merely waiting for the opportunity to revolt and to reconquer land that was once theirs. They live to destroy social institutions such as medical care and education. They dilute the privileges and rights of citizenship for legitimate members of society.

When I coined the term "Latino Threat Narrative," I did so to show that what might appear as random or idiosyncratic comments, characterizations, tirades, images, and other representations of Latinos, both immigrants and U.S.-born, are actually part of a more cohesive set of ideas. The Latino Threat Narrative is a discourse that has developed over time and, as such, expresses a consistent set of assumptions. I also believed that it was necessary to discuss the Latino Threat Narrative in relation to a crisis in the meaning of citizenship today. In a world of widespread movement across national borders, citizenship becomes an ambiguous concept, not contained by purely legalistic definitions. The rights and privileges of citizenship, the possibility of trans-border citizens, the practices of social citizenship, and the sentiments of cultural citizenship are all on the table as we try to understand what a sense of belonging and community membership mean today.

Although powerful and productive in its own domain, the Latino Threat Narrative is also meaningful in a discourse on citizenship. Indeed, it plays an important role in public debates over the dilution of rights and privileges of citizenship. Citizenship is about inclusion and exclusion, and the Latino Threat Narrative helps bring those concepts into relief. Struggles over the meaning of citizenship occur every day in many public contexts. Some of these events become media spectacles, generating extensive coverage on TV, radio, and the Internet. Ideas about fertility and reproduction, confrontations over organ transplants, the Minuteman Project's anti-immigration activities, and immigrant-rights marches provide windows into the way the Latino Threat Narrative informs debates over immigration and citizenship. Latinos are represented as societal threats, thus causing them to be cast as illegitimate members of the community and undermining their claims for social and cultural citizenship. Importantly, the Latino Threat Narrative not only frames these events but also serves as a catalyst for action, such as the Minuteman Project's spectacle of surveillance on the Arizona-Mexico border and proposals to eliminate birthright citizenship.

In each of these media spectacles, the effect of characterizing Latino lives along the lines of the Latino Threat Narrative is to raise questions about citizenship. Are Latino immigrants and their children worthy of citizenship if they are unwilling to integrate into U.S. society? Are Latinos born in the United States suspect as citizens because of the disloyalty to the nation implied by the reconquest narrative? The immigrant marches in the spring of 2006 were, in effect, an attempt to address these questions with a spectacular display of belonging and assertions of social and cultural citizenship. The immigrants displayed their intention of becoming part of American society. They waved U.S. flags, recited the Pledge of Allegiance, and marched in orderly fashion. However, asserting social and cultural citizenship is not enough. The larger society must also recognize their membership in the community of citizens. The way the Minutemen and other anti-immigrant groups responded to the immigrants' marches suggests that many people remained unconvinced by such performances of citizenship. By referring to the marchers as "invaders" and "mobs" who were unwilling to speak English, some commentators on the immigrant marches signaled their dogged adherence to the images of the virtual lives of immigrants so pervasive in the media and public discourse. They invoked the Latino Threat Narrative despite the marchers' attempt to counter the assumptions about their lives.

I have attempted to provide evidence from my research that undercuts the Latino Threat Narrative. Over generations in the United States, Latinos increasingly use English in daily life. They increasingly have non-Latino friends and intermarry with non-Latinos. As Latino immigrants move along a path to citizenship, they are increasingly more integrated in terms of income, levels of education, and political engagement. Latinas are not slaves to childbearing. Rather, they are subject to history and economic pressures just as other women with decreasing fertility levels. Latino immigrants are not a drain on organ transplants and other medical resources for citizens. These trends may not be able to destroy the Latino Threat Narrative, but they do undermine some of its basic premises.

How resilient will the Latino Threat Narrative prove to be in the future? Immigration from Mexico has essentially flatlined since the Great Recession began in 2008, especially for California. A lack of jobs in the United States combined with declining fertility rates in Mexico means there are fewer incentives for going to "El Norte." Will this affect the pervasiveness of the Latino Threat Narrative? It's hard to say. But one thing is clear: attitudes should change, if only because of self-interest. As immigrants become a smaller proportion of the workforce, their children, the second generation, will increasingly become the homegrown workforce.[1] But how much they achieve and the quality of the work they can perform will depend on the investment we make in their education. We can't afford to continue to see them as foreign or a threat. Rather, they are us, and their integration into society is good for them and for the nation.

Although the data presented here suggest strongly that Latinos are integrating into U.S. society, this does not mean that Latinos are undergoing a process of homogenization, or what is often called assimilation in the classic, linear sense of a complete loss of identity and one-way adoption of U.S. culture. Latinos are also contributing to a constantly changing U.S. culture and society. They have played a role in helping to shape what America is today and what it will become in the future. Latinos will change, but they will also remain a richly varied population stemming from national backgrounds and regional histories in the United States. In this sense, they are no different from other Americans. The United States is not a homogenous country. Texans extol their local identity as strongly as New Englanders, southerners, and midwesterners.[2] So, too, Latinos in different regions of the country have their own cultural variations on a theme, as do various generations of Latinos.

The linear assumption of assimilation has other problems as well.[3] The assimilation model posits a one-way change as immigrants lose their culture and acquire "American culture." However, what exactly is American culture? Although there are many generally shared cultural beliefs and behaviors across a national community, there are also some very real local and regional cultural differences in what it means to be American. An immigrant in Los Angeles learns a different version of American culture than an immigrant who has landed in New York or Ohio. Even in different parts of the greater Los Angeles metropolitan area, local cultural variations are important.

But perhaps more important is that the assimilation model assumes that American culture is static and unchanging; it is a fixed target. But American culture has never been static. It has always undergone transformations as a result of internal innovations, generational experiences, contributions from its internally diverse inhabitants, and the inclusion of new immigrant populations. Rather than being linear, cultural change is occurring in many directions all the time.

In addition, the assimilation model assumes not only that immigrant assimilation is a linear change but also that a change toward the mainstream is always positive and must be achieved at all costs. However, this thinking can blind us to the downside of assimilation. There is now a great deal of research showing that rapid assimilation—becoming more "American"—can lead to immigrants losing positive and healthy beliefs and practices, such as a decrease in healthy dietary practices and an increase in fast-food consumption, a loss of family values and an increase in the number of divorces), and a reduced respect for parents.[4] Assimilation can also lead to increases in unhealthy behaviors such as alcohol consumption, smoking, and risky sexual practices.[5] With more time in the United States, Latinos become more obese, experience more birth complications, and do less well in school.[6] Moreover, less concern for assimilation and more tolerance for multiculturalism can have positive effects. Irene Bloemraad found that Canada provides much greater institutional support for multiculturalism, as well as support for community-based programs assisting with citizenship processing, than does the United States, which has resulted in much higher rates of naturalization by immigrants in Canada than in the United States.[7]

Furthermore, even though over time Latinos increasingly use English, have more non-Latino friends, and intermarry with non-Latinos, these trends tell us little about changes Latinos are introducing into U.S. culture. Increasing social and linguistic integration of Latinos underscores a process in which Latinos are also introducing new ideas and ways of being to the United States. Latino ideas of family, work, friendship, emotions, trust, music, humor, sports, artistic expression, and so on are already blending into U.S. culture, both nationally and at local levels. The fact that salsa is a more popular condiment than ketchup is an example of how Mexican culinary culture is changing U.S. culture. Burritos are as much or more an American invention than Mexican, as is much of Tex-Mex food. Then there are sushirritos (sushi burritos) and other hybrid foods occurring as Latinos and other ethnic groups interact. Let us not forget, moreover, that tomatoes, corn, avocados, chilis, beans, certain squashes, peanuts, potatoes, and many more foods are a pre-Columbian contributions to U.S. cuisine, reflecting an earlier period of intercultural exchanges. Because the Latino Threat Narrative views Latinos as a destructive force rather than a creative one, Latino contributions to U.S. culture are obscured or given negative, even paranoid, meanings.

The real danger posed by the Latino Threat Narrative, and the acrimonious debate over Latino immigration that it informs, is that it blinds us to the reality that Latinos are a vital part of U.S. society. Latino integration into society therefore goes unrecognized, either willfully or because of the taken-for-granted assumptions of the narrative. Just as lacking in recognition are Latino contributions to social and cultural life, to what we think of as being American. Perhaps this is because such changes are difficult to observe in process. They are slow and often imperceptible. Also, when so dominant a discourse pervades public culture as does the Latino Threat Narrative, it is difficult for other discourses to blossom, especially when radio and TV talk-show hosts use the supposed Latino threat to bolster their ratings.[8] What about the Latino Contribution Narrative? For over four hundred years Latinos have been contributing to the social, economic, and cultural life of what is now the U.S. Southwest. Where are the media spectacles celebrating those contributions? In a sense, those who worry about U.S. culture being changed by Latino immigrants and their descendants are correct. Latinos are changing U.S. culture and will continue to change it even as they themselves change, which is a strong argument for Latino cultural citizenship. Anthropologists often take the long view of culture change. Immediate reactions to newcomers (immigrants) in a society often focus on difference. New people in the neighborhood who speak a different language, practice a different religion, and put up signs on stores in foreign languages all raise ethnocentric responses and even fears. Over time, these differences may become less pronounced, because what was once new and strange can become part of the accepted way things are or even become central to a people's identity and symbols of that identity.

Anthropologists are likely to speak of the culture changes that occur in a world of moving people, ideas, and products as blending, fusion, syncretism, hybridization, or creolization.[9] These concepts reflect the multidimensional, multidirectional, and often unpredictable changes that take place as people and ideas, beliefs, and behaviors collide and interweave into new cultural formations. Culture is always an emergent form of life.[10] Anthropologists prefer these concepts to the more unidirectional flow of changes presented by models of assimilation, which are often inadequate to capture the complex process of culture change.[11] A couple of examples make the point.

For years, a statue of John Wayne dressed as a cowboy has been displayed prominently at Orange County's John Wayne Airport (Figure E.1). But where does the "cowboy" come from? The image of the cowboy that John Wayne personifies has not always existed. The cowboy is a far cry from the image of Daniel Boone and the frontiersman of the colonial states in the late eighteenth and early nineteenth centuries.

When whites and blacks from the colonial states moved west, they encountered people in what is now Texas and New Mexico who were living a life well adapted to cattle ranching and herding. They were vaqueros, Mexican cowboys from whom the Americans learned the cowboy way of life. Imagine how foreign the first American cowboys—with their sombreros, bandannas, ponchos, leather leggings over their pants, boots, ropes, and general demeanor—must have looked. And the words these new types of Americans used for the items and techniques of their trade were essentially foreign too, because many of them were borrowed from Spanish (some of which were in turn borrowed from the Moors in Spain).[12] Following are some cowboy words and their origins:

Spanish	English
vaquero (literally, "man who works with cows")	buckaroo (cowboy)
chaparreras (pant leg coverings)	chaps
la reata (rope)	lariat
lazo (noose on rope)	lasso
reinda (ropes riders used to guide horse)	reins
mecate (rope made of horse-tail hairs)	McCarty

Figure E.1. Statue of John Wayne at Orange County's airport. Photo by author.

jaquima (bitless bridle to tame horses)	hackamore
bronco (wild horse)	bronc
mesteño (trained horse)	mustang
corral (pen)	corral
darle vuelta (to rope and stop cattle in their tracks by quickly snubbing a rope around the saddle horn)	dolly roping
rodeo	rodeo
juzgado (local jail)	hoosegow

But perhaps just as important as the words cowboys borrowed and adapted from the vaqueros were the lifestyle and personal characteristics they adopted: the strong, silent type of man whose time alone on the range made him independent and self-reliant. Is this not the image John Wayne the cowboy exudes? In a few short years, the foreign-looking and -sounding cowboy became the central figure in the myth of the West, and his qualities and characteristics came to epitomize the quintessential elements of what it means to be an American male. Did migrating west, encountering Mexican vaquero culture, and constructing the cowboy destroy American culture? Or did American culture change and in the process incorporate novelty? The answer is the statue standing at John Wayne Airport.

Latinos in the United States have also experienced culture change, incorporating new ideas and behaviors into their lives and identities. For example, generations of Mexicans lived in Texas before it became part of the United States. When thousands of Germans migrated into Texas in the 1800s, they had a profound and lasting effect on Tejanos (Texans of Mexican descent).[13] German immigrants brought with them the accordion and their fondness for the polkas that they played during their parties. Local Tejanos heard the music and picked up the accordion, adapting it to fit their preferences. Soon Tejanos were playing a new style of music in Texas that came to be known as conjunto, Tex-Mex, Tejano, or norteño music.[14] To many Americans, it was just "Mexican music," and yet this music was a real American invention, blending German polkas, Mexican ballads, and other song styles.[15] The late Texas singer Selena Perez was one of the most nationally famous performers of this style. In the long run, Tejanos did not lose their culture because they incorporated aspects of German culture into their lives. Their culture changed and was enriched in many ways because of such exchanges.

The Latino Threat Narrative distracts us from understanding culture change. It casts Latinos, whites, and everyone else into immutable categories of race, ethnicity, and culture. But the borders of these categories are not fixed; they are permeable. They will not break or be destroyed as they are transformed. What will constitute "Latino" or "white" fifty or a hundred years from now is anyone's guess. Most likely, the changes that occur will be unanticipated, least of all by the Latino Threat Narrative, because the transformations that cultures undergo are difficult to predict.

In the short term, however, the Latino Threat Narrative creates divisiveness and, by representing Latinos as a threat, undermines the integration of Latinos into society. The Latino Threat Narrative obscures the strides Latinos are making and at the same time masks the obstacles many of them face as they struggle to get an education and gain a modicum of economic mobility. But even more, it suggests they deserve the obstacles they face because the threats they allegedly pose render them undeserving and illegitimate members of the community. The Latino Threat Narrative rationalizes actions and public policies targeting Latinas and their children, making it problematic to gain access to prenatal care for Latina mothers, quality schools for Latino children, jobs that provide economic mobility, and a path to citizenship for unauthorized residents living and working in our society.

What is needed as Latinos integrate into U.S. society is a commitment to equal opportunity. This would signal society's recognition of, and pragmatic support for, Latino social and cultural citizenship. Access to schools, medical care, and good jobs is essential for economic and social mobility. Making a commitment to improving opportunities for Latinos requires that we, as a society, move beyond the Latino Threat Narrative. Latinos would not be the only beneficiaries of such a dramatic shift. By moving beyond the Latino Threat Narrative, non-Latinos would be better able to recognize shared ambitions, to appreciate novelty provided by cultural differences, and to be less afraid of change.

What type of policy recommendations does this analysis suggest? Latinos already engage in practices of social citizenship, and they exhibit a sense of belonging that underscores their cultural citizenship. But more is needed to break down the barriers to social integration and economic mobility that Latinos routinely encounter. Here are concrete policies that we, as a society, could pursue to alleviate the damage caused by the Latino Threat Narrative and to ensure a rapid integration of Latino immigrants and their children:

- Active and persistent neutralization of the Latino Threat Narrative by members of the media, government, and academia.
- A comprehensive approach to labor market needs and immigration policy. This would reduce the tendency to blame Latino immigrants as "the problem" when they come to the United States to satisfy its labor needs.
- Elimination of the "illegal alien" as a social type. "Illegal alien" is a concept that represents a thoroughly immoral relationship between those who labor and those who benefit from that labor. If the economy needs more workers than we produce through births, then let those workers and their families live under the protection of law. Recognize their economic and social contributions to the general welfare.

- Provision of a path to citizenship for undocumented immigrants leading productive and law-abiding lives. The 1.5 generation in particular should be provided legal residence, recognizing that they have grown up and attended school in the United States and most likely will continue to live in the United States. This is the best way to guarantee their rapid integration into society.
- Investment in 1.5- and second-generation Latinos by guaranteeing access to quality education and health care. This is an investment that would benefit all of society in terms of economic productivity, physical and mental well-being, and cultural creativity.
- Improvement of the second-chance opportunities for the 1.5- and second-generation Latinos who did not receive an adequate education or whose schooling was cut short. Provide greater support for community colleges and job training programs that allow for a modicum of mobility for those who have experienced major social obstacles. This includes minor brushes with the law. Those desiring to rehabilitate their lives deserve education, not incarceration.

It is time to put the Latino Threat Narrative to rest. It is counterproductive and divisive and creates self-fulfilling prophecies. It is an inaccurate depiction of the everyday lives of Latino immigrants and Latinos in general. Citizenship in all its manifestations is hard enough to construct, and it deserves honest, productive, clear-eyed representations of all members of society, as well as public policies that reduce obstacles to integration and social and economic mobility. Perhaps it is naive to say it all begins with attitudes; an inclusive society is one in which a sense of belonging blooms freely and unhindered, fostered by widespread recognition that we are all in this thing called society together. Pitting one group against another to maintain privileges may have short-term benefits for some, but it creates long-term problems for all of *us*.

REFERENCE MATTER

NOTES

Introduction

1. For the full quotation, see http://www.dailykostv.com/w/001046/.

2. Sullivan, "Officials See Rise in Militia Groups across US."

3. Barnes, "Supreme Court Rejects Much of Arizona Immigration Law."

4. Arizona's HB 2281 is available at www.azleg.gov/legtext/49leg/2r/bills/hb2281s.pdf.

5. *Washington Independent*, October 18, 2010, http://washingtonindependent.com/100958/angle-defends-her-anti-illegal-immigration-ads; Price, "Republican Senate Nominee Uses Picture of Mexicans—in Mexico—to Scare Us about Illegal Immigrants."

6. Wyatt, "Cain Proposes Electrified Border Fence."

7. Chavez, "Immigration Reform and Nativism"; Faegin, "Old Poison in New Bottles"; Higham, *Strangers in the Land*; Perea, *Immigrants Out!*

8. I consider this book, as well as most of my publications and public speeches, as the work of an anthropological cultural critic. Handler defines such critics as anthropologists "who expend at least some of their professional effort in dissecting the commonsense presuppositions of their own world and in disseminating the results of that work to as wide an audience of other citizens as they can reach." Handler, *Critics against Culture*, 4.

9. B. Anderson, *Imagined Communities*, 15–16.

10. B. Anderson, *Imagined Communities*.

11. Habermas, *Structural Transformation*; Lee and LiPuma, "Cultures of Circulation," 193–94.

12. For a discussion of immigrants represented as outside the imagined community of the nation, see Chavez, "Outside the Imagined Community."

13. Kellner, *Media Spectacles*.

14. On the media and immigration, see Bailey, "Mexico in the U.S. Media"; Coutin and Chock, "'Your Friend, the Illegal'"; Fernandez and Pedroza, "Border Patrol"; Keogan, "Sense of Place"; Santa Ana, *Brown Tide Rising*; Santa Ana, "'Like an Animal'"; Santa Ana, Moran, and Sanchez, "Awash under a Brown Tide"; Simon and Alexander, *Ambivalent Welcome*; White and White, *Immigrants and the Media*.

15. *Merriam-Webster Online Dictionary*, http://www.m-w.com, s.v. "spectacle."

16. Debord, *Society of the Spectacle*, 14.

17. For examples of the ways in which the media frame events, see Benford and Snow, "Framing Processes and Social Movements"; Ensink and Sauer, "Social-Functional and Cognitive Approaches"; German, "Role of the Media in Political Socialization"; and Coutin and Chock, "'Your Friend, the Illegal.'"

18. As Ella Shohat has observed, "In a transnational world typified by the global circulation of images and sounds, goods and peoples, media spectatorship impacts complexly on national identity, communal belonging, and political affiliations." Shohat, "Post-Third-Worldist Culture."

19. For a discussion of the theory of virtualism, see Carrier and Miller, *Virtualism*.

20. Debord, *Society of the Spectacle*, 13.

21. Media spectacles become a technique of governmentality by contributing to the development of systems of knowledge to control the conduct of populations.

22. Ngai, *Impossible Subjects*.

23. See table 1 of the Pew Hispanic Center report *Foreign Born at Mid-Decade*, http://pewhispanic.org/files/other/foreignborn/Table-1.pdf.

24. Asia accounted for 10 percent of the undocumented immigrants, Europe and Canada 5 percent, and Africa and other countries 5 percent. Passel, Capps, and Fix, *Undocumented Immigrants*.

25. Hing, *Deporting Our Souls*.

26. Chavez, *Covering Immigration*, 95.

27. S. A. Mohanty et al., "Health Expenditures of Immigrants," 1436.

28. Shogren, "Clinton's Signature."

29. Personal Responsibility and Work Opportunity Reconciliation Act, Public Law 104-193, *U.S. Statutes at Large* 110 (1996), is available at http://wdr.doleta.gov/readroom/legislation/pdf/104-193.pdf.

30. McDonnell, "Mexico Latest to Grant Rights."

31. HR 4437, the Border Protection, Antiterrorism, and Illegal Immigration Control Act, is available at http://thomas.loc.gov.

32. Curtius, "House Moving to Tighten Immigration."

33. Debates over immigration policies lend themselves to political grandstanding and political symbolism; see Kitty Calavita, "New Politics of Immigration."

34. *Los Angeles Times*, "Immigration's Endless Summer."

35. Gerstenzang, "Bush Strongly Defends Deal on Immigration."

36. The concept of citizenship is in a state of crisis, not just in the United States but worldwide. See Balibar, "Is There a 'Neo-Racism'?"; Castles and Davidson, *Citizenship and Migration*; Reed-Danahay and Brettell, *Citizenship, Political Engagement, and Belonging*; Sadiq, *Paper Citizens*; Tsuda, *Local Citizenship*.

37. Cowan, Dembour, and Wilson, introduction to *Culture and Rights*; Roman, "Members and Outsiders"; Turner, "Contemporary Problems." As Carlos Vélez-Ibáñez has argued, in the United States "citizenship, nationality, and ethnic identity reflect the dominant ethnic group of Anglo-Saxon Americans." Vélez-Ibáñez, "Se me acabó la canción."

38. Karst, *Belonging to America*.

39. Ngai, *Impossible Subjects*.

40. Luibheid, *Entry Denied*.

41. Gerstle, *American Crucible*; Molina, *Fit to Be Citizens?*; Stern, *Eugenic Nation*.

42. Appadurai, "Disjuncture and Difference"; Ritzer, *McDonaldization of Society*.

43. Inda and Rosaldo, "Introduction"; Zhan, "Does It Take a Miracle?"

44. Bosniak, "Universal Citizenship"; A. Gordon and Stack, "Citizenship beyond the State"; Hall and Held, "Citizens and Citizenship."

45. C. Gordon, "Governmental Rationality"; Rocco, "Transforming Citizenship."

46. J. Anderson, *Transnational Democracy*; Basch, Schiller, and Blanc, *Nations Unbound*; Bosniak, "Citizenship Denationalized"; Brettell, "Political Belonging and Cultural Belonging"; A. Castaneda, "Roads to Citizenship"; Fitzgerald, *Negotiating Extra-Territorial Citizenship*; Fox, "Unpacking Transnational Citizenship"; Inda, "Flexible World"; Ong, *Flexible Citizenship*; Schiller, "Transborder Citizenship"; Schiller and Fouron, *Georges Woke Up Laughing*.

47. Hammer, *Democracy and the Nation State*; Varsanyi, "Interrogating 'Urban Citizenship.'"

48. Bernal, "Diaspora, Cyberspace and Political Imagination," 164.

49. Ong, *Buddha Is Hiding*.

50. Flores and Benmayor, *Latino Cultural Citizenship*; Inda and Mirón, "Migrant Voices"; Ong, "Cultural Citizenship as Subject-Making"; Rosaldo, "Cultural Citizenship, Inequality, and Multiculturalism"; Stephen, "Cultural Citizenship and Labor Rights"; Stevenson, *Cultural Citizenship*; Torres, Mirón, and Inda, introduction to *Race, Identity, and Citizenship*.

51. Ortner, "On Key Symbols."

52. Aleinikoff, "Tightening Circle of Membership"; Hollinger, "How Wide the Circle?"

53. Aleinikoff and Klusmeyer, *Citizenship Policies*; Coutin, *Nations of Emigrants*; Yuval-Davis, "'Multi-Layered Citizen.'"

54. For a discussion of the theory of virtualism, see Carrier and Miller, *Virtualism*.

55. Bosniak, "Citizenship Denationalized," 455.

56. Ibid., 456.

57. Ibid.

58. Bosniak, "Universal Citizenship"; Schuck, *Citizens, Strangers, and In-Betweens.* For a discussion of the upsurge in pro-regularization movements in immigrant communities across Europe, see Laubenthal, "Emergence of Pro-Regularization Movements." In the mid-1990s, illegal migrants from sub-Saharan Africa, Latin America, and the former Yugoslavia occupied churches and initiated demonstrations in France, Spain, and Switzerland. The aim of these social movements was to protest the illegality of migrants and to push for means to legalize, or regularize, their status.

59. James Holston and Arjun Appadurai observe that legally resident noncitizens and citizens often possess essentially the same civil and socioeconomic rights. Holston and Appadurai, "Introduction," 4.

60. Bosniak, "Universal Citizenship."

61. Schuck, "Law and the Study of Migration"; Soysal, *Limits of Citizenship.* The Universal Declaration of Human Rights was adopted and proclaimed by UN General Assembly Resolution 217 A(III), December 10, 1948. See http://www.un.org/Overview/rights.html.

62. Bosniak, "Citizenship Denationalized." For the European context, see Balibar, "Is There a 'Neo-Racism'?"; Baubock and Rundell, *Blurred Boundaries*; Bhabha, "'Get Back'"; Kristeva, *Crisis of the European Subject*; Soysal, *Limits of Citizenship*; Suárez-Navaz, *Rebordering the Mediterranean.*

63. For examples of citizenship rights being viewed as diluted in the U.S. context, see Geyer, *Americans No More*; Huntington, *Who We Are*; and Maxwell and Jacobson, *Marketing Disease to Hispanics.* For an example of similar views in Spain as a result of immigration from North Africa and South America, see Suárez-Navaz, *Rebordering the Mediterranean.*

64. In January of 2007, the U.S. Supreme Court ruled that auto theft is a felony that warrants deporting a legal immigrant, a provision of the 1996 immigration law. Savage, "Justices Ease Deporting of Car Thieves."

65. Bosniak, "Citizenship Denationalized," 470. See also Bloemraad, *Becoming a Citizen.*

66. M. D. Gupta, *Unruly Immigrants.*

67. B. Anderson, *Imagined Communities*; Bosniak, "Citizenship Denationalized," 477; Coll, "'No Estoy Perdida.'"

68. Bosniak, "Citizenship Denationalized," 477.

69. For a discussion of civic participation and noncitizen citizenship, see Gordon, *Suburban Sweatshops.*

70. Schiller, "Transborder Citizenship." See also Del Castillo, "Illegal Status and Social Citizenship."

71. Schiller, "Transborder Citizenship," 31.

72. B. Anderson, *Imagined Communities*; Bosniak, "Citizenship Denationalized," 479; Menjívar, "Liminal Legality"; Turner, "Contemporary Problems." As Caroline Brettell notes, such subjective sentiments of belonging have also been defined as "nationality." Brettell, "Political Belonging and Cultural Belonging," 97.

73. Nagel and Staeheli argue that because of transnationalism some can claim citizenship in a country without "being part of" or "belonging to" that country. Nagel and Staeheli, "Citizenship, Identity, and Transnational Migration." See also Yuval-Davis, "Belonging and the Politics of Belonging."

74. Coutin, *Legalizing Moves*.

75. Chavez, "Power of the Imagined Community." For an example of the effect of positive sentiments on immigrant behavior, see Hook, Brown, and Bean, who found that immigrants were significantly more likely to become U.S. citizens in states where people have generally positive attitudes about immigrants. Hook, Brown, and Bean, "For Love or Money?"

76. Foucault, *Discipline and Punish*; J. Mohanty, "Status of the Subject in Foucault."

77. Flores and Benmayor, "Constructing Cultural Citizenship," 15.

78. Rosaldo and Flores, "Identity, Conflict, and Evolving Latino Communities," 57.

79. Rosaldo, "Cultural Citizenship, Inequality, and Multiculturalism."

80. It is on this point that Aihwa Ong criticizes Renato Rosaldo's conceptualization of cultural citizenship. Rather than assuming that the assertion of cultural citizenship by a particular social group is sufficient for that group to acquire that subject status, Ong maintains that cultural citizenship is a dialectical process, in that it is asserted as well as being a status subject to construction by the nation-state. See Ong, "Cultural Citizenship as Subject-Making."

81. Ibid., 738.

82. Foucault, "Governmentality."

83. Inda, *Targeting Immigrants*.

84. For a discussion of the media, political citizenship, and consumer subjectivity among Mexican Americans, see Mayer, *Producing Dreams, Consuming Youth*.

85. Ong, "Cultural Citizenship as Subject-Making," 738. As Michael Samers has observed, "if undocumented immigration is produced by stricter regulations, then the state is not so much *controlling* it, the popular press not so much *reporting* it, as they are both *creating* it." Samers, "Invisible Capitalism," 576.

86. Ong, "Cultural Citizenship as Subject-Making," 738.

87. Bandhauer, "Global Trend in Racism"; Brettell, "Wrestling with 9/11."

88. Adams, *Greasers and Gringos*; De Leon, *They Called Them Greasers*.

89. For a discussion of the power of myths in contemporary life, see Barthes, *Mythologies*; Hall, *Representation*; and Kertzer, *Politics and Symbols*.

90. Kellner, *Media Spectacles*.

91. Foucault, "Birth of Biopolitics."

92. For an interdisciplinary examination of the Jesica Santillan case, see Wailoo, Livingston, and Guarnaccia, *Death Retold*.

93. Stepputat, "Marching for Progress." The idea of "performing citizenship" is influenced by Judith Butler's work on gender as an ongoing performance, constantly improvised, rather than an essential identity that is fixed and immutable. Butler, *Bodies That Matter*.

94. Taylor, *Archive and the Repertoire*.

95. For an example of how race is performed among Andean women, see Weismantel, *Cholas and Pishtacos*.

Chapter 1

1. Reagan, "Speech Announcing Ronald Reagan's Presidential Candidacy."

2. Rosaldo, "Cultural Citizenship, Inequality, and Multiculturalism."

3. Chavez, *Covering Immigration*.

4. Buck-Morss, *Thinking Past Terror*; Bush, *National Security Strategy*; Chishti et al., "America's Challenge"; Hardt and Negri, *Empire*.

5. Cole, *Enemy Aliens*; Johnson and Trujillo, "Immigration Reform"; Maher, "Who Has a Right to Rights?"; Volpp, "Citizen and the Terrorist."

6. Huntington, "Hispanic Challenge," 30.

7. Ibid., 42, 32.

8. Huntington, "Special Case of Mexican Immigration," 22.

9. Foucault, *Power/Knowledge*; Hall, introduction to *Representation*.

10. Hall, introduction to *Representation*, 6.

11. Ngai, *Impossible Subjects*, 4.

12. Ibid., 71.

13. For a discussion of U.S. differentiations between "color race" (e.g., the "brown race") and race as groups of people, even what are termed nationalities today (e.g., the "Italian race," the "Mexican race," the "Nordic race"), see Guglielmo, *White on Arrival*.

14. Ibid., 6.

15. For a discussion of racialization, see Torres, Mirón, and Inda, introduction to *Race, Identity, and Citizenship*.

16. Small, "Contours of Racialization."

17. Ngai, *Impossible Subjects*, 7.

18. Stern, "Buildings, Boundaries, and Blood," 75.

19. Ngai, *Impossible Subjects*, 8.

20. Ibid., 89.

21. For a discussion of the public's ambivalent position in relation to undocumented immigrants as criminals and to enforcement, see also Schuck, "Law and the Study of Migration," 197–200.

22. Ngai, *Impossible Subjects*.

23. Geyer, *Americans No More*; Tancredo, *In Mortal Danger*. See also Peter Schuck's views on a "devaluation" of citizenship. Schuck, *Citizens, Strangers, and In-Betweens*.

24. De Genova, "Migrant 'Illegality.'"

25. Inda, *Targeting Immigrants*.

26. Coutin, "Being En Route."

27. For a discussion of the "immigrant invasion" in the Spanish context, see Suárez-Navaz, *Rebordering the Mediterranean*.

28. *U.S. News and World Report*, "How Millions Sneak into U.S."

29. Research by Jeffrey Passel and his associates showed that the INS estimates were too high. See Passel and Woodrow, "Change in the Undocumented Alien Population."

30. Chavez, *Covering Immigration*.

31. Handler, *Nationalism*.

32. Chavez, "Culture Change and Cultural Reproduction."

33. Ngai, *Impossible Subjects*.

34. Buchanan, "What Will America Be in 2050?"

35. Ibid.

36. Brimelow, *Alien Nation*, 218–19.

37. Ibid., 219.

38. Geyer, *Americans No More*, 304–5.

39. Ibid., 305.

40. Kennedy, "Can We Still Afford to Be a Nation of Immigrants?"

41. Ibid., 68.

42. Massey and Pren, "Unintended Consequences of US Immigration Policy," 6. Massey and Pren's analysis builds upon Chavez's findings in *Covering Immigration*.

43. Passel, *Unauthorized Migrants*; Robinson, *ESCAP II*.

44. Grieco, "Foreign Born from Mexico."

45. Will, "We Have Been Here Before."

46. Cleeland, "AFL-CIO Calls for Amnesty."

47. Scheer, "Surprise!"

48. J. F. Smith and Chen, "Bush to Weigh Residency."

49. Tancredo, *In Mortal Danger*.

50. Krikorian, "Dealing with Illegal Immigrants."

51. DeSipio and Masuoka, "Opportunities Lost?"

52. Arellano, "Fear of a Brown Planet."

53. See Arizona's HB 2281 at www.azleg.gov/legtext/49leg/2r/bills/hb2281s.pdf.

54. *Los Angeles Times*, "Lesson for Arizona."

55. Serrano and Castellanos, "Federal Officials Sue Arizona Lawman."

56. Puwar, *Space Invaders*. On the politics of Latina fertility, see also Chavez, "Immigration Reform and Nativism."

57. Gramsci, *Selections from the Prison Notebooks*. See also Chavez, *Covering Immigration*, 45.

58. Ong, *Buddha Is Hiding*.

59. B. Anderson, *Imagined Communities*.

60. LiPuma, "Cultures of Circulation."

61. Ibid., 8.

62. Carrier and Miller, *Virtualism*.

63. Carrier, introduction to Carrier and Miller, *Virtualism*, 2.

64. D. Miller, "Conclusion," 200.

Chapter 2

1. The three people upon whom the cases in this chapter are based were interviewed by the author (Rocío) and Roberto Gonzales (Juan and Carlos), at the time a graduate student in sociology at the University of California, Irvine.

2. Chavez, *Shadowed Lives*; Chavez, "Settlers and Sojourners."

3. The Orange County Survey was conducted in 2006 under the auspices of the Center for Research on Latinos in a Global Society (CRLGS), University of California, Irvine. Interviewing Service of America conducted the telephone survey between January 4 and 31, 2006, using trained interviewers in both English and Spanish. The survey used random-digit dialing on a sample from a database that includes all U.S. directory-published household numbers, both listed and unlisted, combined with a sample that had identified Hispanic markers. Both listed and unlisted numbers were included, avoiding potential bias as a result of exclusion of households with unlisted numbers (see Survey Sampling Inc., *Statistical Analysis of Sample*). The cooperation rate was 70 percent. Interviews were in the interviewee's language of choice. Eligible participants were English- or Spanish-speaking men and women, 18 years of age or older, who were not institutionalized and who identified themselves as white (Anglo, Caucasian, non-Hispanic white) or Latino (Hispanic or more specific ethnic identifiers such as Mexican, Mexican American, Salvadoran, etc.).

4. See U.S. Census Bureau, *State and County Quickfacts*.

5. The Immigration and Intergenerational Mobility in Metropolitan Los Angeles (IIMMLA) project was supported by a grant from the Russell Sage Foundation. Co-principal investigators were Rubén G. Rumbaut, Frank D. Bean, Susan K. Brown, Leo R. Chavez, Louis DeSipio, Jennifer Lee, and Min Zhou. Conducted in 2004, the

study targeted the young-adult children of immigrants from large immigrant groups in the five-county metropolitan Los Angeles area (from Ventura County in the north to San Bernardino County in the south) and used a random telephone survey to gather information from 4,780 persons ages 20 to 40 who had at least one immigrant parent. The study was designed to be a random probability sample of persons whose parents' national origin was Mexican, Chinese (from both the mainland and Taiwan), Filipino, Korean, Vietnamese, or Central Americans (Salvadoran or Guatemalan) residing in households with telephones in the greater Los Angeles area. Because of the centrality of the Mexican-origin group to the immigrant experience in Los Angeles, we oversampled the Mexican population. The sample included individuals other than these national groups who are not considered here, including U.S. whites, African Americans, other Latin Americans, other Asians, and Middle Easterners.

6. Of the 805 Latinos surveyed, 6 were missing values on this question. The percentages cited in the discussion here are based on the total of 799 who answered the question.

7. Rumbaut, "Origins and Destinies."

8. $\chi^2 = 8.349$; $p < .01$.

9. For a discussion of similar gains by the new second-generation children of immigrants more generally, see Bean and Stevens, *America's Newcomers and the Dynamics of Diversity*.

10. $\chi^2 = 29.819$; $p < .001$.

11. $\chi^2 = 16.444$; $p < .01$.

12. Portes and Bach, *Latin Journey*.

13. Brown, "Delayed Spatial Assimilation."

14. There were thirteen interviews with missing information on citizenship status, making the total of respondents to this question 794.

15. Of the 396 Anglos surveyed, one had a missing value on this variable.

16. Bean et al., "Chasing the American Dream"; Bean et al., "Pathways to Legal Status." These works are based on data collected by the IIMMLA project.

17. $\chi^2 = 435.134$; $p < .001$.

18. The IIMMLA project surveyed Mexican immigrants ($N = 125$), 1.5/second-generation Mexican Americans ($N = 844$), and third-plus-generation Mexican Americans ($N = 400$) in the greater Los Angeles area, from Ventura County to San Bernardino County.

19. Hakimzadeh and Cohn," English Usage among Hispanics in the United States."

20. $\chi^2 = 378.705$; $p < .001$.

21. $\chi^2 = 212.835$; $p < .001$.

22. $\chi^2 = 253.765$; $p < .001$.

23. Tatalovich, "Official English as Nativist Backlash."

24. Citrin, "Testing Huntington"; Portes and Rumbaut, *Legacies*; Portes and Schauffler, "Language Acquisition and Loss"; Rumbaut, Massey, and Bean, "Linguistic Life Expectancies"; Suro, *Strangers among Us.*

25. Appadurai, *Modernity at Large*; Inda and Rosaldo, *Anthropology of Globalization.*

26. $\chi^2 = 140.335; p < .001$.

27. For a discussion of intermarriage and integration, see Hollinger, "Amalgamation and Hypodescent."

28. The percentages of Latinos who claimed atheism, agnosticism, or no affiliation varied less across the generations: 6.6 percent in the first generation, 4.8 percent in the second generation, and 7.6 percent in the third-plus generation. Also expressing these preferences were 11.5 percent of the whites in the sample.

29. The change from Catholicism to other religions across Latino generations was statistically significant: $\chi^2 = 47.329; p < .001$.

30. The IIMMLA study found that among the Mexican-origin interviewees in the greater Los Angeles area, 86 percent of the first generation claimed to be Catholics, dropping to 68 percent in the second generation and to 45 percent in the third-plus generations.

31. Hondagneu-Sotelo, *Religion and Social Justice*; Menjívar, "Religion and Immigration"; Suro et al., *Changing Faiths.*

32. Schiller and Caglar, "'And Ye Shall Possess It.'"

33. According to the IIMMLA study cited above, 52.7 percent of first-generation Mexicans in the greater Los Angeles area attended a place of worship with all or mostly people of their own ethnic background, as did 45.3 percent of the 1.5- and second-generation Mexican Americans and only 23.8 percent of the third-plus-generation Mexican Americans.

34. For more on Latinos and civic engagement, see DeSipio, "Pressure of Perpetual Promise"; Zlolinski, *Janitors, Street Vendors and Activists*; and Zlolinski, "Political Mobilization and Activism."

35. A statistically significant difference ($\chi^2 = 27.809; p < .001$).

36. A statistically significant difference ($\chi^2 = 8.044; p < .05$).

37. A statistically significant difference ($\chi^2 = 10.108; p < .01$).

38. A statistically significant difference ($\chi^2 = 18.516; p < .001$).

39. A statistically significant difference ($\chi^2 = 10.372; p < .01$).

40. The difference is not statistically significant ($\chi^2 = 3.969$).

41. The difference across Latino generations is statistically significant ($\chi^2 = 26.161; p < .001$).

42. Putnam, *Bowling Alone.*

43. The increase in civic engagement across the path to citizenship is statistically significant ($\chi^2 = 31.913$; $p < .001$).

44. Waldinger, *Between Here and There*.

45. Aparicio, *Dominican Americans and the Politics of Empowerment*; Basch, Schiller, and Blanc, *Nations Unbound*; Levitt and Schiller, "Conceptualizing Simultaneity"; Menjívar, "Living in Two Worlds?"; R. Rouse, "Mexican Migration"; Schiller and Fouron, *Georges Woke Up Laughing*.

46. For an ethnography that shows the uses of digital technology among Oaxacans in Mexico, California, and Oregon, see Stephen, *Transborder Lives*.

47. Responses to these language questions varied along a five-point scale: Spanish only, mostly Spanish, both Spanish and English equally, mostly English, English only. Each respondent's answers to these questions were summed and then divided by 4 to arrive at the total score. The language assimilation variable had a Cronbach's alpha score of .87.

48. Marin et al., "Development of a Short Acculturation Scale."

49. For each yes answer, one additional value was added. For example, if interviewees had visited their parents' country of origin at least once, a score of 1 was added to their sum.

50. Similarly, transnational activities foster Chinese immigrant entrepreneurs in the Silicon Valley's involvement in the U.S. political arena. Wong, "Globalization and Citizenship."

51. Bean et al., "Pathways to Legal Status."

52. According to the National Immigration Law Center (http://www.nilc.org/immlawpolicy/DREAM/Dream001.htm), the Development, Relief, and Education for Alien Minors (DREAM) Act (S1545), introduced on July 31, 2003, provides a path to citizenship for 1.5-generation undocumented immigrants if they meet certain conditions. Under DREAM 2003, most students of good moral character who came to the United States before they were 16 years old and at least five years before the date of the bill's enactment would qualify for conditional permanent resident status upon acceptance to college, graduation from high school, or being awarded a GED. Students would not qualify for this relief if they had committed crimes, were a security risk, or were inadmissible or removable on certain other grounds. At the end of the conditional period, regular lawful permanent resident status would be granted if, during the conditional period, the immigrant had maintained good moral character, avoided lengthy trips abroad, and met at least one of the following three criteria: (1) graduated from a two-year college or a vocational college that meets certain criteria, or studied for at least two years toward a bachelor's or a higher degree; (2) served in the U.S. armed forces for at least two years; or (3) performed at least 910 hours of volunteer community service. The DREAM Act was reintroduced in the Senate on

November 18, 2005, and it passed the Senate Judiciary Committee on March 27, 2006. However, Congress failed to pass immigration reform, including the DREAM Act, in either 2006 or 2007, and has yet to do so as of 2012.

53. Daniels, *Coming to America*.

54. For an analysis of the integration of the children of immigrants into New York City and a critique of segmented assimilation theory, see Kasinitz et al., *Inheriting the City*. This study also finds that despite expectations as suggested by segmented assimilation, the children of immigrants in New York City are integrating rapidly and experiencing upward mobility. See also Portes and Rumbaut, *Legacies*; and Rumbaut, "Assimilation and Its Discontents."

Chapter 3

1. Longley, "U.S. Population to Hit 300 Million." The U.S. Census Bureau's POP-Clock Projection for the resident population of the United States can be seen at http://www.census.gov/population/www/popclockus.html.

2. S. Roberts, "Come October."

3. Ibid.

4. One has only to Google "300 million population" to get an array of stories on this event from mainstream media such as ABC, CBS, NBC, National Public Radio, MSNBC, Fox News, the daily newspapers, and many other sources, including blogs and newsletters. Some examples are Associated Press, "U.S. Population to Hit 300 Million"; Harden, "America's Population Set to Top 300 Million"; O'Sullivan, "US Copes with Growing Population"; Potter, "America Approaches 300 Million Population"; D. Smith, "Countdown to 300 Million"; and Thomas, "Stopping the Census Clock."

5. Harden, "America's Population Set to Top 300 Million."

6. Mitchell, *Coyote Waits*.

7. Historical accounts often present immigrant women struggling against public attitudes and stereotypes. For example, see Gabaccia, *From the Other Side*; and Ruiz, *From Out of the Shadows*.

8. Gerstle, "Immigrant as Threat"; Gould, *Mismeasure of Man*; Marks, *What It Means to Be 98% Chimpanzee*; D. E. Roberts, "Who May Give Birth to Citizens?"

9. Gardner, *Qualities of a Citizen*; Luibheid, *Entry Denied*.

10. Chavez, "Glass Half Empty"; Chavez, "Immigration Reform and Nativism"; Chock, "No New Women"; Gutiérrez, "Racial Politics of Reproduction"; Hondagneu-Sotelo, "Women and Children First"; Inda, "Biopower"; T. D. Wilson, "Anti-Immigrant Sentiment"; Zavella, "'Playing with Fire'"; Zavella, "Tables Are Turned."

11. Chavez, *Covering Immigration*. See also Fregoso, *MeXicana Encounters*, especially the chapter "Haunted by Miscegenation," for an analysis of Latinas' racialized sexuality, particularly in films.

12. For an analysis of metaphors of women and nation, see Probyn, "Bloody Metaphors."

13. For a discussion of immigrants as threats and the construction of citizens in relation to sexual politics, see Alexander, *Pedagogies of Crossing.*

14. For a discussion of the discourse surrounding Proposition 187, see Ono and Sloop, *Shifting Borders.*

15. Kadetsky, "'Save Our State' Initiative."

16. Lesher and McDonnell, "Wilson Calls Halt."

17. Fix and Passel, *Trends.*

18. Fraser and Gordon, "Genealogy of *Dependency.*"

19. This examination builds upon my earlier work on this topic: Chavez, *Covering Immigration*; Chavez, "Glass Half Empty"; Chavez, "Immigration Reform and Nativism."

20. Ginsburg and Rapp, "Politics of Reproduction."

21. Abramovitz, "Welfare Reform"; Bhuyan, "Production of the 'Battered Immigrant'"; Horn, *Social Bodies*; Lock and Kaufert, *Pragmatic Women.*

22. Ginsburg and Rapp, "Politics of Reproduction," 314.

23. For a thorough discussion of the racial politics of Latina reproduction, see Gutiérrez, "Racial Politics of Reproduction."

24. Colen, "'Housekeeping' for the Green Card."

25. Ginsburg and Rapp, *Conceiving the New World Order*, 3. For a discussion of multilayered citizenship from a feminist perspective, see Yuval-Davis, "'Multi-Layered Citizen.'"

26. Fraser and Gordon, "Genealogy of *Dependency.*" See also Rank, *Living on the Edge.*

27. D. E. Roberts, *Killing the Black Body*, 3.

28. Ibid., 7.

29. Link, "Fanatics, Fundamentalists," 40.

30. Rabinow and Rose, "Biopower Today."

31. Vance, "Anthropology Rediscovers Sexuality," 876. For a discussion of research on transnationalism and sexuality from a feminist theoretical framework, see Grewal and Kaplan, "Global Identities."

32. Glenn, "Social Constructions of Mothering." For a discussion of sexuality in relation to migrant farm labor, see X. Castaneda and Zavella, "Changing Constructions."

33. For an in-depth discussion of Latina reproduction in relation to control of immigration from Mexico, see T. D. Wilson, "Anti-Immigrant Sentiment."

34. For more on how Latinas have been objectified for their sexuality and fecundity, see Fregoso, *MeXicana Encounters*; Negrón-Muntaner, "Jennifer's Butt"; C. E. Rodriguez, *Latin Looks*; Zavella, "'Playing with Fire.'"

35. Ehlers, "Debunking Marianismo."

36. Salladay, "Governor's Candid Moments."

37. Silverstein, "Racist Video Game Incites Anger."

38. Branson, "Racist Video Game Targets Immigrants." Neo-Nazi websites played a large role in making the *Border Patrol* game available; see Anti-Defamation League, "Extremists Declare 'Open Season.'"

39. Gutiérrez, "Racial Politics of Reproduction."

40. Amaro, "Women in the Mexican-American Community," 6.

41. For research on China's one-child policy, see Greenhalgh and Winckler, *Governing China's Population*. For research on sterilization of Latinas, see Lopez, "An Ethnography"; Vélez-Ibáñez, "Non-Consenting Sterilization"; Vélez-Ibáñez, "Se me acabó la canción."

42. Ehrlich, *Population Bomb*, 45.

43. Ibid., 140–41.

44. *U.S. News and World Report*, "How Millions Sneak into U.S."

45. Alvirez and Bean, "Mexican American Family," 271.

46. Ibid., 280–81.

47. Ehrlich, Bilderback, and Ehrlich, *Golden Door*.

48. Ibid., 235.

49. Ibid., 268.

50. Ibid., 236 (emphasis in the original).

51. For a discussion of the infinityline as a visual metaphor for quantity, see Chavez, *Covering Immigration*.

52. Conniff, "War on Aliens."

53. Otto Santa Ana refers to this as a "brown tide rising." Santa Ana, *Brown Tide Rising*.

54. Henry, "Beyond the Melting Pot."

55. Brimelow, "Time to Rethink Immigration?"

56. Hanson, *Mexifornia*, 53.

57. Geyer, *Americans No More*, 304.

58. Huntington, "Hispanic Challenge."

59. Eberstadt, "Population Implosion."

60. Armbruster, "Gibson."

61. For age information in the U.S. Census, see U.S. Census Bureau, *State and County Quickfacts*. In addition, the Orange County Health Care Agency estimates that the fertility rate, in 2002, was about 92 births per 1,000 Hispanic females and about 50 births per 1,000 white females. County of Orange Health Care Agency, *2002 Birth Outcomes Fact Sheet*.

62. Massey, *Return to Aztlan*; Massey et al., *Worlds in Motion*; Piore, *Birds of Passage*.

63. Richard Alba and Hui-shien Tsao have recently argued that the retirement of large numbers of U.S. baby boomers will free up jobs for immigrants and the children of immigrants, thus allowing more economic mobility with less social friction. Alba and Tsao, "Connecting Past, Present and Future."

64. The Population Reference Bureau defines total fertility rate as the average number of children a woman would have, assuming that current age-specific birthrates remain constant throughout her childbearing years (usually considered to be ages 15 to 49).

65. For more on foreign-born in these countries, see Kashiwazaki and Akaha, "Japanese Immigration Policy"; Muenz, "Europe."

66. Checa, Arjona, and Checa, *La integración social de los inmigrados.*

67. Kashiwazaki and Akaha, "Japanese Immigration Policy."

68. Arifin, "Population, Policies and Programmes"; Chivers, "Russians Busy Making Shrouds"; French, "Japan Fails to Cope"; Mitton, *Endangered Species*; Murphy, "EU's Baby Blues"; *Newsweek*, "Perspectives"; *The Telegraph*, "Where Have All the Bambini Gone?"

69. Joyce, "Missing."

70. Bean, Swicegood, and Berg, "Mexican-Origin Fertility."

71. Marchi and Guendelman, "Gender Differences."

72. Ibid., 210.

73. Amaro, "Women in the Mexican-American Community."

74. Stroup-Benham and Trevino, "Reproductive Characteristics."

75. Browner, "Politics of Reproduction."

76. Hirsch, "Migration, Modernity, and Mexican Marriage." For 1990, see CONAPO, "[Mexican] National Fertility Rates"; and Zúñiga, Zubieta, and Araya, "Cuadernos de salud reproductiva." See also Gonzalez-Lopez, *Erotic Journeys*, 28.

77. Population Reference Bureau, *World Population Data Sheet.*

78. CONAPO, "[Mexican] National Fertility Rates."

79. Hirsch, *Courtship after Marriage*; Hirsch, "Migration, Modernity, and Mexican Marriage."

Chapter 4

1. Chavez et al., "Undocumented Immigrants in Orange County, California"; Chavez et al., "Beliefs Matter"; Hubbell et al., "Beliefs about Sexual Behavior"; Hubbell et al., "Influence of Knowledge and Attitudes."

2. See Chapter 2 for information on the methods used in the 2006 study. In the early 1990s study, the Field Research Corporation in San Francisco conducted the telephone survey from September 1992 to March 1993. This survey used a cross-sectional sample of random-digit telephone listings to identify eligible subjects. Both listed and unlisted numbers were included, avoiding potential bias due to exclusion

of households with unlisted numbers (Survey Sampling Inc., *Statistical Analysis of Sample*). The cooperation rate for the early 1990s study was 78.5 percent. Both surveys randomly selected both households and respondents within households—the woman 18 years or older who had the most recent birthday. We pilot-tested the questionnaire, tested its content validity, and translated it from English to Spanish and back to English. Telephone survey findings may not be generalizable to families without telephones. In Orange County, however, approximately 94 percent of Latinos and 99 percent of whites have telephones (see California State Census Data Center, "1990 Census"). Another potential limitation of telephone surveys is hard-to-reach members of the population, the homeless, and those engaged in street-corner employment and migrant agricultural labor. This may be more of a bias, however, for male than female Latinas, who are less likely to be homeless or to seek day work by standing on street corners (see Chavez, *Shadowed Lives*).

3. Marin et al., "Development of a Short Acculturation Scale."

4. Solis et al., "Acculturation."

5. t-value = −3.71; $p < .001$.

6. t-value = 0.63; $p = .530$.

7. t-value = −5.07; $p < .001$.

8. S. M. Harvey et al., "Context and Meaning."

9. t-value = 8.78; $p < .001$.

10. t-value = 1.61; $p = .11$.

11. t-value = 10.36; $p < .001$.

12. t-value = 6.78; $p < .001$.

13. t-value = 4.11; $p < .001$.

14. t-value = 6.90; $p < .001$.

15. $\chi^2 = 5.504$; $p < .05$.

16. $\chi^2 = 0.098$.

17. Bean, Swicegood, and Berg, "Mexican-Origin Fertility."

18. t-value = −2.14; $p = .033$.

19. t-value = 0.30; $p = .768$.

20. t-value = −1.08; $p = .280$.

21. Bean, Swicegood, and Berg, "Mexican-Origin Fertility."

22. D. E. Roberts, "Who May Give Birth to Citizens?" 8.

23. This is not to minimize the issue of teenage pregnancies. Latinas have relatively more teen births than Anglo and non-Hispanic African Americans, but here too, there has been a decline. Pregnancy rates for black and white teenagers between 15 and 19 years of age fell 23 and 26 percent, respectively, from 1990 to 1997. Latina teen pregnancy rates began falling only in 1994, but they fell 11 percent from that time to 1997. Ventura et al., "Trends in Pregnancy Rates." These data do not indicate marital

status, the father's involvement, or extended family relations for the mother and child, important factors when considering life opportunities.

24. Chavez, "Glass Half Empty"; Chavez, "Immigration Reform and Nativism."

25. Kelley, "California Cuts Its Population Projections." See also Pitkin and Myers, "Generational Projections of the California Population by Nativity and Year of Immigrant Arrival."

26. Colon, "Mexican Migration to Drop"; Martin, "Mexico-U.S. Migration."

27. Parrado and Morgan, "Intergenerational Fertility."

28. Ibid., 26–27.

29. Zitner, "Nation's Birthrate Drops."

Chapter 5

1. For an anthropological study of organ transplant recipients, clinical specialists, and surviving kin of deceased organ donors, see Sharp, *Strange Harvest*.

2. Lai, Saldinger, and Spruyt, *Healing Health Care*.

3. Bixler, "Immigrant Boy Gets Kidney Transplant."

4. Bickel and Martinez, "Girl Needs Kidney Transplant."

5. Wang, "Stuck in the Middle."

6. *Saturday Post*, "Madeeha Faryad's Story."

7. Frith, "Immigration." The film *Dirty Pretty Things* captures the plight of undocumented immigrants in Britain, who sometimes resort to selling organs for money or visas.

8. Danna, "Undocumented Immigrants Fight for Lifesaving Liver Transplants."

9. Bernstein, "For Illegal Immigrant, Line Is Drawn at Transplant."

10. Wailoo, Livingston, and Guarnaccia, *Death Retold*.

11. Grady, "Donor Mix-up."

12. Villarosa, "Jesica Was One of 80,000."

13. Archibold, "Girl in Transplant Mix-up Dies."

14. Chavez, "Imagining the Nation."

15. Bickel and Martinez, "Girl Needs Kidney Transplant."

16. The issue of organs for immigrants is not the only controversy related to organ transplants. For example, a proposal in South Carolina to allow inmates to trade an organ for consideration of an early release from prison has also received critical attention. Jarvie, "Inmates Could Trade an Organ."

17. For an analysis of the importance of metaphors in our lives, see Lakoff and Johnson, *Metaphors We Live By*.

18. For examples of the face metaphor for the nation, see the covers of *U.S. News and World Report*, February 20, 1978; *Time*, July 8, 1985, and October 1993 (special issue); and *National Review*, February 21, 1994.

19. Borneman, "Emigres as Bullets"; Inda, "Foreign Bodies"; Kraut, *Silent Travelers*; Shah, *Contagious Divides*.

20. The metaphor of the body of the nation digesting immigrants has had surprising longevity. In 1880 the *New York Times* editorialized, "There is a limit to our powers of assimilation and when it is exceeded the country suffers from something very like indigestion." Simon, *Public Opinion and the Immigrant*, 186. One hundred and twelve years later, Peter Brimelow discussed assimilation as a process of "swallowing and digesting" immigrant groups. Brimelow, "Time to Rethink Immigration?"

21. That which is excreted from the body becomes a polluting force, much like excrement. As Judith Butler has noted, "the boundary of the body as well as the distinction between internal and external is established through the ejection and transvaluation of something originally part of identity into a defiling otherness." Butler, *Gender Trouble*, 170.

22. Ibid.

23. I am reminded here of Walter Benjamin's apt observation: "History dissolves into images." Benjamin, *Illuminations*.

24. Barthes, *Mythologies*.

25. K. J. Wilson, "Transplant Details Raise Cruel Questions."

26. Carnell, "Organ Donation."

27. Briggs and Hallin, "Biocommunicability"; Dunn, Aragones, and Shivers, "Recent Mexican Migration"; Ong, *Buddha Is Hiding*; Ong, "Making the Biopolitical Subject"; Rocco, "Transforming Citizenship"; Sjoberg, Gill, and Williams, "Sociology of Human Rights."

28. Farmer, *Pathologies of Power*.

29. Petryna, *Life Exposed*. See also Rose and Novas, "Biological Citizenship."

30. Chavez, "Outside the Imagined Community."

31. *Border Alert*, "Girl's Death Exposes Transplant Tragedy."

32. Carnell, "Organ Donation."

33. Ibid.

34. *Siskind's Immigration Bulletin*, "Duke Case Raises Questions."

35. Gupta, "Immigrants and Organ Sharing."

36. Danna, "Undocumented Immigrants Fight for Lifesaving Liver Transplants."

37. Butler, *Bodies That Matter*, 2.

38. Chavez, *Covering Immigration*.

39. Hoffman, "Access to Health Care," 242. See also Buescher, "Review of Available Data."

40. Larrubia, "Delivering Dual Benefits."

41. Berk et al., "Health Care Use."

42. Hoffman, "Access to Health Care," 238.

43. Federation for American Immigration Reform, "Immigration Policies."

44. Ibid.

45. For Congressman Rohrabacher's views on health care reform, go to http://rohrabacher.house.gov/Issues/Issue/?IssueID=5033.

46. Berk et al., "Health Care Use." Moreover, new receiving states, such as Georgia, typically offer less access to medical and other social services than do California and New York. See Yang and Wallace, *Expansion of Health Insurance in California.*

47. Malkin, "America."

48. Berk et al., "Health Care Use."

49. In a 2002 survey of hospitals by the National Association of Counties, thirty-seven of forty-three hospitals reported an increase in uncompensated health care costs, with most (67 percent) citing immigrants as a reason. Bixler, "Illegal, Uninsured . . . but Alive."

50. M. A. Rodriguez, Ward, and Perez-Stable, "Breast and Cervical Cancer Screening."

51. Farmer, *Pathologies of Power.*

52. Dumenil and Levy, *Capital Resurgent*; D. Harvey, *Brief History of Neoliberalism.*

53. D. Harvey, *Brief History of Neoliberalism.*

54. Goode and Maskovsky, *New Poverty Studies.*

55. D. Harvey, *Brief History of Neoliberalism.* How low-income and poor people have managed under neoliberal policies has been a recent concern of anthropologists; see Goode and Maskovsky, *New Poverty Studies*; and Lyon-Callo, *Inequality, Poverty, and Neoliberal Governance.*

56. Chavez, "Immigration and Medical Anthropology"; Chavez, "Immigration Reform and Nativism"; Inda, *Targeting Immigrants*; Zavella, "Tables Are Turned."

57. Quotes are from an earlier study by the author. See Chavez, "Wasting Away in Neoliberal-ville"; and Chavez et al., "Models of Cancer Risk Factors."

58. Nguyen and Peschard, "Anthropology, Inequality and Disease," 447.

59. Cunningham, "What Accounts for Differences?"

60. S. A. Mohanty et al., "Health Expenditures."

61. Ortega et al., "Health Care Access."

62. Griffith, "Rural Industry."

63. Migration Policy Institute, "Fact Sheet on the Foreign Born."

64. Ibid.

65. Ibid.

66. Buescher, "Review of Available Data," 67.

67. Ibid., 97.

68. Pressley, "Hispanic Immigration Boom Rattles South."

69. Schmitt, "Pockets of Protest."

70. For a discussion of how children become symbols for organ transplantation and other innovative medical treatments, see C. Rouse, "Jesica Speaks?"; and Sharp, "Babes and Baboons."

71. For example, Brimelow, "That Santillan Saga"; and K. J. Wilson, "Transplant Details Raise Cruel Questions."

72. The site's address is http://www.geocities.com/americanorgans (accessed May 4, 2004).

73. It is important to observe here that this discourse of citizen/foreigner/illegal immigrant masks a racial discourse. Organ transplantation combines body parts from different people across crucial lines of difference. Though not explicit in this discourse on immigration, this transmogrification may be an underlying subtext fueling racial/ethnic tensions in the Santillan case. For a discussion of the issue of race in transplants, see Lederer, "Tucker's Heart." See also Briggs, "Communicability, Racial Discourse, and Disease."

74. Headrick and Cheng, "Some Link Citizenship, Transplants."

75. Hall, "Spectacle of the 'Other,'" 258.

76. Foucault, *Order of Things*, xxiv.

77. Morgan et al., "America's Angel or Thieving Immigrant?"

78. See Foucault's discussion of biopower in his *Discipline and Punish*, 25–31, and his discussion of "biopolitics" and "biopower" in his *History of Sexuality*, 139–41. See also Rabinow and Rose, "Biopower Today."

79. Paul Rabinow and Nikolas Rose provide a sharper definition to Foucault's rather vague concept of "biopolitics": "We can use the term 'biopolitics' to embrace all the specific strategies and contestations over problematizations of collective human vitality, morbidity and mortality; over the forms of knowledge, regimes of authority and practices of intervention that are desirable, legitimate and efficacious." Rabinow and Rose, "Biopower Today," 197.

80. See Inda, *Targeting Immigrants*; and Petryna, *Life Exposed*.

81. Vedantam, "U.S. Citizens Get More Organs."

82. Headrick and Cheng, "Some Link Citizenship, Transplants."

83. Kaushik Sunder Rajan defines surplus health as "the market value that resides for pharmaceutical companies in the potential for future illness in those who might one day consume their drugs (which includes anyone with the buying power to constitute a market for therapeutics)." He adds, "As with surplus value, which, for [Karl] Marx, is not equivalent to material profit, but rather the abstraction that animates the wage- and profit-mediated social interaction between worker and capitalist, surplus health is the animating abstraction of pharmaceutical risk logic." Rajan, "Experimental Values"; Rajan, *Biocapital*. See also Dumit, "Drugs, Algorithms, Markets and Surplus Health."

84. Rose and Novas go on to say, "The bodies and vitality of individual and collective subjects have long had a value that is as much economic as political—or, rather, that is both economic and political." Rose and Novas, "Biological Citizenship," 454.

85. Mauss, *Gift*.

86. Porter, "Illegal Immigrants."

87. Gupta, "Immigrants and Organ Sharing."

88. For a discussion related to ethics and the Jesica Santillan case, see Meslin, Salmon, and Eberl, "Eligibility for Organ Transplantation." For a discussion of the international trade in organs, see Scheper-Hughes, "Global Traffic in Human Organs."

89. Farmer, *Pathologies of Power*.

90. DeVille, "Parties to the Social Contract?"; Dunn, Aragones, and Shivers, "Recent Mexican Migration"; Sjoberg, Gill, and Williams, "Sociology of Human Rights."

91. Agamben, *Homo Sacer*, 126.

92. Ong, *Buddha Is Hiding*.

Chapter 6

1. LoMonaco, "Minutemen Gather in Tombstone."

2. Andreas, *Border Games*; Andreas, "U.S. Immigration Control Offensive"; Dunn, *Militarization of the Border*; Dunn, "Military Collaboration."

3. Massey, Durand, and Malone, *Beyond Smoke and Mirrors*.

4. Stephen, *Transborder Lives*, 29–31.

5. Dunn, "Military Collaboration."

6. Strohm, "Activists to Flock to Border."

7. Ibid.

8. Minuteman Project website at http://minutemanproject.com/Aboutmmp .html.

9. Kertzer, *Ritual, Politics, and Power*.

10. Enloe, *Maneuvers*.

11. Argetsinger, "Immigration Opponents."

12. Comaroff and Comaroff, "Figuring Crime," 212.

13. Inda, *Targeting Immigrants*.

14. *Democracy Now!* "Vigilantes or Civilian Border Patrol?"

15. Strohm, "Activists to Flock to Border."

16. Ibid.

17. J. F. Smith and Chen, "Bush to Weigh Residency."

18. Kelly, "Border Watchers Capture Their Prey."

19. Marizco, "Abusive Acts."

20. Strohm, "Activists to Flock to Border."

21. Ibid.

22. Alonso-Zaldivar, "U.S. to Bolster Arizona Border Security."

23. Argetsinger, "Immigration Opponents."

24. Alonso-Zaldivar, "U.S. to Bolster Arizona Border Security."

25. LoMonaco, "Minutemen Gather in Tombstone."

26. Kelly, "Citizens Border Patrols Hurry Up."

27. Talev, "Minuteman Volunteers Give Motives."

28. Riley, "1,000 Activists"; Rotstein, "Volunteer Border Watchers Cause Concern."

29. Grillo, "Minute Patrol Off to a Slow Start."

30. Delson, "Profile of James Gilchrist."

31. Kelly, "Minutemen Prepare to Lay Down the Law."

32. Talev, "Minuteman Volunteers Give Motives."

33. Ibid.

34. Kelly, "Citizens Border Patrols Hurry Up."

35. Ngai, *Impossible Subjects.*

36. Utley, *Lone Star Justice.*

37. Webb, *Texas Rangers.*

38. G. C. Anderson, *Conquest of Texas.*

39. Kelly, "Border Watchers Capture Their Prey."

40. Ibid.

41. Ibid.

42. Levine, "Border Guard Shift Questioned."

43. Ibid.

44. Coronado, "Wary Groups in Border Watch."

45. Ibid.

46. Richard, "Buzz on the Border."

47. Kelly, "Border Watchers Capture Their Prey."

48. Coronado, "Minutemen Quit Patrol Early."

49. Carroll, "Border Watch to Widen"; Seper, "Border Patrols Inspire Imitation."

50. Sample, "Governor Talks of Closing Mexico Border."

51. Gaouette, "Border Troubles Divide U.S., States."

52. Pasco and Weikel, "OC Race a Border Skirmish."

53. Pasco, "Campbell Wins Seat."

54. Jim Gilchrist for Congress, "Truth about John Campbell and Illegal Immigration," http://www.jimgilchrist.com/article.php?id=119 (accessed December 6, 2005).

55. Barabak and Pasco, "Election as Immigration Bellwether."

56. Ibid.

57. Rosaldo, "Cultural Citizenship, Inequality, and Multiculturalism."

58. For discussion of surveillance and power in relation to the sanctuary movement, which also occurred in Arizona, see Coutin, *Culture of Protest.*

59. Foucault, *Discipline and Punish.*

60. Ibid., 48–49.

61. Ibid., 49.

62. Richard, "Buzz on the Border."

63. Wood, "Minutemen's Message on Immigration."

64. From the Minuteman Salsa website at http://www.minutemansalsa.com/.

65. A. Gupta and Ferguson, "Beyond 'Culture.' "

66. Appadurai, *Modernity at Large*; Inda and Rosaldo, *Anthropology of Globalization*.

67. Tsuda, *Strangers in the Ethnic Homeland*, 358.

68. Castells, *Power of Identity*, 27.

69. Coutin, "Being En Route."

70. Butler, *Bodies That Matter*; Cassell, "Doing Gender, Doing Surgery."

71. Puwar, *Space Invaders*.

72. Delson, "Minuteman Meets His Hour of Crisis"; Holthouse, "Minute Mess."

73. Holthouse, "Dangerous Levels of Overlap."

74. Friedersdorf, "What the Minuteman Project Taught Its Founder."

75. Beirich, "Year in Nativism."

76. Schabner, "Border Vigilante Shawna Forde Sentenced to Death."

77. Ricker, "Gaxiola Sentenced to Life in Arivaca Shootings"; Schabner, "Border Vigilante Shawna Forde Sentenced to Death"; Smith, "Bush Sentenced to Die in Arivaca Killings."

78. Goodwin, "End of the Minutemen."

79. Ibid.

80. Holthouse, "Dangerous Levels of Overlap."

81. Ibid.

82. Goodwin, "End of the Minutemen."

Chapter 7

1. For more on the immigrant marches, see Barreto et al., "Mobilization, Participation, and Solidaridad"; Hing and Johnson, "Immigrant Rights Marches of 2006"; and Voss and Bloemraad, *Rallying for Immigrant Rights*.

2. Ong, "Cultural Citizenship as Subject-Making," 740.

3. Gaouette, "Bush Signs Fence Bill."

4. Chavez, *Covering Immigration*; Kolsto, "National Symbols."

5. Kertzer, *Ritual, Politics, and Power*, 6.

6. Ibid., 7.

7. Kertzer, *Politics and Symbols*, 6.

8. Ibid.

9. Ibid.

10. Watanabe, "Immigrants Gain Pulpit."

11. Ibid.

12. Ibid.

13. Ibid.

14. Watanabe, "Catholic Leaders."

15. Groves, "Day-Labor Group Starts Trek."

16. Ibid.

17. Bernstein, "In the Streets"; Newbart and Thomas, "In Overwhelming Display, Immigrants Protest Bill."

18. Newbart and Thomas, "In Overwhelming Display."

19. Ibid.

20. Ibid.

21. Ibid.

22. Avila and Olivo, "Immigration Supporters, Foes View Chicago March."

23. For research on the relationship between Spanish-language media and Latino attitudes toward immigration, see Abrajano and Singh, "Examining the Link."

24. Avila, "Shooting for a Big Turnout."

25. Avila and Olivo, "Immigration Supporters, Foes View Chicago March."

26. Keller and Gorman, "High School Students Leave School."

27. Leal and McDonald, "4,700 O.C. Students Walk Out."

28. Keller and Gorman, "High School Students Leave School."

29. For a discussion of social citizenship as a function of contributions to society, see Marshall, "Citizenship and Social Class."

30. Friedman, "Immigrant Rights Activists Hopeful."

31. Leal and Sforza, "Issue May Bring More Latino Activism."

32. Dobuzinskis, "Thousands Rally for UFW March."

33. Aguila, "Protesters Turn to Internet"; Cho and Gorman, "Immigration Debate"; Gold, "Student Protests Echo the '60s"; Leal and McDonald, "4,700 O.C. Students Walk Out."

34. Marcucci, "Thousands in Bay Area Protest."

35. Bunis, "Debate with No Clear Lines"; Leal and McDonald, "4,700 O.C. Students Walk Out."

36. Suarez and Kennedy, "L.A.'s Top Officers Vow Crackdown."

37. Gorman, "Flag's Meaning."

38. Ibid.

39. G. Miller, "Immigration Activists on March Again."

40. Gorman, "Flag's Meaning."

41. Rutten, "Lou Dobbs Is All Bully and Bluster."

42. Goffard, Delson, and Covarrubias, "Small, Orderly Immigration Rally in O.C."

43. G. Miller, "Immigration Activists on March Again."

44. An extensive database on the immigrant marches beginning on April 10, 2006, was put together by Xóchitl Bada, Jonathan Fox, Elvia Zazueta, and Ingrid García and is available on the Wilson Center website at http://www.wilsoncenter.org/news/docs/Spring%202006%20Protests.xls.

45. G. Miller, "Immigration Activists on March Again."

46. Ibid.

47. Gorman, "Flag's Meaning"; Prengaman, "Across California, Thousands March."

48. Prengaman, "Across California, Thousands March."

49. Levitt and Schiller, "Conceptualizing Simultaneity," 9.

50. Oppenheimer, "'Transnational Citizens' Emerge."

51. Ibid.

52. http://www.minutemanproject.com/news/?p=16 (accessed April 18, 2006).

53. Ibid.

54. http://www.minutemanproject.com/news/?p=19 (accessed April 18, 2006).

55. Reynolds and Fiore, "Across the U.S., 'We Are America.'"

56. Ibid.

57. Fiore, "Job Can Wait."

58. Reynolds and Fiore, "Across the U.S., 'We Are America.'"

59. Ibid.

60. Fiore, "Job Can Wait."

61. Reynolds, "Call to Shed 'Poison Pill' Immigration Rule."

62. Reynolds and Fiore, "Across the U.S., 'We Are America.'"

63. Brownstein, "Most Back Tighter Border."

64. Becerra and Blankstein, "L.A. Authorities Brace for Marches."

65. Ibid.; Reynolds, "Bush Asks Immigrants."

66. Watanabe, Gorman, and Cleeland, "National Boycott Plans Creating Divide."

67. Archibold, "Immigrants Take to U.S. Streets."

68. Ibid.; Gorman, Miller, and Landsberg, "Marchers Fill L.A. Streets."

69. Archibold, "Immigrants Take to U.S. Streets."

70. Gorman, Miller, and Landsberg, "Marchers Fill L.A. Streets."

71. *Los Angeles Times*, "Primero de Mayo."

72. *New York Times*, "They Are America."

73. Buchanan, *State of Emergency*, 125.

74. Archibold, "Immigrants Take to U.S. Streets."

75. Montgomery, "Anthem's Discordant Notes."

76. Wides-Munoz, "Spanish Version of 'Star-Spangled Banner.'"

77. Carcamo, "Spanish Anthem Adds Fuel to Debate."

78. Chavez, *Covering Immigration*; Kertzer, *Politics and Symbols*.

79. Translation and additional lyrics by Adam Kidron and Eduardo Reyes.

80. Some examples of the controversy that may be found online include "Spanish Version of 'Star-Spangled Banner' Draws Protests," http://www.foxnews.com/story/0,2933,193533,00.html; "Bush: Sing National Anthem In English," http://www.cbsnews.com/stories/2006/04/28/entertainment/main1555938.shtml; "Whose National Anthem?" by Michelle Malkin, http://michellemalkin.com/archives/005056.htm; and "Bush Enters Anthem Fight on Language," by Jim Rutenberg, http://www.nytimes.com/2006/04/29/washington/29bush.html?ex=1303963200&en=b5cdcbf5129c5d6e&ei=5088&partner=rssnyt&emc=rss.

81. Carcamo, "Spanish Anthem Adds Fuel to Debate."

82. Montgomery, "Anthem's Discordant Notes."

83. Ibid.

84. Rutenberg, "Bush Enters Anthem Fight"; Wides-Munoz, "Spanish Version of 'Star-Spangled Banner.'"

85. Wides-Munoz, "Spanish Version of 'Star-Spangled Banner.'"

86. Shaffer and Coombs, "Our Discordant Anthem."

87. Baker, "Administration Is Singing More Than One Tune."

88. Ibid.

89. "So Long, Texas—Hello, Mexico!" Rita W. Jones, author/composer; performed by Johnny Tex and the Texicans. Copyright 2006, Rita Jones Music, Inc.—ASCAP, 308 Longhorn Pkwy., Axtell, TX 76624, all rights reserved. Released on Texas Star Records, http://www.johnnytex.com. The song was cited on the Lou Dobbs website: http://edition.cnn.com/CNN/Programs/lou.dobbs.tonight/.

90. Amaya, "Performing Acculturation."

91. Lyon-Callo, *Inequality, Poverty, and Neoliberal Governance*.

92. Calavita, *California's "Employer Sanctions"*; Calavita, "New Politics of Immigration."

93. Rabinow and Rose, "Biopower Today," 197. The full quote is as follows: "[Biopower includes] modes of subjectification, through which individuals are brought to work on themselves, under certain forms of authority, in relation to truth discourses, by means of practices of the self, in the names of their own life or health, that of their family or some other collectivity, or indeed in the name of the life or health of the population as a whole."

94. Ong, *Neoliberalism as Exception*, 6.

Chapter 8

1. *Huffington Post*, "Alamo Heights Basketball Fans Reprimanded."

2. Boren, "NCAA Tournament: Southern Mississippi Apologizes."

3. Portes and Rumbaut, *Legacies*; Rumbaut, "Ages, Life Stages, and Generational Cohorts."

4. Passel and Cohn, *Portrait of Unauthorized Immigrants in the United States*. In comparison, there are about 120,000 undocumented migrant children in the United Kingdom, where their plight has not received much public attention; see Sigona and Hughes, *No Way Out, No Way In*.

5. Passel, Capps, and Fix, *Undocumented Immigrants: Facts and Figures*.

6. Bean et al., *Chasing the American Dream*.

7. Bunis and Garcia. "New Illegal-Immigration Law Casts Too Wide a Net."

8. Coutin, *Nations of Emigrants*, 9. See also Coutin, "Confined Within"; and Menjívar, "Power of the Law."

9. For more on subjectivity and immigrants, see Coutin, *Legalizing Moves*; De Genova, "Migrant 'Illegality' and Deportability"; Gonzales and Chavez, "'Awakening to a Nightmare'"; Menjívar, "Liminal Legality"; Suárez-Navaz, *Rebordering the Mediterranean*; and Willen, "Toward a Critical Phenomenology of 'Illegality.'"

10. For a discussion of the condition of abjectivity in relation to illegality, see Willen, "Toward a Critical Phenomenology of 'Illegality.'" See also Butler, *Gender Trouble*, 169–70; and Gonzales and Chavez, "'Awakening to a Nightmare.'"

11. *American Heritage Dictionary of the English Language*, 4th ed., s.v. "abject."

12. Butler, *Gender Trouble*, 169.

13. Chavez, "Outside the Imagined Community"; Chavez, *Latino Threat*, 115–16.

14. This is more than the 10 percent of undocumented high school graduates who enroll in college nationwide, according to Fortuny, Capps, and Passel, *Characteristics of Unauthorized Immigrants*. The IMMLA study interviewed 70 1.5-generation undocumented Latinos, 398 legally resident Latinos, 751 second-generation Latinos, and 401 third-plus-generation Latinos.

15. After 2001, according to the National Immigration Law Center, the Development, Relief, and Education for Alien Minors (DREAM) Act (S1545) was introduced on July 31, 2003, and was reintroduced in the Senate on November 18, 2005. It passed the Senate Judiciary Committee on March 27, 2006. However, Congress failed to pass immigration reform, and with it the Dream Act, in either 2006 or 2007. http://www.nilc.org/immlawpolicy/DREAM/Dream001.htm. It is still under consideration in Congress.

16. Abrego, "Legal Consciousness of Undocumented Latinos"; Abrego, "'I Can't Go to College Because I Don't Have Papers'"; Gonzales, "Left Out but Not Shut Down"; Negrón-Gonzales, "Hegemony, Ideology and Oppositional Consciousness"; Olivas, "Political Economy of the DREAM Act."

17. Reston, "California Dream Act Signed into Law."

18. Wolgin and Edelstein. "Keeping the DREAM Alive."

19. Batalova and McHugh, "DREAM vs. Reality."

20. For a list of DREAM Act–related sites, see http://www.google.com/maps/ms?ie=UTF8&source=embed&oe=UTF8&msa=0&msid=104184449682652234459.00 0467fe552f4b837d305.

21. Posters seen at the 2008 mock graduation ceremony in Washington, D.C.: http://www.globalvisas.com/blog/dream-act-protest-enacts-graduation-ceremony .html.

22. Vargas, "Shadow Americans," 34.

23. Text of speech available at http://www.whitehouse.gov/the-press-office/ 2011/01/25/remarks-president-state-union-address.

24. Medrano, "Obama as Border Cop."

25. Preston, "Deportations Go On."

26. Preston, "Federal Policy Resulting in Wave of Deportations Draws Protests."

27. Goffard, Esquivel, and Watanabe. "U.S. Will Review Cases."

28. Preston, "Deportations Go On."

29. Parsons, Bennett, and Tanfani, "Obama Opens New Door."

30. Gabriel, "Florida's Crucial Hispanic Voters Remain Wary of Romney."

31. Oliphant, "Mitt Romney Would Veto DREAM Act."

32. Liptak, "Romney Defends DREAM Act Stance."

33. The quote is available at http://www.youtube.com/watch?v=5bHRzeaYYCM.

34. Passel and Cohn, *Portrait of Unauthorized Immigrants in the United States.*

35. http://caselaw.lp.findlaw.com/data/constitution/amendment14/.

36. *Los Angles Times Magazine*, "Profile of a Lost Generation." For a summary of the history of the term "anchor baby," see http://en.wikipedia.org/wiki/Anchor _baby.

37. Chavez, *Shadowed Lives*, 179.

38. Malkin, "What Makes an American?"

39. Malkin, "No More Drive-by Citizenship."

40. For Lou Dobbs's comments and a discussion of anchor babies and the efforts to repeal the Fourteenth Amendment and birthright citizenship, see *Lou Dobbs Tonight*, April 15, 2006, http://www.youtube.com/watch?v=o6x1t8ej-Tk.

41. Barr, "Graham Eyes 'Birthright Citizenship' "; Conant, "Next Front on Immigration."

42. Santa Ana, "'Like an Animal I Was Treated.' "

43. Berk et al., "Health Care Use among Undocumented Latino Immigrants."

44. Hochschild and Mollenkopf, *Bringing Outsiders In.*

45. Rawle, *View of the Constitution of the United States of America.* See also http:// en.wikipedia.org/wiki/Natural-born_citizen.

46. Justia.com, "US Supreme Court: United States v. Wong Kim Ark."

47. Ibid. See also http://en.wikipedia.org/wiki/Wong_Kim_Ark.

48. Lacey, "New Task Force."

49. Gallegly, "Gallegly Seeks to End Automatic Citizenship"; Lacey, "New Task Force."

50. Lowy, "GOP Congressman Seeks to Limit Citizenship Birthright."

51. Ibid. HR698, the Citizenship Reform Act of 2005, was dropped at the end of that legislative session and never became law; http://www.govtrack.us/congress/billtext.xpd?bill=h109-698. In its place is HR1940, the Birthright Citizenship Act of 2007, which was introduced by Representative Nathan Deal (R-Georgia) and would also amend the Immigration and Nationality Act to eliminate birthright citizenship; http://www .govtrack.us/congress/bill.xpd?bill=h110-1940.

52. Boyle, "Congressman Steve King Rolls Out Plan."

53. The text of HR140, the Birthright Citizenship Act of 2011, is available at http://www.govtrack.us/congress/billtext.xpd?bill=h112-140.

54. *Newser*, "Arizona Bills Target Birthright Citizenship"; Preston, "State Lawmakers Outline Plans to End Birthright Citizenship."

55. Preston, "State Lawmakers Outline Plans to End Birthright Citizenship."

56. Fischer, "Who Is a Citizen?"

57. Bentley, "Sen. Russell Pearce to Introduce 14th Amendment Bill."

58. Schwartz, "Russell Pearce Loses Election."

59. *American Heritage Dictionary of the English Language*, 5th ed., s.v. "anchor baby."

60. http://ahdictionary.com/word/search.html?q=anchor+baby.

61. Lou Dobbs's statement on Fox News is available at http://www.dailykos.com/story/2010/08/03/889930/-Even-Lou-Dobbs-believes-in-the-14th-amendment.

62. Aujla, "Steve King Unveils Birthright Bill."

63. D. Roberts, "Who May Give Birth to Citizens?" 212.

64. *Rasmussen Reports*. "61% Oppose U.S. Citizenship for Children Born to Illegal Immigrants."

65. Agamben, *Homo Sacer*, 130.

66. Tormey, "'Everyone with Eyes Can See the Problem.'" See also Moran, "Immigrant Appearances"; and A. Smith, "Irish Citizenship Referendum."

67. Barnes, "Supreme Court Rejects Much of Arizona Immigration Law."

Epilogue

1. Myers, "California Futures"; Pitkin and Myers, "Generational Projections of the California Population."

2. For a discussion of regional and national identities, see Hayes-Bautista, *La Nueva California*.

3. Alba and Nee, *Remaking the American Mainstream*.

4. Rumbaut, "Assimilation and Its Discontents"; M. M. Suarez-Orozco, "Everything You Wanted to Know."

5. Gutmann, "Ethnicity, Alcohol, and Acculturation"; Hayes-Bautista, *La Nueva California*; Hirsch et al., "Social Constructions of Sexuality"; Marchi and Guendelman, "Gender Differences"; Rumbaut, "Assimilation and Its Discontents."

6. Markides and Coreil, "Health of Hispanics"; Rumbaut, "New Californians"; Rumbaut and Weeks, "Children of Immigrants"; C. Suarez-Orozco and M. Suarez-Orozco, *Transformations*.

7. Bloemraad, *Becoming a Citizen*.

8. For example, the audience of the *Lou Dobbs Tonight* show on CNN increased 72 percent between 2003 and 2007, largely because of Dobbs's anti-immigrant, and particularly anti-Mexican, editorializing. He frequently asserted that a reconquest is occurring and that immigrants have U.S.-born children as anchor babies to help them acquire legal status. Perhaps his most outrageous assertion has been his patently false claim that immigrants are causing an epidemic of leprosy. Leonhardt, "Truth, Fiction, and Lou Dobbs"; Rutten, "Lou Dobbs."

9. Carlos Vélez-Ibáñez refers to a process of "cultural bumping" as people and cultures interact. Vélez-Ibáñez, *Border Visions*.

10. Fischer, *Emergent Forms of Life*.

11. Foner, "Introduction."

12. Graham, *El Rancho in South Texas*. See also Hayes-Bautista, *La Nueva California*, 178–79; McWilliams. *North from Mexico*.

13. Jordan, *German Seed in Texas Soil*.

14. San Miguel, *Tejano Proud*.

15. For more information on this style of music, see the excellent PBS documentary *Accordion Dreams*, produced and directed by Hector Galán and available from Galán Inc., Austin, Texas.

BIBLIOGRAPHY

Abrajano, Marisa, and Simran M. Singh. "Examining the Link between Issue Attitudes and News Source: The Case of Latinos and Immigration Reform." *Social Science Research Network*, 2007. http://ssrn.com/abstract=1017858.

Abramovitz, Mimi. "Welfare Reform in the United States: Gender, Race and Class Matter." *Critical Social Policy* 26, no. 2 (2006): 336–64.

Abrego, Leisy Janet. "Legal Consciousness of Undocumented Latinos: Fear and Stigma as Barriers to Claims-Making for First- and 1.5 Generation Immigrants." *Law & Society Review* 45, no. 2 (2011): 337–70.

———. "'I Can't Go to College Because I Don't Have Papers': Incorporation Patterns of Latino Undocumented Youth." *Latino Studies* 4 (2006): 212–31.

Adams, Jerome R. *Greasers and Gringos: The Historical Roots of Anglo-Hispanic Prejudice*. Jefferson, NC: McFarland and Co., 2006.

Agamben, Giorgio. *Homo Sacer: Sovereign Power and Bare Life*. Stanford, CA: Stanford University Press, 1998.

Aguila, Justino. "Protesters Turn to Internet to Organize Rallies." *Orange County Register*, March 28, 2006, News section, 4.

Alba, Richard D., and Victor Nee. *Remaking the American Mainstream: Assimilation and Contemporary Immigration*. Cambridge, MA: Harvard University Press, 2003.

Alba, Richard D., and Hui-shien Tsao. "Connecting Past, Present and Future: Reflections on Immigration and the Possibilities for Racial and Ethnic Change in the U.S." Paper prepared for the Huggins Lectures, Harvard University, Cambridge, MA, 2008.

Aleinikoff, T. Alexander. "The Tightening Circle of Membership." In Perea, *Immigrants Out!* 324–32.

Aleinikoff, T. Alexander, and Douglas Klusmeyer. *Citizenship Policies for an Age of Migration*. Washington, DC: Carnegie Institute for International Peace, 2002.

Alexander, M. Jacqui. *Pedagogies of Crossing: Meditations on Feminism, Sexual Politics, Memory, and the Sacred.* Durham, NC: Duke University Press, 2005.

Alonso-Zaldivar, Ricardo. "U.S. to Bolster Arizona Border Security." *Los Angeles Times,* March 30, 2005, A12.

Alvirez, David, and Frank D. Bean. "The Mexican American Family." In *Ethnic Families in America: Patterns and Variations,* edited by Charles H. Mindel and Robert W. Habenstein, 271–92. New York: Elsevier, 1976.

Amaro, Hortensia. "Women in the Mexican-American Community: Religion, Culture, and Reproductive Attitudes and Experiences." *Journal of Community Psychology* 16 (1988): 6–20.

Amaya, Hector. "Performing Acculturation: Rewriting the Latina/o Immigrant Self." *Text and Performance Quarterly* 27, no. 3 (2007): 194–212.

Anderson, Benedict. *Imagined Communities.* London: Verso, 1983.

Anderson, Gary Clayton. *The Conquest of Texas: Ethnic Cleansing in the Promised Land, 1820–1875.* Norman: University of Oklahoma Press, 2005.

Anderson, James, ed. *Transnational Democracy: Political Spaces and Border Crossings.* London and New York: Routledge, 2002.

Andreas, Peter. *Border Games: Policing the U.S.-Mexico Divide.* Ithaca, NY: Cornell University Press, 2000.

———. "The U.S. Immigration Control Offensive: Constructing an Image of Order on the Southwest Border." In *Crossings: Mexican Immigration in Interdisciplinary Perspectives,* edited by Marcelo Suárez-Orozco, 343–56. Cambridge, MA: Harvard University Press for the David Rockefeller Center for Latin American Studies, 1998.

Anti-Defamation League. 2006. "Extremists Declare 'Open Season' on Immigrants: Hispanics Target of Incitement and Violence." http://www.adl.org/main_Extremism/immigration_extremists.htm.

Aparicio, Ana. *Dominican Americans and the Politics of Empowerment.* Gainesville: University Press of Florida, 2006.

Appadurai, Arjun. "Disjuncture and Difference in the Global Cultural Economy." In Appadurai, *Modernity at Large,* 27–47.

———. *Modernity at Large: Cultural Dimensions of Globalization.* Minneapolis: University of Minnesota Press, 1996.

Archibold, Randal C. "Girl in Transplant Mix-up Dies after Two Weeks." *New York Times,* February 23, 2003.

———. "Immigrants Take to U.S. Streets in Show of Strength." *New York Times,* May 2, 2006, 1.

Arellano, Gustavo. "Fear of a Brown Planet." *OC Weekly,* September 5, 2003, 16–21.

Argetsinger, Amy. "Immigration Opponents to Patrol U.S. Border: Rights Groups Condemn 'Minuteman' Project." *Washington Post,* March 31, 2005, A3.

Arifin, Evi Nurvidya. "Population, Policies and Programmes in Singapore (Review)." *Population Review* 45, no. 1 (2006): 71–73.

Armbruster, Benjamin J. "Gibson: 'Make More Babies' Because in '[T]wenty-Five Years . . . the Majority of the Population Is Hispanic.'" *Media Matters for America*, May 12, 2006. http://mediamatters.org//items/200605120006.

Arpaio, Joe, and Len Sherman. *Joe's Law: America's Toughest Sheriff Takes on Illegal Immigration, Drugs, and Everything That Threatens America.* New York: AMA-COM, 2008.

Associated Press. "U.S. Population to Hit 300 Million This Fall." FOXNews.com, June 25, 2006. http://www.foxnews.com/story/0,2933,200875,00.html.

Aujla, Simmi. "Steve King Unveils Birthright Bill." *Politico*, January 5, 2011. http://www.politico.com/news/stories/0111/47125.html.

Avila, Oscar. "Shooting for a Big Turnout: 'Pistolero' Steps Away from Shock Jock Persona to Push Immigrants' March, Rally." *Chicago Tribune*, March 10, 2006, Metro section, 1.

Avila, Oscar, and Antonio Olivo. "Across U.S., Immigration Supporters, Foes View Chicago March as Catalyst." *Chicago Tribune*, March 12, 2006, Metro section, 1.

Bailey, John. "Mexico in the U.S. Media, 1979–88: Implications for the Bilateral Relation." In *Images of Mexico in the United States*, edited by John H. Coatsworth and Carlos Rico, 55–87. La Jolla: Center for U.S.-Mexican Studies, University of California, San Diego, 1989.

Baker, Peter. "Administration Is Singing More than One Tune on Spanish Version of Anthem." *Washington Post*, May 3, 2006, A6.

Balibar, Etienne. "Is There a 'Neo-Racism'?" In *Race, Nation, Class: Ambiguous Identities*, edited by Etienne Balibar and Immanuel Wallerstein, 17–28. New York: Verso, 1991.

Bandhauer, Carina A. "A Global Trend in Racism: The Late 20th Century Anti-Immigrant Movement in Southern California." Ph.D. thesis, Binghamton University, State University of New York, 2001.

Barabak, Mark Z., and Jean O. Pasco. "Election as Immigration Bellwether." *Los Angeles Times*, December 8, 2005, B1.

Barnes, Robert. "Supreme Court Rejects Much of Arizona Immigration Law." *Washington Post*, June 25, 2012.

Barr, Andy. "Graham Eyes 'Birthright Citizenship.'" *Politico*, July 29, 2011. http://www.politico.com/news/stories/0710/40395.html#ixzz0v5pFRNr4.

Barreto, Matt A., Sylvia Manzano, Ricardo Ramirez, and Kathy Rim. "Mobilization, Participation, and Solidaridad: Latino Participation in the 2006 Immigration Protest Rallies." *Urban Affairs Review* 44, no. 5 (2009): 736–64.

Barthes, Roland. *Mythologies.* London: Cape, 1972.

Basch, Linda, Nina Glick Schiller, and Cristina Szanton Blanc. *Nations Unbound: Transnational Projects, Postcolonial Predicaments, and Deterritorialized Nation-States*. Amsterdam: Gordon and Breach, 1994.

Batalova, Jeanne, and Margie McHugh. "DREAM vs. Reality: An Analysis of Potential DREAM Act Beneficiaries." *Insight: National Center on Immigrant Integration Policy*, Migration Policy Institute, July 2010. http://www.migrationpolicy.org/pubs/.

Baubock, Rainer, and John Rundell, eds. *Blurred Boundaries: Migration, Ethnicity, Citizenship*. Brookfield, VT: Ashgate, 1998.

Bean, Frank D., Susan K. Brown, Mark Leach, Jim Bachmeier, Leo R. Chavez, Louis DeSipio, Rubén G. Rumbaut, Jennifer Lee, and Min Zhou. *Chasing the American Dream: The Incorporation of Mexican Immigrants*. Washington, DC: Pew Hispanic Center, 2006.

———. *How Pathways to Legal Status and Citizenship Relate to Economic Attainment among the Children of Mexican Immigrants*. Washington, DC: Pew Hispanic Center, 2006.

Bean, Frank D., and Gillian Stevens. *America's Newcomers and the Dynamics of Diversity*. New York: Russell Sage Foundation, 2003.

Bean, Frank D., C. Gray Swicegood, and Ruth Berg. "Mexican-Origin Fertility: New Patterns and Interpretations." *Social Science Quarterly* 81 (2000): 404–20.

Becerra, Hector, and Andrew W. Blankstein. "L.A. Authorities Brace for Huge Immigration Marches." *Los Angeles Times*, April 28, 2006, A1.

Beirich, Heidi. "The Year in Nativism." *Intelligence Report*, no. 137 (2010). http://www.splcenter.org/get-informed/intelligence-report/browse-all-issues/2010/spring/the-year-in-nativism.

Benford, Robert, and David Snow. "Framing Processes and Social Movements: An Overview and Assessment." *Annual Review of Sociology* 26 (2000): 611–39.

Benjamin, Walter. *Illuminations: The Work of Art in the Age of Mechanical Reproduction*. New York: Harcourt Brace and World, 1955.

Bentley, Linda. "Sen. Russell Pearce to Introduce 14th Amendment Bill." *Phoenix Examiner*, January 4, 2011.

Berk, Marc L., Claudia L. Schur, Leo R. Chavez, and Martin Frankel. "Health Care Use among Undocumented Latino Immigrants: Is Free Health Care the Main Reason Why Latinos Come to the United States? A Unique Look at the Facts." *Health Affairs* 19, no. 4 (2000): 51–64.

Bernal, Victoria. "Diaspora, Cyberspace and Political Imagination: The Eritrean Diaspora Online." *Global Networks* 6, no. 2 (2006): 161–79.

Bernstein, Nina. "For Illegal Immigrant, Line Is Drawn at Transplant." *New York Times*, December 20, 2011.

———. "In the Streets, Suddenly, an Immigrant Groundswell." *New York Times*, March 27, 2006, A14.

Bhabha, Jacqueline. "'Get Back to Where You Once Belonged': Identity, Citizenship, and Exclusion in Europe." *Human Rights Quarterly* 20, no. 3 (1998): 592–627.

Bhuyan, Rupaleem. "The Production of the 'Battered Immigrant' in Public Policy and Domestic Violence Advocacy." *Journal of Interpersonal Violence* 23, no. 2 (2008): 153–70.

Bickel, Nardy Baeza, and Shandra Martinez. "Girl Who's Here Illegally Needs Kidney Transplant." *Grand Rapids Press*, December 7, 2006.

Bixler, Mark. "Illegal, Uninsured . . . but Alive." *Atlanta Journal-Constitution*, April 25, 2004, A1.

———. "Immigrant Boy Gets Kidney Transplant." *Atlanta Journal-Constitution*, January 6, 2005, C3.

Bloemraad, Irene. *Becoming a Citizen: Incorporating Immigrants and Refugees in the United States and Canada.* Berkeley: University of California Press, 2006.

Border Alert. "Girl's Death Exposes Transplant Tragedy," September 2003. Published by U.S. Border Control. http://www.usbc.org/info/newslet/BA0903.pdf.

Boren, Cindy. "NCAA Tournament: Southern Mississippi Apologizes for 'Where's Your Green Card?' Chant." *WP Sports, The Early Lead* (blog), *Washington Post*, March 3, 2012.

Borneman, John. "Emigres as Bullets / Immigration as Penetration: Perceptions of the Marielitos." *Journal of Popular Culture* 20, no. 3 (1986): 73–92.

Bosniak, Linda. "Citizenship Denationalized." *Indiana Journal of Global Legal Studies* 7 (2000): 447–509.

———. "Universal Citizenship and the Problem of Alienage." *Northwestern University Law Review* 94, no. 3 (2000): 963–84.

Boyle, Matthew. "Congressman Steve King Rolls Out Plan to Unmoor 'Anchor Babies,'" January 6, 2011. http://dailycaller.com/2011/01/06/congressman-steve-king-rolls-out-plan-to-unmoor-anchor-babies/.

Branson, Serene. "Racist Video Game Targets Immigrants." *CBS 13* (Sacramento, CA), April 14, 2006. http://cbs13.com/local/Immigration.Racism.Border.2.469530.html.

Brettell, Caroline B. "Political Belonging and Cultural Belonging." *American Behavioral Scientist* 50, no. 1 (2006): 70–99.

———. "Wrestling with 9/11: Immigrant Perceptions and Perceptions of Immigrants." *Migration Letters* 3, no. 2 (2006): 107–24.

Briggs, Charles L. "Communicability, Racial Discourse, and Disease." *Annual Review of Anthropology* 34 (2005): 269–91.

Briggs, Charles L., and Daniel C. Hallin. "Biocommunicability: The Neoliberal Subject and Its Contradictions in News Coverage of Health Issues." *Social Text* 25, no. 4/93 (2007): 43–66.

Brimelow, Peter. *Alien Nation: Common Sense about America's Immigration Disaster.* New York: Random House, 1995.

———. "That Santillan Saga: Lies, Damned Lies, Immigration Enthusiasts and Neo-socialist Health Bureaucrats." VDARE.com, May 31, 2003. http://www.vdare.com/pb/santillan.htm.

———. "Time to Rethink Immigration?" *National Review*, June 22, 1992, 30–46.

Brown, Susan K. "Delayed Spatial Assimilation: Multigenerational Incorporation of the Mexican-Origin Population in Los Angeles." *City and Society* 6, no. 3 (2007): 193–209.

Browner, Carol H. "The Politics of Reproduction in a Mexican Village." *Signs: Journal of Women in Culture and Society* 11, no. 4 (1986): 710–24.

Brownstein, Ronald. "Most Back Tighter Border and a Guest-Worker Plan." *Los Angeles Times*, April 13, 2006, A1.

Buchanan, Patrick J. *The Death of the West: How Dying Populations and Immigrant Invasions Imperil Our Country and Civilization*. New York: St. Martin's Press, 2002.

———. *State of Emergency: The Third World Invasion and Conquest of America*. New York: St. Martin's Press, 2006.

———. *Suicide of a Superpower: Will American Survive to 2025?* New York: St. Martin's Press, 2011.

———. "What Will America Be in 2050?" *Los Angeles Times*, October 28, 1994, B7.

Buck-Morss, Susan. *Thinking Past Terror: Islamism and Critical Theory on the Left*. London: Verso, 2003.

Buescher, Paul A. "A Review of Available Data on the Health of the Latino Population in North Carolina." *North Carolina Medical Journal* 64, no. 3 (2003): 97–105.

Bunis, Dena. "Debate with No Clear Lines." *Orange County Register*, March 29, 2006, News section, 3.

Bunis, Dena, and Guillermo X. Garcia. "New Illegal-Immigration Law Casts Too Wide a Net, Critics Say." *Orange County Register*, March 31, 1997, News section, 1.

Bush, George W. *The National Security Strategy of the United States of America*. September 2002. http://www.whitehouse.gov/nsc/nss.pdf.

———. *Securing America's Borders Fact Sheet: Border Security*. January 2002. http://www.whitehouse.gov/news/releases/2002/01/20020125.html.

Butler, Judith P. *Bodies That Matter: On the Discursive Limits of "Sex."* New York: Routledge, 1993.

———. *Gender Trouble: Feminism and the Subversion of Identity*. New York: Routledge: 1999.

Calavita, Kitty. *California's "Employer Sanctions": The Case of the Disappearing Law*. La Jolla: Center for U.S.-Mexican Studies, University of California, San Diego, 1982.

———. "The New Politics of Immigration: 'Balanced-Budget Conservatism' and the Symbolism of Proposition 187." *Social Problems* 43 (1996): 284–305.

California State Census Data Center. "1990 Census of the Population and Housing: Summary Tape File 4." Sacramento: California State Data Center, 1995.

Carcamo, Cindy. "Spanish Anthem Adds Fuel to Debate." *Orange County Register*, April 27, 2006, News section, 1.

Carnell, Brian. 2003. "Organ Donation: Should National Origin Matter?" *Brian .Carnell.com* (blog), February 24, 2003. http://brian.carnell.com/articles/2003/organ-donation-should-national-origin-matter/.

Carrier, James G. "Introduction." In Carrier and Miller, *Virtualism*, 1–24.

Carrier, James G., and Daniel Miller, eds. *Virtualism: A New Political Economy.* Oxford: Berg, 1998.

Carroll, Susan. "Border Watch to Widen: Minuteman Project Plans to Patrol More States." *Arizona Republic*, April 19, 2005, 1.

Cassell, Joan. "Doing Gender, Doing Surgery: Women Surgeons in a Man's Profession." *Human Organization* 56, no. 1 (1997): 274–80.

Castaneda, Alejandra. "Roads to Citizenship: Mexican Migrants in the United States." *Latino Studies* 2, no. 1 (2004): 70–89.

Castaneda, Xochitl, and Patricia Zavella. "Changing Constructions of Sexuality and Risk: Migrant Mexican Women Farmworkers in California." *Journal of Latin American Anthropology* 8, no. 2 (2003): 126–51.

Castells, Manuel. *The Power of Identity.* Malden, MA: Blackwell, 1997.

Castles, Stephen, and Alastair Davidson. *Citizenship and Migration.* New York: Routledge, 2000.

Chavez, Leo R. *Covering Immigration: Popular Images and the Politics of the Nation.* Berkeley: University of California Press, 2001.

———. "Culture Change and Cultural Reproduction: Lessons from Research on Transnational Migration." In *Globalization and Change in Fifteen Cultures: Born in One World and Living in Another,* edited by Janice Stockard and George Spindler, 283–303. Belmont, CA: Thomson-Wadsworth, 2006.

———. "A Glass Half Empty: Latina Reproduction and Public Discourse." *Human Organization* 63, no. 2 (2004): 173–88.

———. "Imagining the Nation, Imagining Donor Recipients." In Wailoo, Livingston, and Guarnaccia, *A Death Retold,* 276–96.

———. "Immigration and Medical Anthropology." In *American Arrivals: Anthropology Engages the New Immigration,* edited by Nancy Foner, 197–227. Santa Fe, NM: School of American Research Press, 2003.

———. "Immigration Reform and Nativism: The Nationalist Response to the Transnationalist Challenge." In Perea, *Immigrants Out!* 61–77.

———. *The Latino Threat: Constructing Immigrants, Citizens, and the Nation.* Stanford, CA: Stanford University Press, 2008.

———. "Outside the Imagined Community: Undocumented Settlers and Experiences of Incorporation." *American Ethnologist* 18 (1991): 257–78.

———. "The Power of the Imagined Community: The Settlement of Undocumented Mexicans and Central Americans in the United States." *American Anthropologist* 96 (1994): 52–73.

———. "Settlers and Sojourners: The Case of Mexicans in the United States." *Human Organization* 47 (1988): 95–108.

———. *Shadowed Lives: Undocumented Immigrants in American Society.* 2nd ed. Fort Worth, TX: Harcourt Brace and Jovanovich College Publishers, 1998.

———. "Wasting Away in Neoliberal-ville: Mexican Immigrant Women's Views of Cervical Cancer, Social Inequality, and Gender Relations." In *Cultural Perspectives on Cancer: From Metaphors to Advocacy*, edited by Juliet McMullin and Diane Weiner. Santa Fe, NM: School of American Research, forthcoming.

Chavez, Leo R., F. Allan Hubbell, Juliet M. McMullin, Rebecca G. Martinez, and Shiraz I. Mishra. "Structure and Meaning in Models of Breast and Cervical Cancer Risk Factors: A Comparison of Perceptions among Latinas, Anglo Women and Physicians." *Medical Anthropology Quarterly* 9 (1995): 40–74.

Chavez, Leo R., F. Allan Hubbell, Shiraz I. Mishra, and R. Burciaga Valdez. "Undocumented Immigrants in Orange County, California: A Comparative Analysis." *International Migration Review* 31, no. 2 (1997): 88–107.

Chavez, Leo R., Juliet M. McMullin, Shiraz I. Mishra, and F. Allan Hubbell. "Beliefs Matter: Cultural Beliefs and the Use of Cervical Cancer Screening Tests." *American Anthropologist* 103, no. 4 (2001): 1114–29.

Checa, Francisco, Ángeles Arjona, and Juan Carlos Checa. *La integración social de los inmigrados: Modelos y experiencias.* Barcelona: Icaria Editorial, 2003.

Chishti, Muzaffer A., Doris Meissner, Demetrios G. Papademetriou, Jay Peterzell, Michael J. Wishnie, and Stephen W. Yale-Loehr. *America's Challenge: Domestic Security, Civil Liberties, and National Unity after September 11.* Washington, DC: Migration Policy Institute, 2003.

Chivers, C. J. "Russians Busy Making Shrouds, Are Asked to Make Babies." *New York Times*, May 14, 2006, A1.

Cho, Cynthia H., and Anna Gorman. "The Immigration Debate: Massive Student Walkout Spreads across Southland." *Los Angeles Times*, March 28, 2006, A1.

Chock, Phyllis Pease. "No New Women: Gender, 'Alien,' and 'Citizen' in the Congressional Debate on Immigration." *Political and Legal Anthropology Review* 19 (1996): 1–9.

Citrin, Jack, Amy Lerman, Michael Murikami, and Kathryn Pearson. "Testing Huntington: Is Latino Immigration a Threat to American Identity?" *Perspectives in Politics* 5, no. 1 (2007): 31–48.

Cleeland, Nancy. "AFL-CIO Calls for Amnesty for Illegal U.S. Workers." *Los Angeles Times*, February 17, 2000, A1.

Cole, David. *Enemy Aliens: Double Standards and Constitutional Freedoms in the War on Terrorism*. New York: Free Press, 2003.

Colen, Shellee. "'Housekeeping' for the Green Card: West Indian Household Workers, the State, and Stratified Reproduction in New York." In *At Work in Homes: Household Workers in World Perspective*, American Ethnological Society Monograph 3, edited by Roger Sanjek and Shellee Colen, 89–118. Washington, DC: American Anthropological Association, 1990.

Coll, Kathleen M. "'No Estoy Perdida': Immigrant Women (Re)Locating Citizenship." In *Passing Lines: Sexuality and Immigration*, edited by Brad Epps, Keja Valens, and Bill Johnson Gonzales, 389–410. Cambridge, MA: Harvard University Press, 2005.

Colon, Vanessa. "Mexican Migration to Drop." *Fresno Bee*, January 17, 2005, A1.

Comaroff, Jean, and John L. Comaroff. "Figuring Crime: Quantifacts and the Production of the Un/Real." *Public Culture* 18 (2006): 209–46.

Conant, Eve. "The Next Front on Immigration." *Newsweek*, August 9, 2010, 9.

CONAPO (Consejo Nacional de Población). "[Mexican] National Fertility Rates, 1960–2000." In *A Report of the Mexican Government*. Federal Institute for Access to Public Information, 2003. http://www.conapo.gob.mx.

Conniff, Ruth. "The War on Aliens: The Right Calls the Shots." *Progressive*, October 1993, 22–29.

Coronado, Michael. "Minutemen Quit Patrol Early but Declare Victory." *Orange County Register*, April 19, 2005, B1.

———. "Wary Groups in Border Watch." *Orange County Register*, April 5, 2005, News section, 1.

County of Orange Health Care Agency (COHCA). *2002 Birth Outcomes Fact Sheet*. http://www.ochealthinfo.com/docs/public/epi/2002-Birth_Data_Factsheet.pdf.

Coutin, Susan Bibler. "Being En Route." *American Anthropologist* 107, no. 2 (2005): 195–206.

———. "Confined within: National Territories as Zones of Confinement." *Political Geography* 29, no. 4 (2010): 200–208.

———. *The Culture of Protest: Religious Activism and the U.S. Sanctuary Movement*. Boulder, CO: Westview Press, 1993.

———. *Legalizing Moves: Salvadoran Immigrants Struggle for U.S. Residency*. Ann Arbor: University of Michigan Press, 2000.

———. *Nations of Emigrants: Shifting Boundaries of Citizenship in El Salvador and the United States*. Ithaca, NY: Cornell University Press, 2007.

Coutin, Susan Bibler, and Phyllis Pease Chock. "'Your Friend, the Illegal': Definition and Paradox in Newspaper Accounts of U.S. Immigration Reform." *Identities* 2 (1995): 123–48.

Cowan, Jane K., Marie-Benedicte Dembour, and Richard A. Wilson. Introduction to *Culture and Rights*, edited by Jane K. Cowan, Marie-Benedicte Dembour, and Richard A. Wilson, 1–26. Cambridge: Cambridge University Press, 2001.

Cunningham, Peter J. "What Accounts for Differences in the Use of Hospital Emergency Departments across U.S. Communities?" *Health Affairs* 25 (2006): 324–36.

Curtius, Mary. "House Moving to Tighten Immigration." *Los Angeles Times*, December 16, 2005, A22.

Daniels, Rogers. *Coming to America: A History of Immigration and Ethnicity in American Life*. New York: Harper Perennial, 2002.

Danna, Jeff. "Undocumented Immigrants Fight for Lifesaving Liver Transplants." *Chicago Tribune*, June 11, 2012.

Debord, Guy. *The Society of the Spectacle*. New York: Zone Books, 1995 [1965].

De Genova, Nicholas P. "Migrant 'Illegality' and Deportability in Everyday Life." *Annual Review of Anthropology* 31 (2002): 419–47.

Del Castillo, Adelaida R. "Illegal Status and Social Citizenship: Thoughts on Mexican Immigrants in a Postnational World." In *Women and Migration in the U.S.-Mexico Borderlands*, edited by Denise A. Segura and Patricia Zavella, 92–105. Durham, NC: Duke University Press, 2007.

De Leon, A. *They Called Them Greasers*. Austin: University of Texas Press, 1983.

Delson, Jennifer. "A Minuteman Meets His Hour of Crisis: Jim Gilchrist, Co-Founder of the Anti-Illegal Immigrant Group, Battles Three Board Members for the Organization's Control." *Los Angeles Times*, March 11, 2007, B1.

———. "Profile of James Gilchrist." *Los Angeles Times*, April 11, 2005, B2.

Democracy Now! "Vigilantes or Civilian Border Patrol? A Debate on the Minuteman Project." TV/radio news program, April 5, 2005. http://www.democracynow.org/article.pl?sid=05/04/05/1334206.

DeSipio, Louis. "The Pressure of Perpetual Promise: Latinos and Politics, 1960–2003." In *The Columbia History of Latinos in the United States since 1960*, edited by David G. Gutiérrez, 421–65. Berkeley: University of California Press, 2004.

DeSipio, Louis, and Natalie Masuoka. "Opportunities Lost? Latinos, Cruz Bustamante, and California's Recall." In *Clicker Politics: Essays on the California Recall*, edited by Shaun Bowler and Bruce Cain, 112–27. Upper Saddle River, NJ: Pearson, 2006.

DeVille, Kenneth. "Parties to the Social Contract? Justice and Health Care for Undocumented Immigrants." In *Intervention and Reflection*, edited by Ronald Munson, 306–11. Belmont, CA: Wadsworth/Thomson Learning, 2000.

Dobuzinskis, Alex. "Thousands Rally for UFW March—Legal Status for Undocumented Workers Sought." *Daily News of Los Angeles*, March 27, 2006, N4.

Douglas, Mary. *Purity and Danger*. London: Routledge and Kegan Paul, 1966.

Dumenil, Gerard, and Dominique Levy. *Capital Resurgent: Roots of the Neoliberal Revolution*. Cambridge, MA: Harvard University Press, 2004.

Dumit, Joseph. "Drugs, Algorithms, Markets and Surplus Health." Paper presented at the conference "Lively Capital 2.0: Ethnographic Method and Techno-Corporate Critique," Center for Ethnography, University of California, Irvine, October 23–24, 2005.

Dunn, Timothy J. *The Militarization of the U.S.-Mexico Border, 1978–1992: Low-Intensity Conflict Doctrine Comes Home*. Austin: CMAS Books, Center for Mexican American Studies, University of Texas at Austin, 1996.

———. "Military Collaboration with the Border Patrol in the U.S.-Mexico Border Region: Inter-Organizational Relations and Human Rights Implications." *Journal of Political and Military Sociology* 27 (1999): 257–77.

Dunn, Timothy J., Ana Maria Aragones, and George Shivers. "Recent Mexican Migration in the Rural Delmarva Peninsula: Human Rights versus Citizenship Rights in a Local Context." In *New Destinations: Mexican Immigration in the United States*, edited by Victor Zuniga and Ruben Hernandez-Leon, 155–83. New York: Russell Sage Foundation, 2005.

Eberstadt, Nicholas. "The Population Implosion." *Foreign Policy*, March–April 2001, 42–53.

Ehlers, Tracy Bachrach. "Debunking Marianismo: Economic Vulnerability and Survival Strategies among Guatemalan Wives." *Ethnology* 30, no. 1 (1991): 1–16.

Ehrlich, Paul R. *The Population Bomb*. New York: Ballantine Books, 1968.

Ehrlich, Paul R., Loy Bilderback, and Anne H. Ehrlich. *The Golden Door*. New York: Ballantine Books, 1979.

Enloe, Cynthia. *Maneuvers: The International Politics of Militarizing Women's Lives*. Berkeley: University of California Press, 2000.

Ensink, Titus, and Christoph Sauer. "Social-Functional and Cognitive Approaches to Discourse Interpretation: The Role of Frame and Perspective." In *Framing and Perspectivising in Discourse*, edited by Titus Ensink and Christoph Sauer, 1–21. Philadelphia: John Benjamins, 2003.

Eurostat. "Europa." European Commission, Statistical Office of the European Communities, 2006. http://epp.eurostat.ec.europa.eu.

Faegin, Joe R. "Old Poison in New Bottles: The Deep Roots of Modern Nativism." In Perea, *Immigrants Out!* 13–43.

Farmer, Paul. *Pathologies of Power: Health, Human Rights, and the New War on the Poor*. Berkeley: University of California Press, 2003.

Federation for American Immigration Reform (FAIR). "Immigration Policies Fueling Rise in Health Care Costs, Study Finds." Press release, February 26, 2004. http://www.fairus.org/site/PageServer?pagename=media_mediac9f6.

Fernandez, Celestino, and Lawrence R. Pedroza. "The Border Patrol and the News Media Coverage of Undocumented Mexican Immigration during the 1970's: A Quantitative Content Analysis in the Sociology of Knowledge." *California Sociologist* 5 (1982): 1–26.

Fiore, Faye. "The Job Can Wait, the Protests Can't." *Los Angeles Times*, April 11, 2006, A10.

Fischer, Howard. "Who Is a Citizen? The Battle Is Begun." *Arizona Daily Star*, January 5, 2011, A1.

Fischer, Michael M. J. *Emergent Forms of Life and the Anthropological Voice*. Durham, NC: Duke University Press, 2003.

Fitzgerald, David. *Negotiating Extra-Territorial Citizenship: Mexican Migration and the Transnational Politics of Community*. La Jolla: Center for Comparative Immigration Studies, University of California, San Diego, 2000.

Fix, Michael E., and Jeffrey S. Passel. *Trends in Noncitizens' and Citizens' Use of Public Benefits Following Welfare Reform: 1994–97*. Washington, DC: Urban Institute, 1999.

Flores, William V., and Rina Benmayor. "Constructing Cultural Citizenship." In Flores and Benmayor, *Latino Cultural Citizenship*, 1–23.

———, eds. *Latino Cultural Citizenship: Claiming Identity, Space, and Rights*. Boston: Beacon Press, 1997.

Foner, Nancy. "Introduction: Anthropology and Contemporary Immigration to the United States—Where We Have Been and Where We Are Going." In *American Arrivals: Anthropology Engages the New Immigration*, edited by Nancy Foner, 3–44. Santa Fe, NM: School of American Research, 2003.

Fortuny, Karina, Randy Capps, and Jeffrey S. Passel. *The Characteristics of Unauthorized Immigrants in California, Los Angeles, and the United States*. Washington, DC: Urban Institute, 2007.

Foucault, Michel. "The Birth of Biopolitics." In *Ethics, Subjectivity and Truth*, edited by Paul Rabinow, 73–80. New York: New Press, 1997.

———. *Discipline and Punish*. London: Tavistock, 1977.

———. "Governmentality." In *The Foucault Effect: Studies in Governmentality*, edited by Graham Burchell, Colin Gordon, and Peter Miller, 87–104. Chicago: University of Chicago Press, 1991.

———. *The History of Sexuality*, vol. 1: *An Introduction*. New York: Vintage Books, 1990 [1976].

———. *The Order of Things*. New York: Vintage Books, 1970.

————. *Power/Knowledge*. Brighton, UK: Harvester, 1980.

Fox, Jonathan. "Unpacking Transnational Citizenship." *Annual Review of Political Science* 8 (2005): 171–201.

Fraser, Nancy, and Linda Gordon. "A Genealogy of *Dependency*: Tracing a Keyword of the U.S. Welfare State." *Signs: Journal of Women in Culture and Society* 19, no. 21 (1994): 309–35.

Fregoso, Rosa Linda. *MeXicana Encounters: The Making of Social Identities on the Borderlands*. Berkeley: University of California Press, 2003.

French, Howard W. "Japan Fails to Cope with Its Declining Population." *Orange County Register*, March 14, 2000, News section, 19.

Friedersdorf, Conor. "What the Minuteman Project Taught Its Founder." *Atlantic*, November 11, 2011.

Friedman, Lisa. "Immigrant Rights Activists Hopeful." *Long Beach Press-Telegram*, March 27, 2006, A1.

Frith, Maxine. "Immigration: The Real Scandal." *Independent* (London), May 18, 2006, 40.

Gabaccia, Donna. *From the Other Side: Women, Gender, and Immigrant Life in the U.S. 1820–1990*. Bloomington: Indiana University Press, 1994.

Gabriel, Trip. "Florida's Crucial Hispanic Voters Remain Wary of Romney." *New York Times*, April 28, 2012.

Gallegly, Elton. "Gallegly Seeks to End Automatic Citizenship for Illegal Alien Children." Press release from the Office of U.S. Congressman Elton Gallegly, Washington, DC, 1991.

Gaouette, Nicole. "Border Troubles Divide U.S., States." *Los Angeles Times*, August 18, 2005, A1.

————. "Bush Signs Fence Bill, Pushes Back." *Los Angeles Times*, October 27, 2006, A1.

————. "Talk-Radio Fans Unite on Immigration." *Los Angeles Times*, April 28, 2007, A9.

Gardner, Martha. *The Qualities of a Citizen: Women, Immigration, and Citizenship, 1870–1965*. Princeton, NJ: Princeton University Press, 2005.

German, Daniel B. "The Role of the Media in Political Socialization and Attitude Formation toward Racial/Ethnic Minorities in the U.S." In *Nationalism, Ethnicity, and Identity*, edited by Russell F. Farnen, 285–97. New Brunswick, NJ: Transaction Publishers, 1994.

Gerstenzang, James. "Bush Strongly Defends Deal on Immigration." *Los Angeles Times*, May 20, 2007, A21.

Gerstle, Gary. *American Crucible: Race and Nation in the Twentieth Century*. Princeton, NJ: Princeton University Press, 2001.

———. "The Immigrant as Threat to American Security: A Historical Perspective." In *The Maze of Fear: Security and Migration after 9/11*, edited by John Tirman, 87–108. New York: New Press, 2004.

Geyer, Georgie Ann. *Americans No More*. New York: Atlantic Monthly Press, 1996.

Gilchrist, Jim, and Jerome R. Corsi. *Minutemen: The Battle to Secure America's Borders*. Los Angeles: World Ahead Publishing, 2006.

Ginsburg, Faye D., and Rayna Rapp. *Conceiving the New World Order: The Global Politics of Reproduction*. Berkeley: University of California Press, 1995.

———. "The Politics of Reproduction." *Annual Review of Anthropology* 20 (1991): 311–43.

Glenn, Evelyn Nakano. "Social Constructions of Mothering: A Thematic Overview." In *Mothering: Ideology, Experience, and Agency*, edited by Evelyn Nakano Glenn, Grace Chang, and Linda Rennie Forcey, 1–29. New York: Routledge, 1994.

Goffard, Christopher, Jennifer Delson, and Amanda Covarrubias. "Small, Orderly Immigration Rally in O.C." *Los Angeles Times*, April 2, 2006, B1.

Goffard, Christopher, Paloma Esquivel, and Teresa Watanabe. "U.S. Will Review Cases of 300,000 Illegal Immigrants in Deportation Proceedings." *Los Angeles Times*, August 19, 2011, A1.

Gold, Scott. "Student Protests Echo the '60s, but with a High-Tech Buzz." *Los Angeles Times*, March 31, 2006, A1.

Gonzalez-Lopez, Gloria. *Erotic Journeys: Mexican Immigrants and Their Sex Lives*. Berkeley: University of California Press, 2005.

Gonzales, Roberto G. "Left Out but Not Shut Down: Political Activism and the Undocumented Student Movement." *Northwestern Journal of Law and Social Policy* 3, no. 2 (2008): 219–39.

Gonzales, Roberto G., and Leo R. Chavez. "'Awakening to a Nightmare': Abjectivity and Illegality in the Lives of Undocumented 1.5 Generation Latino Immigrants in the United States." *Current Anthropology* 53, no. 3 (2012): 255–81.

Goode, Judith, and Jeff Maskovsky, eds. *The New Poverty Studies: The Ethnography of Power, Politics, and Impoverished People in the United States*. New York: New York University Press, 2001.

Goodwin, Liz. "The End of the Minutemen: Tea Party Absorbs the Border-Watching Movement." *The Lookout* (blog), *Yahoo! News*, April 16, 2012. news.yahoo.com/blogs/lookout/end-minutemen-tea-party-absorbs-border-watching-movement-173424401.html.

Gordon, Andrew, and Trevor Stack. "Citizenship beyond the State: Thinking with Early Modern Citizenship in the Contemporary World." *Citizenship Studies* 11, no. 2 (2007): 117–33.

Gordon, Colin. "Governmental Rationality: An Introduction." In *The Foucault Effect: Studies in Governmentality*, edited by Graham Burchell, Colin Gordon, and Peter Miller. Chicago: University of Chicago Press, 1991.

Gordon, Jennifer. *Suburban Sweatshops: The Fight for Immigrant Rights.* Cambridge, MA: Belknap Press at Harvard University Press, 2005.

Gorman, Anna. "Flag's Meaning Is in the Eye of the Beholder." *Los Angeles Times,* March 29, 2006, A11.

Gorman, Anna, Marjorie Miller, and Mitchell Landsberg. "Marchers Fill L.A. Streets: Immigrants Demonstrate Peaceful Power." *Los Angeles Times,* May 2, 2006, A1.

Gould, Stephen J. *The Mismeasure of Man.* New York: Norton, 1981.

Grady, Denise. "Donor Mix-up Leaves Girl, 17, Fighting for Life." *New York Times,* February 19, 2003.

Graham, Joe S. *El Rancho in South Texas: Continuity and Change from 1750.* College Station: Texas A&M University Press, 1994.

Gramsci, Antonio. *Selections from the Prison Notebooks.* New York: International Publishers, 1971.

Greenhalgh, Susan, and Edwin A. Winckler. *Governing China's Population: From Leninist to Neoliberal Biopolitics.* Stanford, CA: Stanford University Press, 2005.

Grewal, Inderpal, and Caren Kaplan. "Global Identities: Theorizing Transnational Studies of Sexuality." *GLQ Archive* 7, no. 4 (2001): 663–79.

Grieco, Elizabeth. "The Foreign Born from Mexico in the United States." Migration Information Source, Migration Policy Institute, October 2003. http://www.migrationinformation.org/feature/print.cfm?ID=163.

Griffith, David C. "Rural Industry and Mexican Immigration and Settlement in North Carolina." In *New Destinations: Mexican Immigration in the United States,* edited by Victor Zuniga and Ruben Hernandez-Leon, 50–75. New York: Russell Sage Foundation, 2005.

Grillo, Ioan. "Minute Patrol Off to a Slow Start." *Houston Chronicle,* April 2, 2005, A8.

Groves, Martha. "Day-Labor Group Starts Trek." *Los Angeles Times,* March 5, 2006, B4.

Guglielmo, Thomas A. *White on Arrival: Italians, Race, Color, and Power in Chicago, 1890–1945.* Oxford: Oxford University Press, 2003.

Gupta, Akhil, and James Ferguson. "Beyond 'Culture': Space, Identity, and the Politics of Difference." *Cultural Anthropology* 7, no. 1 (1992): 1–23.

Gupta, Charu. "Immigrants and Organ Sharing: A One-Way Street." *American Medical Association Journal of Ethics* 10, no. 4 (2008): 229–34.

Gupta, Monisha Das. *Unruly Immigrants: Rights, Activism, and Transnational South Asian Politics in the United States.* Durham, NC: Duke University Press, 2006.

Gutiérrez, Elena Rebeca. "The Racial Politics of Reproduction: The Social Construction of Mexican-Origin Women's Fertility." Ph.D. diss., University of Michigan, 1999.

Gutmann, Matthew C. "Ethnicity, Alcohol, and Acculturation." *Social Science and Medicine* 48 (1999): 173–84.

Habermas, Jürgen. *The Structural Transformation of the Public Sphere*. Cambridge, MA: MIT Press, 1986.

Hakimzadeh, Shirin, and D'Vera Cohn. *English Usage among Hispanics in the United States*. Washington, DC: Pew Hispanic Center, 2007.

Hall, Stuart. "Introduction." In Hall, *Representation*, 1–12.

———, ed. *Representation: Cultural Representations and Signifying Practices*. London and Thousand Oaks, CA: Sage Publications, 1997.

———. "Spectacle of the 'Other.'" In Hall, *Representation*, 223–90.

Hall, Stuart, and David Held. "Citizens and Citizenship." In *New Times: The Changing Face of Politics in the 1990s*, edited by Stuart Hall and Martin Jacque, 172–88. New York: Verso, 1989.

Hammer, Tomas. *Democracy and the Nation State: Aliens, Denizens, and Citizens in a World of International Migration*. Aldershot, UK: Avebury, 1990.

Handler, Richard. *Critics against Culture: Anthropological Observers of Mass Society*. Madison: University of Wisconsin Press, 2005.

———. *Nationalism and the Politics of Culture in Quebec*. Madison: University of Wisconsin Press, 1988.

Hanson, Victor Davis. *Mexifornia: A State of Becoming*. San Francisco: Encounter Books, 2003.

Harden, Blaine. "America's Population Set to Top 300 Million." *Washington Post*, October 12, 2006, A1.

Hardt, Michael, and Antonio Negri. *Empire*. Cambridge, MA: Harvard University Press, 2001.

Harvey, David. *A Brief History of Neoliberalism*. Oxford: Oxford University Press, 2005.

Harvey, S. Marie, Linda J. Beckman, Carole Browner, Helen Rodriguez-Trias, Silvia Balzano, Michelle Doty, and Sarah J. Satre. *Context and Meaning of Reproductive Decision-Making among Inner City Couples: Executive Summary; Report to Conrad/Centers for Disease Control*. Los Angeles: Pacific Institute for Women's Health, 1997.

Hayes-Bautista, David E. *La Nueva California: Latinos in the Golden State*. Berkeley: University of California Press, 2004.

Headrick, Christina, and Vicki Cheng. "Some Link Citizenship, Transplants." *News and Observer* (Raleigh, NC), March 4, 2003, A1.

Henry, William A., III. "Beyond the Melting Pot." *Time*, April 9, 1990, 28–31.

Higham, John. *Strangers in the Land: Patterns of American Nativism, 1860–1925*. New Brunswick, NJ: Rutgers University Press, 2002 [1955].

Hing, Bill Ong. *Deporting Our Souls: Values, Morality, and Immigration Policy*. Cambridge: Cambridge University Press, 2006.

Hing, Bill Ong, and Kevin R. Johnson. "The Immigrant Rights Marches of 2006 and the Prospects for a New Civil Rights Movement." *Harvard Civil Rights–Civil Liberties Law Review* 42 (2007): 99–138.

Hirsch, Jennifer S. *A Courtship after Marriage: Sexuality and Love in Mexican Transnational Families.* Berkeley: University of California Press, 2003.

———. "Migration, Modernity, and Mexican Marriage: A Comparative Study of Gender, Sexuality, and Reproductive Health in a Transnational Community." Ph.D. diss., Johns Hopkins University, 1998.

Hirsch, Jennifer S., J. Higgins, M. E. Bentley, and C. A. Nathanson. "The Social Constructions of Sexuality: Marital Infidelity and Sexually Transmitted Disease—HIV." *American Journal of Public Health* 92, no. 8 (2002): 1227–37.

Hochschild, Jennifer L., and John H. Mollenkopf, eds. *Bringing Outsiders In: Transatlantic Perspectives on Immigrant Political Incorporation.* Ithaca, NY: Cornell University Press, 2009.

Hoffman, Beatrix. "Access to Health Care for Undocumented Immigrants in the United States." In Wailoo, Livingston, and Guarnaccia, *A Death Retold*, 237–54.

Hollinger, David. "Amalgamation and Hypodescent: The Quest of Ethnoracial Mixture in the History of the United States." *American Historical Review* 108, no. 5 (2003): 1363–90.

———. "How Wide the Circle of 'We'? American Intellectuals and the Problem of Ethnos since World War II." *American Historical Review* 98, no. 2 (1993): 317–37.

Holston, James, and Arjun Appadurai. "Introduction: Cities and Citizenship." In *Cities and Citizenship*, edited by James Holston, 1–20. Durham, NC: Duke University Press, 1999.

Holthouse, David. "Dangerous Levels of Overlap between Xenophobic 'Minuteman' Movement and Tea Party." *AlterNet*, May 30, 2011.

———. "Minute Mess: Minuteman Leader Ousted, Forms New Group." *Intelligence Report*, Southern Poverty Law Center, Summer 2007. http://www.splcenter.org/intel/intelreport/article.jsp?aid=794.

Hondagneu-Sotelo, Pierrette. *Religion and Social Justice for Immigrants.* Piscataway, NJ: Rutgers University Press, 2006.

———, ed. "Women and Children First: New Directions in Anti-Immigrant Politics." *Socialist Review* 25, no. 1 (1995): 169–90.

Hook, Jennifer Van, Susan K. Brown, and Frank D. Bean. "For Love or Money? Welfare Reform and Immigrant Naturalization." *Social Forces* 85, no. 2 (2006): 643–66.

Horn, David G. *Social Bodies: Science, Reproduction, and Italian Modernity.* Princeton, NJ: Princeton University Press, 1994.

Hubbell, F. Allan, Leo R. Chavez, Shiraz I. Mishra, and R. Burciaga Valdez. "Beliefs about Sexual Behavior and Other Predictors of Pap Smear Screening among Latinas and Anglo Women." *Archives of Internal Medicine* 156 (1996): 2353–58.

———. "The Influence of Knowledge and Attitudes about Breast Cancer on Mammography Use among Latinas and Anglo Women: Brief Report." *Journal of General Internal Medicine* 12 (1997): 505–8.

Huffington Post. "Alamo Heights Basketball Fans Reprimanded after 'U-S-A' Chant Deemed Racist." March 7, 2012. http://www.huffingtonpost.com/2012/03/07/alamo-heights-basketball-_n_1327451.html.

Huntington, Samuel P. "The Hispanic Challenge." *Foreign Policy*, March–April 2004, 30–45.

———. "The Special Case of Mexican Immigration: Why Mexico Is a Problem." *American Enterprise*, December 2000, 20–22.

———. *Who We Are: The Challenges to America's National Identity.* New York: Simon and Schuster, 2004.

Inda, Jonathan Xavier. "Biopower, Reproduction, and the Migrant Woman's Body." In *Decolonial Voices: Chicana and Chicano Cultural Studies in the 21st Century,* edited by Arturo J. Aldama and Naomi H. Quinones, 98–112. Bloomington: Indiana University Press, 2002.

———. "A Flexible World: Capitalism, Citizenship, and Postnational Zones." *PoLAR: Political and Legal Anthropology Review* 23, no. 1 (2000): 86–102.

———. "Foreign Bodies: Migrants, Parasites, and the Pathological Nation." *Discourse: Journal for Theoretical Studies in Media and Culture* 22, no. 3 (2000): 46–62.

———. *Targeting Immigrants: Government, Technology, and Ethics.* Malden, MA: Blackwell, 2006.

Inda, Jonathan Xavier, and Louis F. Mirón. "Migrant Voices: Fashioning Cultural Citizenship in Translocal Spaces." *Plurimondi* 1, no. 1 (1999): 203–26.

Inda, Jonathan Xavier, and Renato Rosaldo, eds. *The Anthropology of Globalization: A Reader.* Malden, MA: Blackwell, 2002.

———. "Introduction: A World in Motion." In Inda and Rosaldo, *The Anthropology of Globalization: A Reader,* 1–34.

Jarvie, Jenny. "Inmates Could Trade an Organ for an Early Out." *Los Angeles Times,* March 9, 2007, A25.

Johnson, Kevin R., and Bernard Trujillo. "Immigration Reform, National Security after September 11, and the Future of North American Integration." *Minnesota Law Review* 91, no. 5 (2007): 1369–1406.

Jordan, Terry G. *German Seed in Texas Soil: Immigrant Farmers in Nineteenth-Century Texas.* Austin: University of Texas Press, 1966.

Joyce, Kathryn. "Missing: The 'Right' Babies." *Nation*, March 3, 2008. http://www.thenation.com/doc/20080303/joyce.

Justia.com. "US Supreme Court: United States v. Wong Kim Ark, 169 U.S. 649 (1898)."

Kadetsky, Elizabeth. "'Save Our State' Initiative: Bashing Illegals in California." *Nation*, October 17, 1994.

Karst, Kenneth. *Belonging to America*. New Haven, CT: Yale University Press, 1989.

Kashiwazaki, Chikako, and Tsuneo Akaha. "Japanese Immigration Policy: Responding to Conflicting Pressures." Migration Information Source, Migration Policy Institute, November 2006. http://www.migrationinformation.org/Profiles/display.cfm?ID=487.

Kasinitz, Philip, John H. Mollenkopf, Mary C. Waters, and Jennifer Holdaway. *Inheriting the City: The Children of Immigrants Come of Age*. Cambridge, MA: Harvard University Press and the Russell Sage Foundation, 2008.

Keller, Michelle, and Anna Gorman. "High School Students Leave School to Protest Immigration Legislation." *Los Angeles Times*, March 25, 2006, A1.

Kelley, Daryl. "California Cuts Its Population Projections." *Los Angeles Times*, October 4, 2004, A1.

Kellner, Douglas. *Media Spectacles*. New York: Routledge, 2003.

Kelly, David. "Border Watchers Capture Their Prey—the Media." *Los Angeles Times*, April 5, 2005, A1.

———. "Citizens Border Patrols Hurry Up . . . and Wait." *Los Angeles Times*, April 3, 2005, A20.

———. "Minutemen Prepare to Lay Down the Law." *Los Angeles Times*, April 2, 2005, A15.

Kennedy, David M. "Can We Still Afford to Be a Nation of Immigrants?" *Atlantic Monthly*, November 1996, 51.

Keogan, Kevin. "A Sense of Place: The Politics of Immigration and the Symbolic Construction of Identity in Southern California and the New York Metropolitan Area." *Sociological Forum* 17, no. 2 (2002): 223–53.

Kertzer, David I. *Politics and Symbols: The Italian Communist Party and the Fall of Communism*. New Haven, CT: Yale University Press, 1996.

———. *Ritual, Politics, and Power*. New Haven, CT: Yale University Press, 1988.

Kolsto, Pal. "National Symbols as Signs of Unity and Division." *Ethnic and Racial Studies* 29, no. 4 (2006): 676–701.

Kovacs, Joe. "Coming to America: Transplants for Illegals Igniting U.S. Firestorm; Case of Smuggled Mexican Teenager Prompting Public to Cry 'Citizens First.'" *WorldNetDaily*, March 6, 2003. http://worldnetdaily.com/index.php?fa=PAGE.view&pageId=17606.

Kraut, Alan M. *Silent Travelers: Germs, Genes, and the "Immigrant Menace."* Baltimore: Johns Hopkins University Press, 1994.

Krikorian, Mark. 2003. "Dealing with Illegal Immigrants Should Be a Top Priority of the War on Terror." *National Review Online*, February 12, 2003. http://www.nationalreview.com/debates/debates021203.asp.

Kristeva, Julia. *Crisis of the European Subject*. New York: Other Press, 2000.

Lacey, Marc. "New Task Force Targets Illegal Immigration." *Los Angeles Times*, March 16, 1995, A3.

Lai, Jules, Adva Saldinger, and Jessica Valadez Spruyt. "Healing Health Care: Immigrants Struggle with Politics, Cost and Culture." Medill at Northwestern University, Student Work, 2005. http://www.medill.northwestern.edu.

Lakoff, George, and Mark Johnson. *Metaphors We Live By*. Chicago: University of Chicago Press, 1980.

Larrubia, Evelyn. "Delivering Dual Benefits: Medi-Cal Spends about $400 Million a Year on Birth-Related Care for Illegal Immigrants." *Los Angeles Times*, December 23, 2006, A1.

Laubenthal, Barbara. "The Emergence of Pro-Regularization Movements in Western Europe." *International Migration* 45, no. 3 (2007): 101–33

Leal, Fermin, and John McDonald. "4,700 O.C. Students Walk Out." *Orange County Register*, March 28, 2006, News section, 4.

Leal, Fermin, and Teri Sforza. "Issue May Bring More Latino Activism." *Orange County Register*, March 31, 2006, News section, 4.

Lederer, Susan E. "Tucker's Heart: Racial Politics and Heart Transplantation in America." In Wailoo, Livingston, and Guarnaccia, *A Death Retold*, 142–57.

Lee, Benjamin, and Edward LiPuma. "Cultures of Circulation: The Imaginations of Modernity." *Public Culture* 14, no. 1 (2002): 191–213.

Leonhardt, David. "Truth, Fiction, and Lou Dobbs." *New York Times*, May 30, 2007, C1.

Lesher, Dave, and Patrick McDonnell. "Wilson Calls Halt to Much Aid for Illegal Immigrants." *Los Angeles Times*, August 28, 1996, A1.

Levine, Samantha. "Border Guard Shift Questioned." *Houston Chronicle*, April 3, 2005, A16.

Levitt, Peggy, and Nina Glick Schiller. "Conceptualizing Simultaneity: A Transnational Social Field Perspective on Society." *International Migration Review* 38, no. 3 (2004): 1002–39.

Link, Jürgen. "Fanatics, Fundamentalists, Lunatics, and Drug Traffickers—the New Southern Enemy Image." *Cultural Critique* 19 (1991): 33–53.

Liptak, Kevin. "Romney Defends DREAM Act Stance." *CNN Politics*, January 1, 2012. http://politicalticker.blogs.cnn.com/2012/01/04/romney-defends-dream-act-stance/.

LiPuma, Edward. "Cultures of Circulation and Imaginaries of the Modern." Paper presented at the Irvine Seminar on the Anthropology of Modernity, University of California, Irvine, 2001.

Lock, Margaret, and Patricia A. Kaufert, eds. *Pragmatic Women and Body Politics*. Cambridge: Cambridge University Press, 1998.

LoMonaco, Claudine. "Minutemen Gather in Tombstone for Border Watch." *Tucson Citizen*, April 1, 2005, A7.

Longley, Robert. "U.S. Population to Hit 300 Million on Oct. 17." About.com, *US Government Info* (blog), 2006. http://usgovinfo.about.com/b/a/217378.htm.

Lopez, Iris. "An Ethnography of the Medicalization of Puerto Rican Women's Reproduction." In Lock and Kaufert, *Pragmatic Women and Body Politics*, 240–59.

Los Angeles Times. "Immigration's Endless Summer." September 2, 2006, B14.

———. "Primero de Mayo." May 2, 2006, B12.

———. "A Lesson for Arizona." June 10, 2012, A29.

Los Angles Times Magazine. "A Profile of a Lost Generation." December 13, 1987.

Lowy, Joan. "GOP Congressman Seeks to Limit Citizenship Birthright." *Arizona Daily Star*, July 30, 1995, A1.

Luibheid, Eithne. *Entry Denied: Controlling Sexuality at the Border*. Minneapolis: University of Minnesota Press, 2002.

Lyon-Callo, Vincent. *Inequality, Poverty, and Neoliberal Governance: Activist Ethnography in the Homeless Sheltering Industry*. Peterborough, ON: Broadview Press, 2004.

Maher, Kristen Hill. "Who Has a Right to Rights? Citizenship's Exclusions in an Age of Migration." In *Globalization and Human Rights*, edited by Alison Brysk, 19–43. Berkeley: University of California Press, 2002.

Malkin, Michelle. "America: Medical Welcome Mat to the World." VDARE.com, February 20, 2003. http://www.vdare.com/malkin/welcome_mat.htm.

———. *Invasion: How America Still Welcomes Terrorists, Criminals, and Other Foreign Menaces to Our Shores*. Washington, DC: Regnery, 2002.

———. "No More Drive-by Citizenship." *Michelle Malkin* (blog), June 13, 2004. http://michellemalkin.com/2004/06/13/no-more-drive-by-citizenship/.

———. "What Makes an American?" *Jewish World Review*, July 4, 2003. http://www.jewishworldreview.com/michelle/malkin070403.asp.

Marchi, Kristen, and Sylvia Guendelman. "Gender Differences in the Sexual Behavior of Latino Adolescents: An Exploratory Study in a Public High School in the San Francisco Bay Area." *International Quarterly of Community Health Education* 15, no. 2 (1994): 209–26.

Marcucci, Michele R. "Thousands in Bay Area Protest Immigration Bills." *Daily Review* (Hayward, CA), March 27, 2006, Local section, 1.

Marin, G., F. Sabogal, B. V. Marin, R. Otero-Sabogal, and E. J. Perez-Stable. "Development of a Short Acculturation Scale for Hispanics." *Hispanic Journal of Behavioral Science* 9 (1987): 183–205.

Marizco, Michael. "Abusive Acts vs. Entrants Are Ignored, Activists Say." *Arizona Daily Star*, March 29, 2005, A1.

Markides, K. S., and J. Coreil. "The Health of Hispanics in the Southwestern United States: An Epidemiological Paradox." *Public Health Reports* 101 (1986): 253–65.

Marks, Jonathan. *What It Means to Be 98% Chimpanzee: Apes, People, and Their Genes.* Berkeley: University of California Press, 2002.

Marshall, T. H. "Citizenship and Social Class." In *Citizenship and Social Class*, edited by T. H. Marshall and Tom Bottomore, 3–51. London: Pluto Press, 1992.

Martin, Philip. "Mexico-U.S. Migration." In *NAFTA Revisited: Achievements and Challenges*, edited by Gary Hufbauer and Jeffrey Schott, 441–86. Washington, DC: Institute for International Economics, 2005.

Massey, Douglas S. *Return to Aztlan: The Social Process of International Migration from Western Mexico.* Berkeley: University of California Press, 1987.

Massey, Douglas S., Joaquin Arango, Graeme Hugo, Ali Kouaouci, Adela Pellegrino, and J. Edward Taylor. *Worlds in Motion: Understanding International Migration at the End of the Millennium.* Oxford: Clarendon Press, 1998.

Massey, Douglas S., Jorge Durand, and Nolan J. Malone. *Beyond Smoke and Mirrors: Mexican Immigration in an Era of Economic Integration.* New York: Russell Sage Foundation, 2002.

Massey, Douglas S., and Karen A. Pren. "Unintended Consequences of US Immigration Policy: Explaining the Post-1965 Surge from Latin America." *Population and Development Review* 38, no. 1 (2012): 1–29.

Mauss, Marcel. *The Gift: Forms and Functions of Exchange in Archaic Societies.* Translated by Ian Cunnison. London: Cohen and West, 1970.

Maxwell, Bruce, and Michael Jacobson. *Marketing Disease to Hispanics.* Washington, DC: Center for Science in the Public Interest, 1989.

Mayer, Vicki. *Producing Dreams, Consuming Youth: Mexican Americans and Mass Media.* New Brunswick, NJ: Rutgers University Press, 2003.

McDonnell, Patrick J. "Mexico Latest to Grant Rights to Expatriates of Other Citizenship." *Los Angeles Times*, March 20, 1998, A9.

McWilliams, Carey. *North from Mexico: The Spanish-Speaking People of the United States.* Philadelphia: J. B. Lippincott, 1948.

Medrano, Lourdes. "Obama as Border Cop: He's Deported Record Number of Illegal Immigrants." *Christian Science Monitor*, August 12, 2010.

Menjívar, Cecilia. "Liminal Legality: Salvadoran and Guatemalan Immigrants' Lives in the United States." *American Journal of Sociology* 111 (2006): 999–1037.

———. "Living in Two Worlds? Guatemalan-Origin Children in the United States and Emerging Transnationalism." *Journal of Ethnic and Migration Studies* 28 (2002): 531–52.

———. "The Power of the Law: Central Americans' Legality and Everyday Life in Phoenix, Arizona." *Latino Studies* 9, no. 4 (2011): 377–95.

———. "Religion and Immigration in Comparative Perspective: Salvadorans in Catholic and Evangelical Communities in San Francisco, Phoenix, and Washington D.C." *Sociology of Religion* 64, no. 1 (2003): 21–45.

Meslin, Eric M., Karen R. Salmon, and Jason T. Eberl. "Eligibility for Organ Transplantation to Foreign Nationals: The Relationship between Citizenship, Justice, and Philanthropy." In Wailoo, Livingston, and Guarnaccia, *A Death Retold*, 255–75.

Migration Policy Institute (MPI). "Fact Sheet on the Foreign Born: North Carolina." Migration Information Source, Migration Policy Institute, n.d. http://www .migrationinformation.org/USFocus/state.cfm?ID=NC.

Miller, Daniel. "Conclusion: A Theory of Virtualism." In *Virtualism: A New Political Economy*, edited by James G. Carrier and Daniel Miller, 187–215. Oxford: Berg, 1998.

Miller, Greg. "Immigration Activists on March Again." *Los Angeles Times*, April 10, 2006, A11.

Mitchell, Pablo. *Coyote Waits: Sexuality, Race, and Conquest in Modernizing New Mexico, 1880–1920*. Chicago: University of Chicago Press, 2005.

Mitton, Roger. "Endangered Species: Singaporeans Need to Have More Babies; but Success Breeds Selfishness." *Asiaweek*, December 1, 2000. http://www-cgi.cnn .com/ASIANOW/asiaweek/magazine/2000/1201/nat.singapore.html.

Mohanty, Jitendra. "The Status of the Subject in Foucault." In *Foucault and the Critique of Institutions*, edited by John D. Caputo and Mark Yount. University Park: Pennsylvania State University Press, 1993.

Mohanty, Sarita A., Steffie Woolhandler, David U. Himmelstein, Susmita Pati, Olveen Carrasquillo, and David H. Bor. "Health Expenditures of Immigrants in the United States: A Nationally Representative Analysis." *American Journal of Public Health* 95 (2005): 1431–38.

Molina, Natalia. *Fit to Be Citizens? Public Health and Race in Los Angeles, 1879–1939*. Berkeley: University of California Press, 2006.

Montgomery, David. "An Anthem's Discordant Notes: Spanish Version of 'Star-Spangled Banner' Draws Strong Reactions." *Washington Post*, April 28, 2006, A1.

Moran, Erin. "Immigrant Appearances and the Emergence of 'Active Citizenship' in Ireland." Paper presented at the annual meeting of the American Anthropological Association, Washington, DC, November 30, 2007.

Morgan, Susan E., Tyler R. Harrison, Lisa Volk Chewning, and Jacklyn B. Habib. "America's Angel or Thieving Immigrant? Media Coverage, the Santillan Story, and Publicized Ambivalence toward Donation and Transplantation." In Wailoo, Livingston, and Guarnaccia, *A Death Retold*, 19–45.

Muenz, Rainer. "Europe: Population and Migration in 2005." Migration Information Source, Migration Policy Institute, June 2006. http://www.migrationinfor mation.org/Feature/display.cfm?ID=402.

Murphy, Clare. "The EU's Baby Blues." *BBC News*, March 27, 2006. http://news.bbc .co.uk/1/hi/world/europe/4768644.stm.

Myers, Dowell. "California Futures." *BOOM* 2, no. 2 (2012): 37–54.

Nagel, C. R., and L. A. Staeheli. "Citizenship, Identity, and Transnational Migration: Arab Immigrants to the United States." *Space and Polity* 8 (2004): 3–23.

Negrón-Gonzales, Genevieve. "Hegemony, Ideology and Oppositional Consciousness: Undocumented Youth and the Personal-Political Struggle for Educational Justice." SSI Fellows Working Papers, Institute for the Study of Societal Issues, University of California, Berkeley, 2009.

Negrón-Muntaner, Frances. "Jennifer's Butt." In *Perspectivas on Las Américas: A Reader in Culture, History, and Representation*, edited by Matthew C. Gutmann, Félix V. Matos Rodríguez, Lynn Stephen, and Patricia Zavella, 291–98. Malden, MA: Blackwell, 2003.

Newbart, Dave, and Monifa Thomas. "In Overwhelming Display, Immigrants Protest Bill: Up to 100,000 March against Plan to Criminalize Undocumented Workers." *Chicago Sun-Times*, March 11, 2006, News section, 6.

Newser. "Arizona Bills Target Birthright Citizenship." 2011. http://www.newser.com/story/110764/arizona-bills-target-birthright-citizenship.html.

Newsweek. "Perspectives." June 12, 2000, 23.

New York Times. "They Are America." May 2, 2006, 24.

Ngai, Mae M. *Impossible Subjects: Illegal Aliens and the Making of Modern America.* Princeton, NJ: Princeton University Press, 2004.

Nguyen, Vinh-Kim, and Karine Peschard. "Anthropology, Inequality and Disease: A Review." *Annual Review of Anthropology* 32 (2003): 447–74.

Oliphant, James. "Mitt Romney Says He Would Veto DREAM Act." *Los Angeles Times*, January 1, 2012, A1.

Olivas, Michael A. "The Political Economy of the DREAM Act and the Legislative Process: A Case Study of Comprehensive Immigration Reform." *Wayne Law Review* 55 (2009): 1757–1810.

Ong, Aihwa. *Buddha Is Hiding: Refugees, Citizenship, the New America.* Berkeley: University of California Press, 2003.

———. "Cultural Citizenship as Subject-Making: Immigrants Negotiate Racial and Cultural Boundaries in the United States." *Current Anthropology* 37, no. 5 (1996): 737–62.

———. *Flexible Citizenship: The Cultural Logics of Transnationality.* Durham, NC: Duke University Press, 1999.

———. "Making the Biopolitical Subject: Cambodian Immigrants, Refugee Medicine, and Cultural Citizenship in California." *Social Science and Medicine* 40 (1995): 1243–57.

———. *Neoliberalism as Exception: Mutations in Citizenship and Sovereignty.* Durham, NC: Duke University Press, 2006.

Ono, Kent A., and John M. Sloop. *Shifting Borders: Rhetoric, Immigration, and California's Proposition 187.* Philadelphia: Temple University Press, 2002.

Oppenheimer, Andres. "'Transnational Citizens' Emerge." *Orange County Register*, April 9, 2006, News section, 34.

Ortega, Alexander N., Hai Fang, Victor H. Perez, John A. Rizzo, Olivia Carter-Pokras, Steven P. Wallace, and Lillian Gelberg. "Health Care Access, Use of Services, and Experiences among Undocumented Mexicans and Other Latinos." *Archives of Internal Medicine* 167, no. 21 (2007): 2354–60.

Ortner, Sherry. "On Key Symbols." *American Anthropologist* 75 (1973): 1228–46.

O'Sullivan, Mike. "U.S. Copes with Growing Population, Approaching 300 Million." Voice of America, March 8, 2006. http://www.voanews.com/english/archive/2006-03/2006-03-08-voa25.cfm.

Parrado, Emilio A., and S. Philip Morgan. "Intergenerational Fertility among Hispanic Women: New Evidence of Immigrant Assimilation." *Demography* (forthcoming).

Parsons, Christi, Brian Bennett, and Joseph Tanfani. "Obama Opens New Door." *Los Angeles Times*, June 16, 2012, A1.

Pasco, Jean O. "Campbell Wins Seat; Gilchrist Takes 3rd." *Los Angeles Times*, December 7, 2005, A1.

Pasco, Jean O., and Dan Weikel. "OC Race a Border Skirmish." *Los Angeles Times*, December 4, 2005, A1.

Passel, Jeffrey S. *Unauthorized Migrants: Numbers and Characteristics*. Washington, DC: Pew Hispanic Center, 2005.

Passel, Jeffrey S., Randolph Capps, and Michael E. Fix. *Undocumented Immigrants: Facts and Figures*. Washington, DC: Urban Institute, 2004.

Passel, Jeffrey S., and D'Vera Cohn. *A Portrait of Unauthorized Immigrants in the United States*. Washington, DC: Pew Hispanic Center, 2009.

Passel, Jeffrey S., and Kathryn A. Woodrow. "Change in the Undocumented Alien Population in the United States, 1979–1983." *International Migration Review* 21 (1987): 1304–34.

Perea, Juan F., ed. *Immigrants Out! The New Nativism and the Anti-Immigrant Impulse in the United States*. New York: New York University Press, 1997.

Petryna, Adriana. *Life Exposed: Biological Citizens after Chernobyl*. Princeton, NJ: Princeton University Press, 2002.

Piore, Michael J. *Birds of Passage: Migrant Labor Industrial Societies*. Cambridge: Cambridge University Press, 1979.

Pitkin, John, and Dowell Myers. "Generational Projections of the California Population by Nativity and Year of Immigrant Arrival." Los Angeles: Population Dynamics Research Group, Sol Price School of Public Policy, University of Southern California, 2012.

Population Reference Bureau (PRB). *World Population Data Sheet, Total Births per Woman, Mexico*. 2003. http://www.prb.org.

Porter, Eduardo. "Illegal Immigrants Are Bolstering Social Security with Billions." *New York Times*, April 5, 2005, A1.

Portes, Alejandro, and Robert L. Bach. *Latin Journey: Cuban and Mexican Immigrants in the United States*. Berkeley: University of California Press, 1985.

Portes, Alejandro, and Rubén G. Rumbaut. *Immigrant America: A Portrait*. 3rd ed. Berkeley: University of California Press, 2006.

———. *Legacies: The Story of the Immigrant Second Generation*. Berkeley: University of California Press, 2001.

Portes, Alejandro, and Richard Schauffler. "Language Acquisition and Loss among Children of Immigrants." In *Origins and Destinies: Immigration, Race, and Ethnicity in America*, edited by Silvia Pedraza and Rubén Rumbaut, 432–43. Belmont, CA: Wadsworth, 1996.

Potter, Ned. "America Approaches 300 Million Population." ABC News, January 13, 2006. http://abcnews.go.com/US/story?id=1503435.

Prengaman, Peter. "Across California, Thousands March: Pro-Immigrant Demonstrators Demand Legislation from Congress to Allow Rights." *Orange County Register*, April 11, 2006, News section, 1.

Pressley, Sue Anne. "Hispanic Immigration Boom Rattles South: Rapid Influx to Some Areas Raises Tensions." *Washington Post*, March 6, 2000, A3.

Preston, Julia. "Deportations Go On Despite U.S. Review of Backlog." *New York Times*, June 7, 2012, A12.

———. "Federal Policy Resulting in Wave of Deportations Draws Protests." *New York Times*, August 17, 2011, A12.

———. "State Lawmakers Outline Plans to End Birthright Citizenship, Drawing Outcry." *New York Times*, January 5, 2011.

Price, Andrew. "Republican Senate Nominee Uses Picture of Mexicans—in Mexico—to Scare Us about Illegal Immigrants." *Good News*, October 9, 2010. http://www.good.is/post/republican-senate-nominee-uses-picture-of-mexicans-in-mexico-to-scare-us-about-illegal-immigrants/.

Probyn, Elspeth. "Bloody Metaphors and Other Allegories of the Ordinary." In *Between Woman and Nation: Nationalisms, Transnational Feminisms, and the State*, edited by C. Kaplan, N. Alarcon, and M. Moallem, 47–62. Durham, NC: Duke University Press, 1999.

Putnam, Robert D. *Bowling Alone: The Collapse and Revival of American Community*. New York: Simon and Schuster, 2001.

Puwar, Nirmal. *Space Invaders: Race, Gender and Bodies Out of Place*. Oxford: Berg, 2004.

Rabinow, Paul, and Nikolas Rose. "Biopower Today." *Biosocieties* 1 (2006): 195–217.

Rajan, Kaushik Sunder. *Biocapital: The Constitution of Postgenomic Life*. Durham, NC: Duke University Press, 2006.

———. "Experimental Values: Indian Clinical Trials and Surplus Health." *New Left Review* 45 (2007): 67–88.

Rank, Mark Robert. *Living on the Edge.* New York: Columbia University Press, 1994.

Rasmussen Reports. "61% Oppose U.S. Citizenship for Children Born to Illegal Immigrants." 2011. http://www.rasmussenreports.com/public_content/politics/current_events/immigration/61_oppose_u_s_citizenship_for_children_born_to_illegal_immigrants.

Rawle, Wiliam. *A View of the Constitution of the United States of America.* Philadelphia: Philip H. Nicklin Law Bookseller, 1829.

Reagan, Ronald. Speech Announcing Ronald Reagan's Presidential Candidacy, November 13, 1979. Available from http://millercenter.org/president/speeches/detail/5852.

Reed-Danahay, Deborah, and Caroline B. Brettell, eds. *Citizenship, Political Engagement, and Belonging: Immigrants in Europe and the United States.* New Brunswick, NJ: Rutgers University Press, 2008.

Reston, Maeve. "California Dream Act Signed into Law." *Los Angeles Times,* July 26, 2011, A1.

Reynolds, Maura. "Bush Asks Immigrants to Reject Work Boycotts." *Los Angeles Times,* April 29, 2006, A5.

———. "A Call to Shed 'Poison Pill' Immigration Rule." *Los Angeles Times,* April 12, 2006, A12.

Reynolds, Maura, and Faye Fiore. "Across the U.S., 'We Are America.'" *Los Angeles Times,* April 11, 2006, A1.

Richard, Chris. "The Buzz on the Border." *Press-Enterprise* (Riverside, CA), April 14, 2005, A1.

Ricker, Dave. "Gaxiola Sentenced to Life in Arivaca Shootings." *Green Valley News and Sun,* August 15, 2011.

Riley, Michael. "1,000 Activists to Patrol Arizona Border for Migrants." *Denver Post,* March 31, 2005, A6.

Ritzer, George. *The McDonaldization of Society.* 3rd ed. Thousand Oaks, CA: Pine Forge Press, 2000.

Roberts, Dorothy E. *Killing the Black Body: Race, Reproduction, and the Meaning of Liberty.* New York: Pantheon Books, 1997.

———. "Who May Give Birth to Citizens? Reproduction, Eugenics, and Immigration." In Perea, *Immigrants Out!* 205–19.

Roberts, Sam. "Come October, Baby Will Make 300 Million or So." *New York Times,* January 13, 2006, A1.

Robinson, J. Gregory. *ESCAP II: Demographic Analysis Results.* Washington, DC: Bureau of the Census, U.S. Department of Commerce, 2001.

Rocco, Raymond. "Transforming Citizenship: Membership, Strategies of Containment, and the Public Sphere in Latino Communities." *Latino Studies* 2, no. 1 (2004): 4–25.

Rodriguez, Clara E. *Latin Looks: Images of Latinas and Latinos in the U.S. Media*. Boulder, CO: Westview Press, 1997.

Rodriguez, M. A., L. M. Ward, and E. J. Perez-Stable. "Breast and Cervical Cancer Screening: Impact of Health Insurance Status, Ethnicity and Nativity of Latinas." *Annals of Family Medicine* 3, no. 3 (2005): 235–41.

Roman, Ediberto. "Members and Outsiders: A Vision of the Models of United States Citizenship and a Few Questions Concerning European Union Citizenship." *University of Miami International and Comparative Law Review* 9 (2001): 81–113.

Rosaldo, Renato. "Cultural Citizenship, Inequality, and Multiculturalism." In Flores and Benmayor, *Latino Cultural Citizenship*, 27–38.

Rosaldo, Renato, and William Flores. "Identity, Conflict, and Evolving Latino Communities: Cultural Citizenship in San Jose, California." In Flores and Benmayor, *Latino Cultural Citizenship*, 57–96.

Rose, Nikolas, and Carlos Novas. "Biological Citizenship." In *Global Assemblages: Technology, Politics, and Ethics as Anthropological Problems*, edited by Aihwa Ong, 439–63. Malden, MA: Blackwell, 2005.

Rotstein, Arthur H. "Volunteer Border Watchers Cause Concern." *Ventura County Star*, March 27, 2005, 1.

Rouse, Carolyn. "Jesica Speaks? Adolescent Consent for Transplantation and Ethical Uncertainty." In Wailoo, Livingston, and Guarnaccia, *A Death Retold*, 329–48.

Rouse, Roger. "Mexican Migration and the Social Space of Postmodernism." *Diaspora* 1 (1991): 8–23.

Ruiz, Vicki L. *From Out of the Shadows: Mexican Women in Twentieth-Century America*. Oxford: Oxford University Press, 1999.

Rumbaut, Rubén G. "Ages, Life Stages, and Generational Cohorts: Decomposing the Immigrant First and Second Generations in the United States." *International Migration Review* 38 (2004): 432–43.

———. "Assimilation and Its Discontents: Between Rhetoric and Reality." *International Migration Review* 31 (1997): 923–60.

———. "The New Californians: Comparative Research Findings on the Educational Progress of Immigrant Children." In *California's Immigrant Children: Theory, Research, and Implications for Educational Policy*, edited by Rubén G. Rumbaut and Wayne A. Cornelius. San Diego: Center for U.S.-Mexican Studies, University of California, San Diego, 1995.

———. "Origins and Destinies: Immigration, Race, and Ethnicity in Contemporary America." In *Origins and Destinies: Immigration, Race, and Ethnicity in America*, edited by Silvia Pedraza and Rubén G. Rumbaut, 21–42. Belmont, CA: Wadsworth, 1996.

Rumbaut, Rubén G., Douglas S. Massey, and Frank D. Bean. "Linguistic Life Expectancies: Immigrant Language Retention in Southern California." *Population and Development Review* 32, no. 3 (2006): 447–60.

Rumbaut, Rubén G., and John R. Weeks. "Children of Immigrants: Is 'Americanization' Hazardous to Infant Health?" In *Children of Color: Research, Health, and Public Policy Issues*, edited by H. E. Fitzgerald, B. M. Lester, and B. Zuckerman. New York: Garland, 1989.

Rutenberg, Jim. "Bush Enters Anthem Fight on Language." *New York Times*, April 29, 2006, A1.

Rutten, Tim. "Lou Dobbs Is All Bully and Bluster." *Los Angeles Times*, April 1, 2006, E1.

Sadiq, Kamal. *Paper Citizens: How Illegal Immigrants Acquire Citizenship in Developing Countries*. New York: Oxford University Press (forthcoming).

Salladay, Robert. "Governor's Candid Moments Caught on Audiotape." *Los Angeles Times*, September 8, 2006, A1.

Samers, Michael. "Invisible Capitalism: Political Economy and the Regulation of Undocumented Immigration in France." *Economy and Society* 32, no. 4 (2003): 555–83.

Sample, Herbert A. "Governor Talks of Closing Mexico Border." *Sacramento Bee*, April 20, 2005, A3.

San Miguel, Guadalupe, Jr. *Tejano Proud: Tex-Mex Music in the Twentieth-Century*. College Station: Texas A&M University Press, 2002.

Santa Ana, Otto. *Brown Tide Rising*. Austin: University of Texas Press, 2002.

———. "'Like an Animal I Was Treated': Anti-Immigrant Metaphors in U.S. Public Discourse." *Discourse and Society* 10, no. 2 (1996): 192–224.

Santa Ana, Otto, Juan Moran, and Cynthia Sanchez. "Awash under a Brown Tide: Immigration Metaphors in California Public and Print Media Discourse." *Aztlan* 23, no. 2 (1998): 137–75.

Sassen, Saskia. "The Repositioning of Citizenship: Emergent Subjects and Spaces for Politics." *New Centennial Review* 3, no. 2 (2003): 41–66.

Saturday Post. "Madeeha Faryad's Story." 2007. http://www.thesaturdaypost.com/rendezvous_45_madeeha.html.

Savage, David G. "Justices Ease Deporting of Car Thieves." *Los Angeles Times*, January 18, 2007, A22.

Schabner, Dean. "Border Vigilante Shawna Forde Sentenced to Death for Home Invasion." ABC News, February 22, 2011. abcnews.go.com/US/minutemen-vigilante-shawna-forde-sentenced-death-deadly-arizona/?id=12976687&page=4#.

Scheer, Robert. "Surprise! Immigration Hasn't Ruined Us." *Los Angeles Times*, February 22, 2000, B11.

Scheper-Hughes, Nancy. "The Global Traffic in Human Organs." *Current Anthropology* 41, no. 2 (2000): 191–224.

Schiller, Nina Glick. "Transborder Citizenship: An Outcome of Legal Pluralism with Transnational Social Fields." In *Mobile People, Mobile Law: Expanding Legal Relations in a Contracting World*, edited by Franz von Benda-Beckmann, Keebet von Benda-Beckmann, and Anne Griffiths, 27–49. Burlington, VT: Ashgate, 2005.

Schiller, Nina Glick, and Ayse Caglar. "'And Ye Shall Possess It, and Dwell Therein': Social Citizenship, Global Christianity, and Non-Ethnic Immigrant Incorporation." In Reed-Danahay and Brettell, *Citizenship, Political Engagement and Belonging*, 203–25.

Schiller, Nina Glick, and Georges Eugene Fouron. *Georges Woke Up Laughing*. Durham, NC: Duke University Press, 2001.

Schlesinger, Arthur M., Jr. *The Disuniting of America*. New York: W. W. Norton, 1992.

Schmitt, Eric. "Pockets of Protest Are Rising against Immigration." *New York Times*, August 9, 2001.

Schuck, Peter H. *Citizens, Strangers, and In-Betweens: Essays on Immigration and Citizenship*. Boulder, CO: Westview Press, 1998.

———. "Law and the Study of Migration." In *Migration Theory*, edited by Caroline Brettell and James F. Hollifield, 187–204. New York: Routledge, 2000.

Schuck, Peter H., and Rogers M. Smith. *Citizenship without Consent: Illegal Aliens in the American Polity*. New Haven, CT: Yale University Press.

Schwartz, David. "Russell Pearce, Architect of Illegal Immigration Law in Arizona, Loses Election." *Christian Science Monitor*, November 9, 2011.

Seper, Jerry. "Border Patrols Inspire Imitation—Other Civilians Take Up Cause." *Washington Times*, April 16, 2005, A1.

Serrano, Richard A., and Dalina Castellanos. "Federal Officials Sue Arizona Lawman." *Los Angeles Times*, May 11, 2012, A14.

Shaffer, Ralph E., and Walter P. Coombs. "Our Discordant Anthem." *Los Angeles Times*, May 2, 2006, B13.

Shah, Nayan. *Contagious Divides: Epidemics and Race in San Francisco's Chinatown*. Berkeley: University of California Press, 2001.

Sharp, Lesley A. "Babes and Baboons: Jesica Santillan and Experimental Pediatric Transplant Research in America." In Wailoo, Livingston, and Guarnaccia, *A Death Retold*, 299–328.

———. *Strange Harvest: Organ Transplants, Denatured Bodies, and the Transformed Self*. Berkeley: University of California Press, 2006.

Shogren, Elizabeth. "Clinton's Signature Launches Historical Overhaul of Welfare." *Los Angeles Times*, August 23, 1996, A1.

Shohat, Ella. "Post-Third-Worldist Culture: Gender, Nation, and the Cinema." In *Feminist Genealogies, Colonial Legacies, Democratic Future*, edited by M. Jacqui Alexander and Chandra Talpade Mohanty, 183–209. New York: Routledge, 1997.

Sigona, Nando, and Vanessa Hughes. *No Way Out, No Way In: Irregular Migrant Children and Families in the UK*. Oxford, UK: ESRC Centre on Migration, Policy and Society, 2012.

Silverstein, Jonathan. "Racist Video Game Incites Anger: Internet Game Lets Players Take Shots at Immigrants." ABC News, May 1, 2006. http://www.abcnews .go.com/Technology/Story?id=1910119&page=1.

Simon, Rita J. *Public Opinion and the Immigrant*. Lexington, MA: Lexington Books, 1985.

Simon, Rita J., and Susan H. Alexander. *The Ambivalent Welcome: Print Media, Public Opinion and Immigration*: Westport, CT: Praeger, 1993.

Siskind's Immigration Bulletin. "Duke Case Raises Questions about Transplants for Immigrants." March 2003. http://www.visalaw.com/03mar1/9mar103.html.

Sjoberg, Gideon, Elizabeth A. Gill, and Norma Williams. "A Sociology of Human Rights." *Social Problems* 48, no. 1 (2001): 11–47.

Small, Stephen. "The Contours of Racialization: Structure, Representations and Resistance in the United States." In *Race, Identity, and Citizenship: A Reader*, edited by Rodolfo D. Torres, Louis F. Mirón, and Jonathan Xavier Inda. Malden, MA: Blackwell, 1999.

Smith, Angèle. "The Irish Citizenship Referendum (2004): Motherhood and Belonging in Ireland." In *Citizenship, Political Engagement, and Belonging: Immigrants in Europe and the United States*, edited by Deborah Reed-Danahay and Caroline B. Brettell, 60–77. New Brunswick, NJ: Rutgers University Press, 2008.

Smith, Doug. "A Countdown to 300 Million." *Los Angeles Times*, October 4, 2006, A1.

Smith, James F., and Edwin Chen. "Bush to Weigh Residency for Illegal Mexican Immigrants." *Los Angeles Times*, September 7, 2001, A1.

Smith, Kim. "Bush Sentenced to Die in Arivaca Killings." *Arizona Daily Star*, April 7, 2011.

Solis, J. M., G. Marks, M. Garcia, and D. Shelton. "Acculturation, Access to Care, and Use of Preventive Services by Hispanics: Findings from HHANES 1982–84." *American Journal of Public Health* 80 (Supplement, 1990): 11–19.

Soysal, Yasemin Hohoglu. *Limits of Citizenship: Migrants and Postnational Membership in Europe*. Chicago: University of Chicago Press, 1995.

Stephen, Lynn. "Cultural Citizenship and Labor Rights for Oregon Farmworkers: The Case of Pineros y Campesinos Unidos del Nordoeste (PCUN)." *Human Organization* 62, no. 1 (2003): 27–38.

———. *Transborder Lives: Indigenous Oaxacans in Mexico, California, and Oregon*. Durham, NC: Duke University Press, 2007.

Stepputat, Finn. "Marching for Progress: Rituals of Citizenship, State and Belonging in a High Andes District." *Bulletin of Latin American Research* 23, no. 2 (2004): 244–59.

Stern, Alexandra Minna. "Buildings, Boundaries, and Blood: Medicalization and Nation-Building on the U.S.-Mexico Border, 1910–1930." *Hispanic American Historical Review* 79, no. 1 (1999): 41–81.

———. *Eugenic Nation: Faults and Frontiers of Better Breeding in Modern America.* Berkeley: University of California Press, 2005.

Stevenson, Nick. *Cultural Citizenship: Cosmopolitan Questions.* Maidenhead, UK: Open University Press, 2003.

Strohm, Chris. "Activists to Flock to Border, Set Up Citizen Patrols." *Government Executive*, March 28, 2005. http://www.govexec.com/dailyfed/0305/032805c1.htm.

Stroup-Benham, Christine A., and Fernando M. Trevino. "Reproductive Characteristics of Mexican-American, Mainland Puerto Rican, and Cuban-American Women." *Journal of the American Medical Association* 265, no. 2 (1991): 222–26.

Suarez, Kelly-Anne, and J. Michael Kennedy. "L.A.'s Top Officers Vow Crackdown on Students." *Los Angeles Times*, March 29, 2006, A11.

Suárez-Navaz, Liliana. *Rebordering the Mediterranean: Boundaries and Citizenship in Southern Europe.* New York: Berghahn Books, 2004.

Suarez-Orozco, C., and Suarez-Orozco, M. *Transformations: Immigration, Family Life and Achievement Motivation among Latino Adolescents.* Stanford, CA: Stanford University Press, 1995.

Suarez-Orozco, Marcelo M. "Everything You Wanted to Know about Assimilation but Were Afraid to Ask." *Daedalus* 129, no. 4 (2000): 1–30.

Sullivan, Eileen, "Officials See Rise in Militia Groups across US." *Huffington Post*, August 12, 2009. http://www.huffingtonpost.com/2009/08/12/officials-see-rise-in-mil_n_257128.html.

Suro, Robert. *Strangers among Us: How Lationo Immigration Is Transforming America.* New York: Knopf, 1998.

Suro, Robert, Gabriel Escobar, Gretchen Livingston, and Shirin Hakimzadeh. *Changing Faiths: Latinos and the Transformation of American Religion.* Washington, DC: Pew Hispanic Center, 2007.

Survey Sampling Inc. (SSI). *Statistical Analysis of Sample.* Fairfield, CT: SSI, 1990.

Talev, Margaret. "Minuteman Volunteers Give Motives: Middle Aged Whites Express Frustrations with Illegal Crossings." *Modesto Bee*, April 4, 2005, A10.

Tancredo, Tom. *In Mortal Danger: The Battle for America's Border and Security.* Nashville, TN: Cumberland House, 2006.

Tatalovich, Raymond. "Official English as Nativist Backlash." In Perea, *Immigrants Out!* 78–102.

Taylor, Diana. *The Archive and the Repertoire: Performing Cultural Memory in the Americas*. Durham, NC: Duke University Press, 2003.

The Telegraph. "Where Have All the Bambini Gone?" April 18, 2004. http://www.tele graph.co.uk/news/main.jhtml?xml=/news/2004/04/18/wbamb18.xml&sSheet=/news/2004/04/18/ixworld.html.

Thomas, Evan. "Stopping the Census Clock: As America's Population Approaches the 300-Million Mark, the Country Isn't in the Mood for Celebrating." *Newsweek*, October 10, 2006. http://www.newsweek.com/id/45281.

Tormey, Anwen. "'Everyone with Eyes Can See the Problem': Moral Citizens and the Space of Irish Nationhood." *International Migration* 45, no. 3 (2007): 69–100.

Torres, Rodolfo D., Louis F. Mirón, and Jonathan Xavier Inda. Introduction to *Race, Identity, and Citizenship*, edited by Rodolfo D. Torres, Louis F. Mirón, and Jonathan Xavier Inda. Malden, MA: Blackwell, 1999.

Tsuda, Takeyuki. *Local Citizenship in Recent Countries of Immigration: Japan in Comparative Perspective*. Lanham, MD: Lexington Books, 2006.

———. *Strangers in the Ethnic Homeland: Japanese Brazilian Return Migration in Transnational Perspective*. New York: Columbia University Press, 2003.

Turner, Bryan S. "Contemporary Problems in the Theory of Citizenship." In *Citizenship and Social Theory*, edited by Bryan S. Turner. London: Sage Publications, 1993.

United Nations Statistics Division. *UNdata: A World of Information*. 2007. http://unstats.un.org/unsd/default.htm.

U.S. Census Bureau. *State and County Quickfacts: Orange County, California*. 2007. http://quickfacts.census.gov/qfd/states/06/06059.html.

U.S. News and World Report. "How Millions of Illegal Aliens Sneak into U.S.: Interview with Leonard F. Chapman Jr., Commissioner, Immigration and Naturalization Service." July 22, 1974, 27.

Utley, Robert M. *Lone Star Justice: The First Century of the Texas Rangers*. Oxford, UK: Oxford University Press, 2002.

Vance, Carole S. "Anthropology Rediscovers Sexuality: A Theoretical Comment." *Social Science and Medicine* 33, no. 8 (1991): 875–84.

Vargas, Jose Antonio. "Shadow Americans." *Time*, June 25, 2012, 34–44.

Varsanyi, Monica W. "Interrogating 'Urban Citizenship' vis-à-vis Undocumented Migration." *Citizenship Studies* 10, no. 2 (2006): 229–45.

Vedantam, Shankar. "U.S. Citizens Get More Organs Than They Give." *Washington Post*, March 3, 2003, A3.

Vélez-Ibáñez, Carlos G. *Border Visions: Mexican Cultures of the Southwest United States*. Tucson: University of Arizona Press, 1996.

———. "The Non-Consenting Sterilization of Mexican Women in Los Angeles: Issues of Psychocultural Rupture and Legal Redress in Paternalistic Behavioral

Environments." In *Twice a Minority*, edited by A. Melville, 235–48. St. Louis: C. V. Mosby Press, 1980.

———. "Se me acabó la canción: An Ethnography of Non-Consenting Sterilizations among Mexican Women in Los Angeles, California." In *Latina Issues: Fragments of Historia(ella) (Herstory)*, edited by Antoinette S. Lopez. New York: Garland Press, 1999.

Ventura, Stephanie J., William D. Mosher, Sally C. Curtin, and Joyce C. Abma. "Trends in Pregnancy Rates for the United States, 1976–97: An Update." *National Vital Statistics Reports* 49, no. 4 (2001): 1–10.

Villarosa, Linda. "Jesica Was One of 80,000 on Organ Waiting List." *New York Times*, February 19, 2003.

Volpp, Leti. "The Citizen and the Terrorist." *UCLA Law Review* 49 (2002): 1575–1600.

Voss, Kim, and Irene Bloemraad. *Rallying for Immigrant Rights: The Fight for Inclusion in 21st Century America*. Berkeley: University of California Press, 2011.

Wailoo, Keith, Julie Livingston, and Peter Guarnaccia, eds. *A Death Retold: Jesica Santillan, the Bungled Transplant, and Paradoxes of Medical Citizenship*. Chapel Hill: University of North Carolina Press, 2006.

Waldinger, Roger. *Between Here and There: How Attached Are Latino Immigrants to Their Native Country?* Washington, DC: Pew Hispanic Center, 2007.

Wang, Justina. 2006. "Stuck in the Middle." *Suburban Chicago News*, December 26, 2006. http://www.suburbanchicagonews.com.

Watanabe, Teresa. "Catholic Leaders Hope to Sway Immigration Debate." *Los Angeles Times*, March 4, 2006, B1.

———. "Immigrants Gain Pulpit." *Los Angeles Times*, March 1, 2006, A1.

Watanabe, Teresa, Anna Gorman, and Nancy Cleeland. "National Boycott Plans Creating Divide." *Los Angeles Times*, April 29, 2006, A1.

Watanabe, Teresa, and Francisco Vara-Orta. "Small Turnout, Big Questions." *Los Angeles Times*, May 2, 2007, A1.

Webb, Walter Prescott. *The Texas Rangers: A Century of Frontier Defense*. Austin: University of Texas Press, 1965.

Weismantel, Mary. *Cholas and Pishtacos: Stories of Race and Sex in the Andes*. Chicago: University of Chicago Press, 2001.

White, Naomi Rosh, and Peter B. White. *Immigrants and the Media*. Melbourne, Australia: Oongman Cheshire, 1983.

Wides-Munoz, Laura. "Spanish Version of 'Star-Spangled Banner' Draws Protests." Associated Press, April 28, 2006, 1.

Will, George F. "We Have Been Here Before." *Newsweek*, June 11, 2001, 64.

Willen, Sarah S. "Toward a Critical Phenomenology of 'Illegality': State Power, Criminality and Abjectivity among Undocumented Migrant Workers in Tel Aviv, Israel." *International Migration* 45, no. 3 (2007): 8–38.

Wilson, Kimberley Jane. 2003. "Transplant Details Raise Cruel Questions." New Visions Commentary paper, National Center for Public Policy Research, Washington, DC, April 2003. http://www.nationalcenter.org/P21NVWilsonOrgans403.html.

Wilson, Tamar D. "Anti-Immigrant Sentiment and the Problem of Reproduction/Maintenance in Mexican Immigration to the United States." *Critique of Anthropology* 20, no. 2 (2000): 191–213.

Wolgin, Philip E., and Maya Edelstein. "Keeping the DREAM Alive: States Continue the Fight to Give Undocumented Students Access to Higher Education." Center for American Progress, June 28, 2011. http://www.americanprogress.org/issues/2011/06/keeping_dream_alive.html.

Wong, Bernard. "Globalization and Citizenship: The Chinese in Silicon Valley." In *Citizenship, Political Engagement, and Belonging: Immigrants in Europe and the United States*, edited by Deborah Reed-Danahay and Caroline B. Brettell, 183–202. New Brunswick, NJ: Rutgers University Press, 2008.

Wood, Daniel B. "Minutemen's Message on Immigration: On a Roll?" *Christian Science Monitor*, May 5, 2006. http://www.csmonitor.com/2006/0505/p02 s02-uspo.html.

WorldNetDaily. "Invasion USA: Illegals Push U.S. to 300 Million Mark." October 2, 2006. http://www.worldnetdaily.com/news/article.asp?ARTICLE_ID=52258.

Wyatt, Edward. "Cain Proposes Electrified Border Fence." *New York Times*, October 15, 2011.

Yang, Joshua S., and Steven P. Wallace. *Expansion of Health Insurance in California Unlikely to Act as Magnet for Undocumented Immigration.* UCLA Health Policy Research Brief. Los Angeles: UCLA Center for Health Policy Research, 2007.

Yuval-Davis, Nira. "Belonging and the Politics of Belonging." *Patterns of Prejudice* 40, no. 3 (2006): 196–213.

———. "The 'Multi-Layered Citizen': Citizenship in the Age of Globalization." *International Feminist Journal of Politics* 1, no. 1 (1999): 119–36.

Zavella, Patricia. "'Playing with Fire': The Gendered Construction of Chicana/Mexicana Sexuality." In *Perspectives on Las Americas*, edited by Matthew C. Guttman, Felix V. Matios Rodriguez, Lynn Stephen, and Patricia Zavella. Malden, MA: Blackwell, 2003.

———. "The Tables Are Turned: Immigration, Poverty, and Social Conflict in California Communities." In Perea, *Immigrants Out!* 136–61.

Zhan, Mei. "Does It Take a Miracle? Negotiating Knowledge, Identities, and Communities of Traditional Chinese Medicine." *Cultural Anthropology* 16, no. 4 (2001): 453–80.

Zitner, Aaron. "Nation's Birthrate Drops to Its Lowest Level since 1909." *Los Angeles Times*, June 26, 2003, A1.

Zlolinski, Christian. *Janitors, Street Vendors and Activists: The Lives of Mexican Immigrants in Silicon Valley*. Berkeley: University of California Press, 2006.

———. "Political Mobilization and Activism among Latinos/as in the United States." In *Latino/a Sourcebook*, edited by H. Rodríguez, R. Saenz, and C. Menjívar. New York: Springer, 2008.

Zúñiga, Elena, Beatriz Zubieta, and Cristina Araya. *Cuadernos de salud reproductiva: República Mexicana*. Mexico City: Consejo Nacional de la Población, 2000.

INDEX

Italic page numbers indicate material in tables or figures.